Kohlhammer

Ann-Stephane Schäfer/Stefan Schäfer/Cory Wanek

The euro and its history

An economic introduction

Verlag W. Kohlhammer

This work, including all of its parts, is protected by copyright. Any use beyond the narrow confines of copyright law is not permitted without the publisher's consent and is liable to prosecution. This applies in particular to reproductions, translations, microfilming, and storage or processing in electronic systems.

First edition 2025

All rights reserved
© W. Kohlhammer GmbH, Stuttgart (Germany)
Production: W. Kohlhammer GmbH, Heßbrühlstr. 69, 70565 Stuttgart, GERMANY
produktsicherheit@kohlhammer.de
Printed in Germany

Print edition:
ISBN 978-3-17-043544-5

E-Books:
pdf: ISBN 978-3-17-043545-2
epub: ISBN 978-3-17-043546-9

The respective website operators are solely responsible for the content of any websites cited or linked in this work. W. Kohlhammer GmbH has no influence over the content of external websites and assumes no liability for them.

Inhalt

	Preface		9
1	Introduction: national money and international trade – a simple thought experiment		11
	1.1	Money and its functions	11
	1.2	International trade and the balance of payments	12
	1.3	Foreign exchange market and currency system	16
	1.4	The design of the international monetary system	18
2	Background: The long road to the euro (1945–1989)		19
	2.1	A new start after the war: Bilateralism, European Payments Union and the Treaty of Rome	19
		2.1.1 The years of so-called 'bilateralism'	19
		2.1.2 The European Payments Union	24
		2.1.3 The "Treaty of Rome"	26
	2.2	Western Europe's currencies in the Bretton Woods era	28
		2.2.1 The gold-dollar standard – an overview	28
		2.2.2 How can fixed exchange rates be achieved?	30
		2.2.3 The EEC currencies in the Bretton Woods system	32
		2.2.4 The trilemma of monetary policy	33
		2.2.5 From the mid-1960s onwards: Problems and collapse	37
	2.3	The 1970s: the Werner plan and the 'European Currency Snake'	40
		2.3.1 The Werner plan: Creating an EC monetary union by 1980?	40
		2.3.2 The 'European Currency Snake'	44
	2.4	The European Monetary System (EMS)	46
		2.4.1 Objectives, functioning and development over time	46
		2.4.2 Analyzing the EMS from the perspective of economic history (1): Was it a success story?	49
		2.4.3 Analyzing the EMS from the perspective of economic history (2): Was it a Deutschmark bloc with the Bundesbank as its central bank?	50
		2.4.4 Analyzing the EMS from the perspective of economic history (3): Was it a precursor to the monetary union?	52

3	**Paving the way: Delors Report, Maastricht Treaty, Stability and Growth Pact (1989–1998)**		54
	3.1	The Delors report	54
	3.2	Economic foundations of the discussion in the 1990s	58
		3.2.1 The theory of optimum currency areas	58
		3.2.2 Endogeneity of the functional conditions of a monetary union?	63
		3.2.3 The political economy perspective	64
		3.2.4 Monetary policy and public debt in a currency union	65
	3.3	The Maastricht Treaty	68
		3.3.1 The ECB as a 'European Bundesbank'?	68
		3.3.2 The convergence criteria	73
	3.4	The Stability and Growth Pact	75
	3.5	Decisive steps on the road to monetary union	78
	3.6	The ECB formulates its strategy	84
4	**Honeymoon: The euro before the financial crisis (1999–2007)**		89
	4.1	The ECB stands the test – and adapts its strategy	89
	4.2	Greece, the Stability and Growth Pact, and international imbalances – dark clouds on the horizon?	97
5	**Crisis years: The monetary union on the brink of collapse (2008–2015)**		100
	5.1	From the global financial crisis to the European sovereign debt crisis	100
	5.2	Dimensions of the euro crisis	102
		5.2.1 The euro crisis as a current account crisis	102
		5.2.2 The euro crisis as a banking crisis	108
		5.2.3 The euro crisis as a sovereign-debt crisis	109
	5.3	The discussion about the institutional causes of the crisis	115
	5.4	The 'rescue packages', the European Stability Mechanism (ESM) and the crisis year 2015	118
	5.5	The reform of the eurozone architecture	123
		5.5.1 Overview of the main features of the discussion	123
		5.5.2 The reorganization of the fiscal and economic policy rules	126
		5.5.3 The reform of the financial architecture	129
6	**'The only game in town:' The ECB in charge of everything? (2015–2022)**		138
	6.1	Overview: The evolution of the ECB's monetary policy since the start of the financial crisis	138
		6.1.1 The ECB's response to the problems on the banking market	138

		6.1.2	The ECB's response to the sovereign debt crisis	143
		6.1.3	"Whatever it takes"	145
	6.2	Quantitative Easing		152
		6.2.1	The Asset Purchase Programme	152
		6.2.2	Criticism of the government bond purchases	157
	6.3	The monetary policy response to the Covid pandemic		160
7	**Present and future**			**162**
	7.1	Inflation is back		162
	7.2	The 2021 revision of the ECB's strategy		165
	7.3	Is the ECB operating under conditions of fiscal dominance?		169
	7.4	The "NextGenEU" program and the future of fiscal policy in the monetary union		172
	7.5	A 'digital euro'?		180
	7.6	When will the eurozone be complete?		183
Literature				**186**

Preface

Since its introduction on January 1, 1999, the euro has become the money more and more Europeans use to make payments. In the beginning, the monetary union involved just under 300 million inhabitants in eleven countries, but the single European currency has grown to be used in twenty member states with around 350 million inhabitants today. To this end, the participants in the monetary union have ceded their responsibility for monetary policy to one supranational institution that is responsible for the euro, namely the European Central Bank (ECB). Since the creation of the monetary union, the eurozone countries have thus been 'moneyless,' and the euro and the ECB are in a sense 'stateless.' In the history of money, this has never been the case before. It is therefore no exaggeration to call the euro a unique experiment.

This book aims to trace how this experiment came about and how it has developed over the past decades. It differs from the vast number of publications dealing with the European single currency in the following respects:

- The euro did not appear out of thin air, neither in 1999 nor during the famous Maastricht Conference in 1991. This book provides a detailed account of the euro's extensive prehistory, tracing back to the end of World War II – an aspect often overlooked in existing literature.
- Many articles dealing with the European currency reflect a particular point of view. In contrast, this book strives for a more balanced view by presenting different perspectives. The aim is to enable readers to understand the pros and cons of the decisive stages that the European monetary integration has gone through from its beginnings in the 1940s to the present day.
- Unlike most publications on the subject, "The Euro and its History" takes an explicitly interdisciplinary perspective. In particular, it is written for a lay readership with a background in history, political science, law or cultural studies as well as for economists who are interested in historical developments.
- Although the book reflects an economic perspective, it does not apply the usual economic methodology. Instead, the central relationships are explained verbally and with the help of clear graphics. Also, the book starts with an introduction that uses a thought experiment to introduce the fundamental relationships of international macroeconomics. While the foundational concepts outlined in this introductory chapter may offer basic orientation for some readers, those seeking a more in-depth exploration of the euro's (pre-)history are encouraged to proceed directly to the subsequent chapters.

The authors are deeply grateful to Lisa Baker for taking the time to read the manuscript and for offering thoughtful feedback that helped shape this book.

Limburg and Milwaukee, June 2025
Ann-Stephane Schäfer   Stefan Schäfer   Cory Wanek

1 Introduction: national money and international trade – a simple thought experiment

1.1 Money and its functions

"Europe is going to be created through the currency, or it is not created at all."[1] As early as 1950, the French politician and economist Jacques Rueff thus claimed that the European integration and monetary cooperation were inherently linked. Rueff was far ahead of his time. At the time, the idea of a European integration process – and in particular of a common currency – existed at best as a thought experiment in the minds of a few visionaries. After all, the continent had just been liberated from the National Socialists and, in the wake of the Second World War, economic activity and international trade had come to a complete standstill in large parts of Europe. Initially, close ties between the former wartime enemies, therefore, seemed almost inconceivable from a political as well as economic perspective. By the end of the 1940s, however, the national economies were growing again – and with them the efforts of the agricultural sector and industry to import primary products and export end products. The prerequisite for such a cross-border exchange of goods and services is, however, that money can flow in the opposite direction, because these trade goods have to be paid for.

But what kind of money is it that flows from one country to another? Since the second half of the 19th century, money had been organized nationally as an economic institution. At the time Jacques Rueff formulated the memorable quote above, every Western European country had its own currency as well as its central bank, which was vested with a monopoly note issue and administered this currency. As a generally accepted legal tender, the respective national money was part of the public infrastructure, fulfilling three basic functions that can be found in every economics textbook (▶ Fig. 1): Firstly, with its function as a means of payment, money is a universal transaction medium, which implies that its use enables trade partners to forgo barter trade, i. e., the direct exchange of goods. Secondly, with its function as a unit of account, money serves as a generally recognized measure of value. Thirdly, money functions as a store of value, i. e., it enables trade partners to separate the production

---

1 Jacques Rueff, L'Europe se fera par la monnaie ou ne se fera pas, in: Synthèses – Revue Mensuelle Internationale, Vol. 4, Fevrier 1950, pp. 267–271 (here: p. 267). Cf. Schäfer, S., "Eine kurze Geschichte der Europäischen Währungsunion", in: Aus Politik und Zeitgeschichte, vol. 72, issue 18–19/22, pp. 32–39.

and consumption of goods. Anyone who produces and sells something does not have to consume it immediately. Instead, they can save the proceeds for later consumption – for example, by simply keeping the money earned as cash at home.

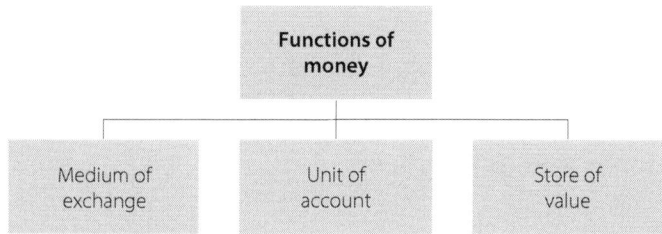

Fig. 1: Functions of money

The use of money is characterized by so-called network externalities: The more people use a certain money, the more likely it is that buyers will find a seller who accepts this money and that sellers will find buyers who want to pay with this money. The provision of money, therefore, tends towards monopolization – not only for the legal and political reasons mentioned above (legal tender, dominant role of the central bank) but also because of these network effects. This is why, in Rueff's time, there were as many currencies as there were nation states, and every nation state in Europe had 'its money.'[2] From an internal perspective, this set-up was efficient for each individual country.

1.2 International trade and the balance of payments

If we leave the national level, the matter becomes more complicated. In order to grasp the basic problem, let us take a mental journey back in time to the Mediterranean region of antiquity and, more precisely, to Ancient Rome and Ancient Athens. We assume that Rome produces wine and Athens produces olive oil and that the two cities trade with each other. Now, if Rome delivers wine to Athens, what money should Athens use to pay? The same question, of course, holds true the other way around: How should Rome settle the bill for the olive oil supplied by Athens? If Rome pays for the Athenian olive oil with sestertii, the Roman currency, this is of little use to the olive oil producers in Athens. This is because their workers and the suppliers of the preliminary products and machinery (e.g., oil mills) expect to be paid in drachmas, the Athenian currency, for their services and goods; after all, they are not able to

---

2   One exception here is Luxembourg, which was part of a monetary union with Belgium until the introduction of the Euro in 1999.

make use of sestertii in Athens. Similarly, Roman winegrowers have nothing to gain from receiving drachmas for their wine.

What is missing here is international money, which can serve as a transaction medium, a unit of account and a store of value for Romans and Athenians alike. In the 19th and 20th centuries, these tasks were fulfilled first by gold, then by the British pound and finally by the US dollar. Anyone who was paid with them knew that they could easily convert them into their own national currency. This still applies today: A German exporter can accept US dollars for his goods without hesitation because there are always euro owners who are willing to exchange their euros for the exporter's dollar earnings due to the high international acceptance of the dollar. The exporter can use the euros acquired in this way to pay his employees and suppliers in Germany. At all times, national and international transactions are – and were – thus linked in monetary terms.

In our thought experiment, Rome and Athens do not (initially) have such options. This is not a problem as long as the wine delivered from Rome to Athens has the same value as the olive oil delivered from Athens to Rome. In this simple case, the two cities do not have to leave the barter economy stage. In economic terms, their respective current accounts (where imports and exports are recorded, among other things) is balanced. In terms of value, both Rome and Athens export as much as they import (▶ Fig. 2).

Fig. 2: Current accounts at barter economy stage

CURRENT ACCOUNTS			
Athens		Rome	
Exports	Imports	Exports	Imports
Value of olive oil delivered	= Value of wine received	Value of wine delivered	= Value of olive oil received

In the next step, we want to move on to a monetary economy and expand our example accordingly. We then assume that the wine ordered by the Athenians in Rome costs 100 sestertii (S) and the olive oil ordered by the Romans in Athens costs 200 drachmas (D). We also assume that there is an exchange rate agreed on between the two cities: One sestertius is worth two drachmas or one drachma is worth half a sestertius. This exchange rate is treated as given (▶ Fig. 3).

1 Introduction: national money and international trade

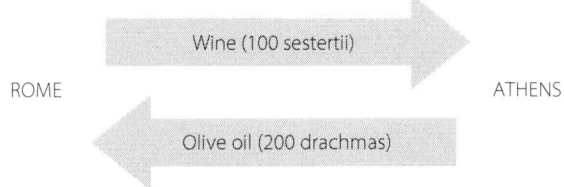

Fig. 3: The monetary value of the traded goods

The exchange rate is the price of a unit of the domestic currency expressed in units of a foreign currency (indirect quotation) or the price of a unit of the foreign currency expressed in units of the domestic currency (direct quotation). The exchange rate according to the indirect quotation thus corresponds to the reciprocal of the exchange rate in direct quotation and vice versa.

Example:

1 sestertius = 2 drachmas (indirect quotation from a Roman perspective, direct quotation from an Athenian perspective)	corresponds to	1 drachma = 0.5 sestertii (direct quotation from the Roman perspective, indirect quotation from the Athenian perspective)

The – still balanced – current account balances then look as follows (▶ Fig. 4).

Fig. 4: Current accounts at the monetary economy stage

CURRENT ACCOUNTS			
Athens		Rome	
Exports	Imports	Exports	Imports
Value of olive oil delivered (200 drachmas) =	Value of wine received (200 drachmas)	Value of wine delivered (100 sestertii) =	Value of olive oil received (100 sestertii)

Even though in this case (▶ Fig. 4) we are pro forma considering a monetary economy, what takes place is de facto still a barter transaction. Rome delivers wine to Athens, receives 200 drachmas in return and buys olive oil with these 200 drachmas. Or expressed in sestertii: Athens supplies Rome with olive oil, receives 100 sestertii in return and buys wine with these 100 sestertii. The entry in the current account is made in the respective national currency.

But what happens if the value of the deliveries from one trading partner exceeds the value of the deliveries from the other? Let us assume that bad weather has severely affected the grape harvest in Rome. In the following example, Rome therefore only delivers half as much wine as before, i.e., the equivalent of 50 sestertii or 100 drachmas (▶ Fig. 5).

1.2 International trade and the balance of payments

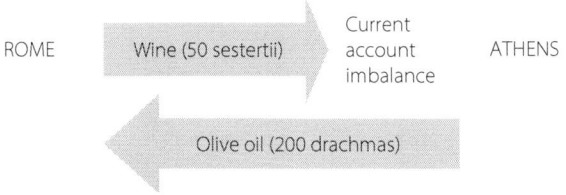

Fig. 5: A current account imbalance

Now Rome only receives 100 drachmas for its wine delivery for which it can buy olive oil. If Rome wants to continue buying olive oil worth the equivalent of 200 drachmas, there is an imbalance. The Roman current account now shows a deficit, the Athenian one a surplus (▶ Fig. 6).

Fig. 6: Current accounts with imbalances

CURRENT ACCOUNTS							
Athens				Rome			
Exports		Imports		Exports		Imports	
Value of olive oil delivered (200 drachmas)	>	Value of wine received (100 drachmas)		Value of wine delivered (50 sestertii)	<	Value of olive oil received (100 sestertii)	
Surplus: 100 drachmas				Deficit: 50 sestertii			

This raises the question of how Rome can finance the (as yet unpaid) olive oil worth the equivalent of 50 sestertii or 100 drachmas. The simplest possibility would be a so-called trade credit: Athens could initially supply Rome with this olive oil without payment, i. e., grant a loan of 100 drachmas. Athens would be the creditor, Rome the debtor.

As soon as the current accounts of the countries involved are no longer balanced, assets and liabilities arise, which are recorded in another balance sheet, the so-called capital account (▶ Fig. 7).

Fig. 7: Capital accounts

CAPITAL ACCOUNTS			
Athens		Rome	
Increase in liabilities	Increase in assets	Increase in liabilities	Increase in assets
	Loan granted to Rome (100 drachmas)	Liability to Athens (50 sestertii)	

A country's balance of payments should record all economic transactions with other countries according to the principle of double-entry bookkeeping. It essentially consists of the current account and the capital account. The current account records the cross-border movement of goods and services, while the capital account records the creation of cross-border receivables and liabilities. In our example, the balance of payments looks as follows (▶ Fig. 8).

Fig. 8: Balances of payments

BALANCE OF PAYMENTS ATHENS		BALANCE OF PAYMENTS ROME	
CURRENT ACCOUNT		CURRENT ACCOUNT	
Exports	Imports	Exports	Imports
Value of olive oil delivered (200 drachmas)	Value of wine received (100 drachmas)	Value of wine delivered (50 sestertii)	Value of olive oil received (100 sestertii)
CAPITAL ACCOUNT		CAPITAL ACCOUNT	
Increase in liabilities	Increase in assets	Increase in liabilities	Increase in assets
	Loan granted to Rome (100 drachmas)	Liability to Athens (50 sestertii)	
TOTAL: 200 drachmas	TOTAL: 200 drachmas	TOTAL: 100 sestertii	TOTAL: 100 sestertii

Both balances of payments are balanced. This is because the balances of the current account and the capital account always balance each other out. The Athenian current account surplus of 100 drachmas is offset by the build-up of receivables from Rome in the amount of 100 drachmas; similarly, the Roman current account deficit of 50 sestertii is balanced ("financed") by the build-up of liabilities in the same amount.

1.3 Foreign exchange market and currency system

The international movement of goods is facilitated if there is a functioning foreign exchange market[3] on which currencies can be freely bought and sold. In our case, the Roman importers could buy the 100 drachmas still required in exchange for 50 sestertii to settle the outstanding olive oil bill. The Athenian oil mill owners would then have received the full 200 drachmas for the olive oil delivered and could pay their workers and suppliers.

---

3   Foreign exchange refers to foreign book money (current account balances in foreign currency) or, more generally, receivables denominated in foreign currency. This is to be distinguished from foreign notes and coins (foreign cash).

However, this raises the question from whom the Roman importers could receive the 100 drachmas in exchange for 50 sestertii. Or, to put it another way, who offers foreign currency and who demands it? To answer this, let us look at the options that Romans and Athenians have in our thought experiment when they want to buy or sell goods or invest capital internationally.

The relationships between the imports and exports of goods and foreign exchange supply and demand are as follows (▶ Fig. 9).

Fig. 9: Current account transactions and the foreign exchange market

	Imports of goods	**Exports of goods**
Principle	...lead to the supply of domestic currency and demand for foreign currency	...lead to the supply of foreign currency and demand for domestic currency
Example	Roman importers offer sestertii and ask for drachmas to buy olive oil with drachmas in Athens Athenian importers offer drachmas and ask for sestertii to buy wine with the sestertii in Rome	Roman exporters receive drachmas for their wine. They offer them and ask for sestertii in order to pay their workers and suppliers with the sestertii. Athenian exporters receive sestertii for their olive oil. They offer them and ask for drachmas so that they can use them to pay their workers and suppliers.

Similarly, capital account transactions create supply and demand on the foreign exchange market (▶ Fig. 10).

Fig. 10: Capital account transactions and the foreign exchange market

	Capital investment abroad	**Raising of funds abroad**
Principle	...leads to supply of domestic currency and demand for foreign currency	...leads to supply of foreign currency and demand for domestic currency
Example	Roman investors offer sestertii and ask for drachmas to acquire assets in Athens (e.g., real estate) Athenian investors offer drachmas and ask for sestertii in order to acquire assets in Rome (e.g., real estate)	Romans receive a drachma loan from Athens. In order to invest in Rome, they offer these borrowed drachmas and ask for sestertii. Athenians receive a loan of sestertii from Rome. In order to invest in Athens, they offer these borrowed sestertii and ask for drachmas

As we will see later, the exchange rate is formed on the foreign exchange market through the interplay of current account and capital account transactions.

1.4 The design of the international monetary system

The thought experiment above has demonstrated the link between international goods and capital transactions, their recording in the balance of payments and the foreign exchange market. The reality is, of course, much more complex. Around the globe, billions of consumers, millions of companies and hundreds of countries are in constant exchange with each other. The cross-border flow of goods and services as well as of capital (defined as receivables and liabilities or assets) cannot take place in a vacuum, just as the trade in foreign exchange cannot. A large number of international agreements regulate the conditions under which current account, capital account and foreign exchange market transactions between residents of different countries are possible. The sum of these agreements is known as the 'international monetary system.' The central question is to what extent and under what conditions exporters, importers and investors have access to foreign exchange in order to sell goods, services and assets abroad or to buy from abroad. There are basically the following options here:

- Foreign exchange control:
  Access to foreign exchange is strictly regulated by the state; there is no free movement of goods and capital abroad.
- Fixed exchange rate system:
  Foreign currency can be bought and sold freely but at rates set by the state. The movement of goods (apart from customs duties) is generally largely free, but there may be restrictions regarding the movement of capital.
- System of flexible exchange rates:
  Foreign currencies can be bought and sold freely; the exchange rates are constantly set based on supply and demand on the foreign exchange market. The movement of goods is generally largely free (apart from customs duties), but there may be restrictions regarding the movement of capital.
- Monetary union:
  Several countries join forces, irrevocably fix the exchange rates of their currencies or introduce a common currency and delegate monetary policy to a supranational central bank. Goods and capital transactions are generally possible without restrictions in the monetary union.

After the Second World War, the European states tried out all four options – both internally, i.e., between the European currencies, and externally, i.e., in relation to the US dollar, for example. As members of the European Monetary Union, 20 of them are currently part of what is possibly the biggest experiment in the history of money: 80 years after the end of the Second World War and 75 years after Jacques Rueff's vision quoted in the beginning of this chapter, 350 million Europeans are paying with one common currency, the euro!

2 Background: The long road to the euro (1945–1989)

2.1 A new start after the war: Bilateralism, European Payments Union and the Treaty of Rome

2.1.1 The years of so-called 'bilateralism'

Nowadays, most of the world's currencies are convertible. They can be bought and sold on the foreign exchange market. In addition, there are international financial service providers with a wide range of services and a cross-border payment transaction infrastructure. This significantly streamlines the process of settling payments for goods, services, and investment assets among importers, exporters, tourists, business travelers, and international investors.

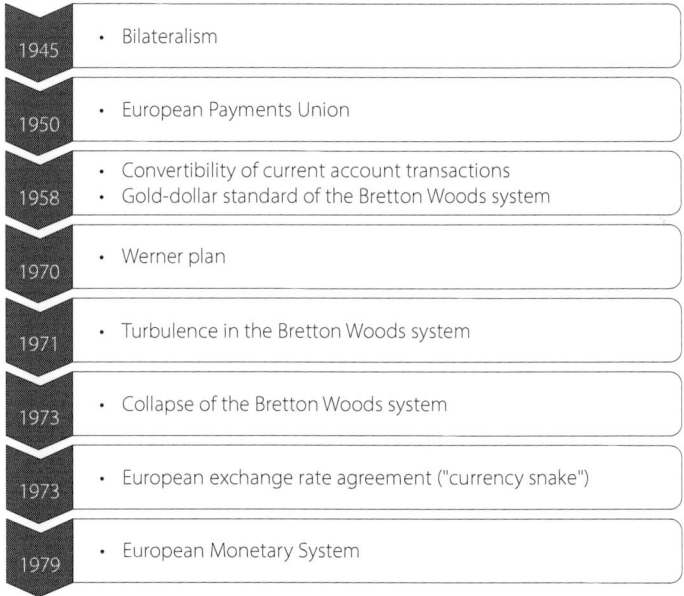

Fig. 11: Historical developments preceding the euro

Europe was far removed from such a monetary situation immediately after the Second World War. There was no foreign exchange market in today's sense nor were there any globally integrated commercial banks. Instead, foreign exchange controls prevailed: cross-border transactions were strictly regulated and generally subject to approval. Fixed exchange rates (known as parities or central rates) were agreed upon internationally and administratively prescribed for importers and exporters. Foreign exchange transactions for the payment of international deliveries of goods generally had to be processed via the central banks of the countries in which the importer and exporter had their registered office.

Figure 12 illustrates this using German-Belgian trade relations as an example. At the center is the agreement between the German Bundesbank and the National Bank of Belgium to provide each other with their own currency (1). Belgian companies wishing to import German products needed Deutschmarks (DM) to do so. Due to foreign exchange controls, they could only obtain these from the National Bank of Belgium. Similarly, German companies had to turn to the Bundesbank if they needed Belgian francs (BEF) to pay for imported products from Belgium (2). The Belgian or German importers could then pay for the imported goods in Deutschmarks or Belgian francs (3).

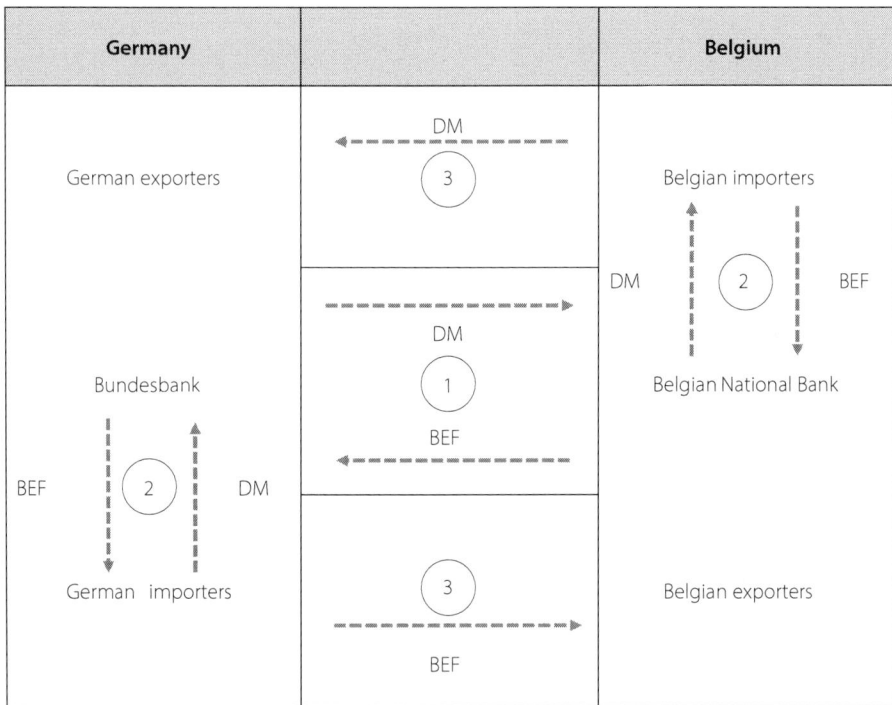

Fig. 12: Example of trade and currency exchange in the era of bilateralism

As long as German and Belgian imports and exports balanced each other out in terms of value, this arrangement was administratively complex yet fundamentally feasible. Converted at the valid exchange rate, the goods that Germany supplied to Belgium cost the same as the Belgian goods that were sold in the opposite direction. In this situation, the German Bundesbank and the Belgian National Bank exchanged DM and BEF volumes, which also balanced each other out in terms of value.

Things became more complicated in the case of current account imbalances, i.e., when the exports of one country were higher than those of the other. If the value of German exports to Belgium exceeded that of Belgian exports to Germany, more DM had to flow from the Bundesbank to the National Bank of Belgium than Belgian francs from the National Bank of Belgium to the Bundesbank. The National Bank of Belgium built up a liability with the Bundesbank in the amount of the Belgian current account deficit; similarly, the Bundesbank booked a credit claim against the National Bank of Belgium in the amount of the German current account surplus.

This configuration could occur between all trading partners in the years after 1945. The legal basis was provided by more than 200 agreements that the (Western) European states concluded bilaterally and with non-European states. This phase of economic relations is therefore referred to as 'bilateralism.' In the bilateral agreements, two countries (or the central banks of these two countries) always granted each other limited credit lines. This means that they were prepared to lend their own currency to the central banks of their trading partners up to a certain maximum amount. These central banks then forwarded the foreign currency to the importers in their country, who could use it to pay their invoices. Within the framework of these credit lines, the two central banks involved bilaterally offset the receivables and liabilities from foreign trade. The internationally agreed exchange rate applied.

If a country's import requirements exceeded its credit line with another country, the difference had to be paid in dollars or gold. Such a situation was to be avoided in order to conserve the already chronically scarce foreign exchange reserves[4]. The only way out was to restrict imports through import quotas and tariffs. Ideally, liabilities to foreign countries are not to be incurred in the first place.

For our example, this means (▶ Fig. 13): The Bundesbank and the National Bank of Belgium could have granted each other a credit line of DM 20 million and BEF 238 million respectively.[5] If German exports in a certain period (e.g., one quarter) had a value of DM 70 million and Belgian exports a value of BEF 476 million, this resulted in a German export surplus of DM 30 million (or BEF 357 million at the exchange rate at the time). This was the balance of the credit relationship between the Bundesbank and the National Bank of Belgium. As the balance exceeded the mutually agreed credit line by DM 10 million, the Belgian National Bank had to deliver gold and/or dollars to the Bundesbank in this amount. In addition, the Bundesbank had a credit claim

---

4 Foreign exchange reserves (also: currency reserves) are the stock of internationally accepted means of payment held by a central bank (primarily gold and dollars).
5 The exchange rate was 1 DM = 11.9 BEF.

of DM 20 million against the National Bank of Belgium. In order to prevent a further depletion of its currency reserves, the Belgian government might in such a situation have tried to reduce Belgian imports from Germany and thus the Belgian current account deficit by imposing tariffs on German products to such an extent that the foreign exchange reserves of the Belgian National Bank would no longer be utilized in the future.

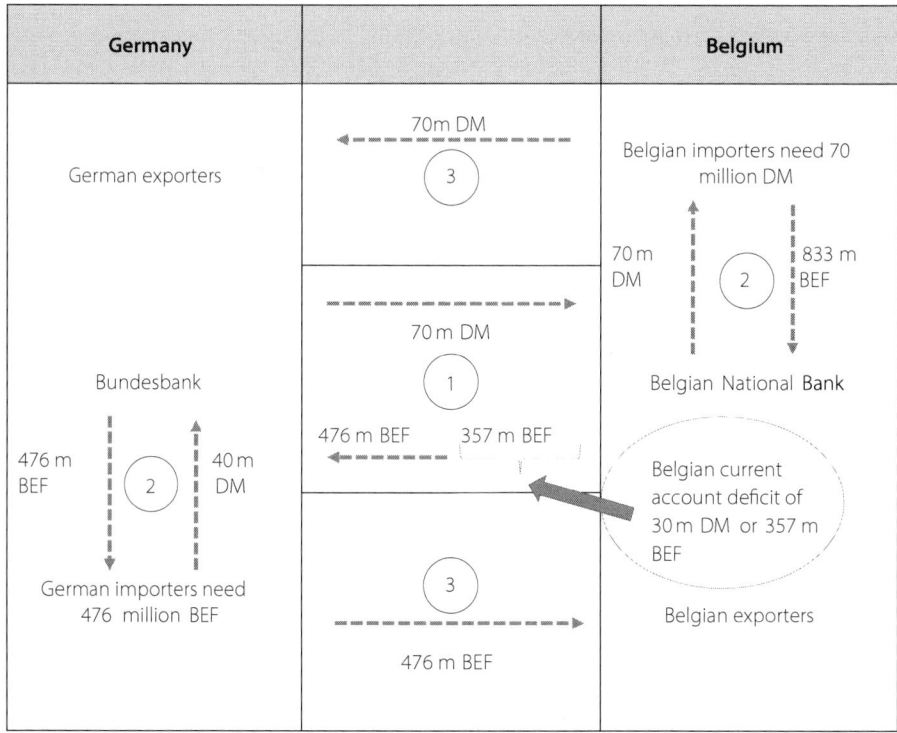

Fig. 13: Financing of current account deficits in the era of bilateralism (exchange rate 1 DM = 11.9 BEF)

The results for the balances of payments of Germany and Belgium are the following: The Belgian current account deficit of BEF 357 million or DM 30 million leads to a liability of the Belgian National Bank to the Bundesbank of BEF 238 million or DM 20 million within the framework of the agreed credit line. The BEF 119 million or DM 10 million in excess of the credit line must be settled in gold and/or dollars and lead to a corresponding decrease in the Belgian foreign exchange reserves and an increase in the German foreign exchange reserves. This is recorded in the official reserves account (▶ Fig. 14).

With the addition of the official reserves account, our stylized example balance of payments is complete (▶ Fig. 8). It now shows the main relationships between the current account on the one hand and the capital account and the official reserves account on the other. The German current account surplus leads to a build-up of foreign assets, in this case in the form of credit claims against the Belgian National Bank and to additional currency reserves. The Belgian current account deficit must be financed, as Belgium receives more German goods in terms of value than it delivers to Germany. In return, Belgium becomes indebted to Germany and also gives up some of its currency reserves.

Fig. 14: Exemplary balances of payments (Germany vs. Belgium)

BALANCE OF PAYMENTS GERMANY		BALANCE OF PAYMENTS BELGIUM	
CURRENT ACCOUNT		CURRENT ACCOUNT	
Exports	Imports	Exports	Imports
DM 70 million	DM 40 million	BEF 476 million	BEF 833 million
CAPITAL ACCOUNT		CAPITAL ACCOUNT	
Increase in liabilities	Increase in receivables	Increase in liabilities	Increase in receivables
	DM 20 million	BEF 238 million	
OFFICIAL RESERVES ACCOUNT		OFFICIAL RESERVES ACCOUNT	
Decrease	Increase	Decrease	Increase
	DM 10 million	BEF 119 million	
TOTAL: DM 70 million	TOTAL: DM 70 million	TOTAL: BEF 833 million	TOTAL: BEF 833 million

This reveals a central relationship in international macroeconomics: surplus countries build up foreign assets, deficit countries borrow abroad and reduce foreign assets (here: foreign exchange reserves).

In reality, economic transactions between a country and other countries are more complex and are recorded in this country's balance of payments according to Figure 15.

The current account is broken down into the balance of trade (goods transactions), the balance of services (balance of cross-border purchases and sales of services, including tourism services), the balance of primary income (cross-border compensation of employees and investment income, e. g., wages or interest earned abroad) and the balance of secondary income (current transfers). The latter refers to cross-border payments without a direct return service from the other country. Examples include remittances from migrant workers to their countries of origin, ongoing development aid payments or payments to international organizations. Due to the quantitative importance of the trade balance within the current account, the terms 'current account' and 'trade balance' are often used interchangeably. This can lead to serious misjudgements, because it is entirely possible for a country with a trade deficit to generate such high surpluses in the three other current account sub-balances that the current account balance is also positive overall.

Fig. 15: The balance of payments and its sub-balances

BALANCE OF PAYMENTS	
CURRENT ACCOUNT	
Exports of goods	Imports of goods
Exports of services	Imports of services
Primary income received from abroad (compensation of employees and investment income)	Primary income paid abroad (compensation of employees and investment income)
Secondary income received from abroad (current transfers)	Secondary income paid abroad (current transfers)
CAPITAL ACCOUNT	
Increase in liabilities	Increase in receivables
Asset transfers from abroad	Transfer of assets abroad
Sale of domestic assets to foreigners ('non-residents')	Purchase of foreign assets by nationals ("residents')
OFFICIAL RESERVE ACCOUNT	
Decrease in foreign exchange reserve	Increase in foreign exchange reserves

In addition to the increase or decrease in cross-border assets and liabilities and the cross-border purchase and sale of assets, the capital account also includes so-called capital transfers. These are one-off changes in the cross-border asset position without a direct return, such as inheritances or debt relief as part of development cooperation.

Contrary to what its name suggests, the balance of payments and its sub-balances are not balance sheets in the sense of a comparison of the stock of assets and capital at a point in time (e.g., month-end, quarter-end or year-end). Rather, the balance of payments is kept over a period of time (e.g., month, quarter or year) and records flows.

2.1.2 The European Payments Union

The more the European economies recovered from the consequences of the war and the more they traded with each other again, the more problematic the bilateral settlement of payments via the two central banks involved became. The convertibility of currencies and the freedom of trade urgently needed to be restored, ideally reaching at least the level of the interwar period. This was the aim of the European Payments Union (EPU), which was established in 1950 under the umbrella of the Organization for European Economic Cooperation (OEEC). The Bank for International Settlements in Basel (BIS) was responsible for the technical implementation. The core of the EPU were bilateral loans between the participating central banks, which were balanced once a month and settled multilaterally by the BIS. This meant that the balances of each country no longer had to be settled with a two-digit number of trading partners, but rather only with the EPU.

Fig. 16: Exemplary settlement of bilateral balances by the EPU (current account balances converted into million $)

	France	Germany	Italy	Balancing by EPU
France		−20	+10	−10
Germany	+20		−10	10
Italy	−10	+10		0

Figure 16 shows how the EPU worked based the example of three countries. Let us assume that Germany has a current account surplus of $20 million with France and a current account deficit of $10 million with Italy.[6] Also, France has a current account surplus of $10 million with Italy. In the era of bilateralism, each country would have had to monitor its balances with all other countries and (if the credit line was exceeded) partially settle them in foreign exchange reserves. The EPU considerably simplified trade and currency relations by netting out all bilateral balances so that only one balance remained for each country, namely the balance with the EPU.

Part of the deficit balances vis-à-vis the EPU was granted as a loan, the rest had to be settled in gold or dollars. The higher the deficits, the higher the proportion that had to be settled with foreign exchange reserves.

If a country consistently recorded high foreign trade deficits, i.e., consistently imported significantly more than it exported, sooner or later it was at risk of running out of foreign exchange reserves. This is referred to as a structural balance of payments problem. In this case, there was the option of adjusting the central rates (i.e., the official exchange rates of the respective country's currency against individual or all ECU currencies). The aim of such an exchange rate adjustment is to make exports cheaper by devaluing the currency of the country with structural balance of payments problems. Here is a simplified example: Let us assume that France wants to reduce its current account deficit with Germany (USD 20 million). To this end, France requests a reduction of the DM price of a franc from 0.8336 DM to 0.75 DM. This makes an exemplary French product with a price of FF 100 cheaper for German buyers. Its DM price falls from DM 83.36 to DM 75. At the same time, it becomes more expensive for French people to buy German products. A German product with a price of 100 DM no longer costs 119.96 FF after the exchange rate adjustment, but 133.33 FF. In the

---

6 The US dollar assumes the function of the international unit of account here. For this purpose, bilateral claims and liabilities between the central banks are converted at the internationally agreed dollar exchange rates.

simplest case, the change in parity causes French exports to rise while the country's imports fall. The current account deficit decreases.

If a deficit country wanted to avoid both a devaluation of its currency and the depletion of its currency reserves, it could restrict imports through direct political intervention. This could be either import duties or direct quantitative restrictions. Import duties, as a tax on imported goods, make their purchase less attractive; direct quantity restrictions set a certain quantity that may be imported annually of a certain good. It would also have been possible for the central bank of the deficit country to refuse or make foreign exchange transactions more difficult as soon as they contributed to an increase in the trade deficit. Importers would then no longer have received foreign currency (at least in the quantity they wanted), which would have limited or possibly even reduced imports and thus the current account deficit.

However, measures of this kind impaired international trade relations. They were thus diametrically opposed to the declared aim of some Western European governments that their countries should grow together economically and politically. The process of growing together in the sense of a Europeanization of national economies reached an initial high point with the 'Treaty of Rome.'

2.1.3 The "Treaty of Rome"

The path to today's European Union began with the "European Coal and Steel Community" (1951). The Treaty of Rome of 1957 then constituted the "European Atomic Energy Community" and, in particular, the European Economic Community (EEC). Both began their activities on January 1, 1958. This gave rise to the "European Communities" (EC) in 1967 and the European Union (EU) in 1993. With the EEC, the six founding members (Belgium, Germany, France, Italy, Luxembourg and the Netherlands) pursued the goal of establishing a common market with free movement of goods, services, people and capital. Later, they also sought to establish a 'Common Agricultural Policy' (CAP). In connection with this, a customs union was to be created, which would be characterized by common tariffs vis-à-vis third countries and the comprehensive abolition of restrictions on trade between the EEC states. The implementation of the plans was to be completed within twelve years, i.e., by 1970.

These economic and trade policy goals, which were ambitious for the time, were contrasted by a conspicuous restraint in monetary policy. In the 'Treaty of Rome,' which constituted the European Economic Community, paragraph 1 of Article 107 states succinctly: "Each Member State shall treat its policy in the field of exchange rates as a matter of common concern." Previously, Article 104 had declared the safeguarding of confidence in the currency to be a national task: "Each Member State shall conduct the economic policies necessary to maintain equilibrium in its overall balance of payments and to maintain confidence in its currency while safeguarding a high level of employment and price stability."

The tension between exchange rate developments as a matter of common interest and national responsibility for monetary policy was reflected institutionally in the

'Monetary Committee' pursuant to Art. 105(2). Its powers hardly went beyond the role of an observer of the monetary, financial and payments system. The same applies to the 'Committee of Governors of the Central Banks of the Member states of the European Economic Community' ('Committee of Governors'). It was set up in 1964. Its task was to promote cooperation between the national central banks through consultations and a regular exchange of information.

Fig. 17: The road to a united Europe

1951	European Coal and Steel Community
1957	European Atomic Energy Community; European Economic Community Members: Belgium, France, Germany, Italy, Luxembourg, Netherlands
1967	The three Communities merge to form the 'European Communities' (EC)
1973	Expansion to include Denmark, Great Britain and Ireland
1981	Accession of Greece
1986	Accession of Spain and Portugal
1992	Maastricht Treaty
1993	European Single Market The EC becomes the European Union (EU)
1995	Expansion by Finland, Austria and Sweden
1999	Monetary union
2003	Eastward enlargement: Estonia, Latvia, Lithuania, Malta, Poland, Slovenia, Slovakia, Czech Republic, Hungary, Cyprus join the EU
2007	Accession of Romania and Bulgaria
2013	Accession of Croatia
2020	Brexit

The importance of monetary policy for the integration of Europe was therefore well known in the 1950s and 1960s; however, there were no significant steps towards monetary integration of the six founding members of the EEC beyond the resolution of practical problems relating to payment transactions and convertibility. Nor did these seem necessary (at first), as the period from the end of the 1950s to the mid/late 1960s was characterized by a stable macroeconomic environment with low inflation and unemployment as well as relative exchange rate stability in the Bretton Woods environment.

2.2 Western Europe's currencies in the Bretton Woods era

2.2.1 The gold-dollar standard – an overview

Until the early 1970s, fixed exchange rates within the framework of the Bretton Woods system characterized the world's currency markets. Fixed exchange rates are intended to give importers, exporters, capital investors and politicians planning security by setting a key macroeconomic variable as essentially unchangeable. The exchange rate can be fixed either by administrative determination or by means of foreign exchange market intervention. In the early years after the Second World War, when there was not yet a developed foreign exchange market in the modern sense; the governments set bilateral central rates administratively. Based on these rates, (almost) all foreign exchange transactions were settled via the two central banks involved (▶ Ch. 2.1.1). Alternatively, if foreign exchange controls are lifted and a foreign exchange market exists, the central banks can influence supply and demand on the foreign exchange market through targeted purchases and sales (interventions) so that exchange rates do not move (too far) away from the desired level (central rate, parity). Currencies are convertible with one another, but at politically determined exchange rates.

This is exactly how fixed exchange rates worked in the Bretton Woods system. The framework for international economic relations negotiated in 1944 in the small US town of Bretton Woods, New Hampshire, provided for the West to trade goods as freely as possible. The shortage economy of the post-war years was to be a thing of the past, as were the economic conflicts of the interwar period. For currency relations in Europe, this meant that a new order for the international exchange of currencies would replace the exchange controls that had been in place in the second half of the 1940s and early 1950s. The increasingly free global foreign exchange market gradually replaced the currency exchange previously managed by the central banks with its administratively fixed exchange rates. The conditions of monetary relations between countries were no longer determined by control and coercion but by the self-commitment of states within a supranational framework.

The liberalization of currency relations initially applied primarily to current account transactions, i.e., essentially cross-border trade in goods and services. In particular, trade in goods and services was to be promoted through fixed exchange rates. Capital account transactions, i.e., the international exchange of ownership of assets (securities, real estate, etc.) were not the focus and could be further restricted by means of government measures. This reflects the view of the global economy at the time: the aim was to achieve the freest trade in goods and services possible and predictable exchange rates; financial globalization as we know it today, on the other hand, seemed unimaginable to most people at the time.

Fig. 18: Structure, objectives and basis the Bretton Woods system

	Institutional set-up	
International Monetary Fund (IMF)	Gold backing of the US dollar (redemption obligation of the Federal Reserve at $35 per troy ounce)	Fixed exchange rates of the member countries' currencies vis-à-vis the dollar
	Objective: Stable framework for the global trade in goods	
	Basis: Currency convertibility for current account transactions	

However, the Bretton Woods system was more than just a system of fixed exchange rates. As an international gold-dollar standard, it rested on three pillars (▶ Fig. 18):

1. As a supranational organization, the International Monetary Fund (IMF) formed the organizational backbone of the Bretton Woods system. It was tasked with monitoring the functioning of the gold-dollar mechanism and analyzing the balance of payments situation of the member countries.
2. The US Federal Reserve ('Fed') guaranteed the other central banks in the system the redemption of dollars in gold at a price of 35 dollars per troy ounce. Its task was also to keep the gold price at 35 dollars per troy ounce by buying and selling gold. This meant that every currency was indirectly backed by gold. This was because they could be exchanged for dollars at a fixed rate, which in turn could be exchanged for gold at 35 US dollars per troy ounce.
3. The exchange rates of the most important currencies had been fixed against the dollar since 1958 at the latest. Each currency had a bilateral central rate ('parity') against the dollar. The actual exchange rate was not allowed to deviate by more than one percent above or below the central rate. The central banks in the system had to keep the exchange rate of their respective currencies against the US dollar within this range. The US Federal Reserve was not obliged to defend the dollar exchange rate. Changes to the bilateral dollar central rates had to be coordinated multilaterally – i.e., with the IMF and the other participating countries. The prerequisite for this was the determination of a 'fundamental imbalance in the balance of payments' for the country that wanted to apply for a parity change. Its current account balance had to be permanently clearly positive or negative.

If such a fundamental balance of payments imbalance[7] existed, there were basically two options: [1] Either the country concerned received a strong recommendation to address the causes of the external imbalance through economic policy measures. For

---

7   Strictly speaking, the term 'balance of payments imbalance' is an oxymoron because, by definition, the balance of payments is always balanced. What is meant here is a positive or negative current account balance that is offset by a balance of the capital account or the balance of foreign exchange reserves with the opposite sign.

example, a deficit country could be required to increase the competitiveness of its export industry (e. g., by lowering taxes and reducing bureaucracy) in order to reduce the current account deficit. The implementation of a corresponding catalog of measures could be a condition for an IMF aid loan ("conditionality" of the aid loan). [2] Or an adjustment of the dollar central rate of the currency of the country with the structural balance of payments imbalance was initiated. If it was a surplus country, the currency was revalued in order to reduce its exports and increase its imports. Whereas the currency of a deficit country was devalued accordingly in order to achieve the opposite effect on exports and imports.

2.2.2 How can fixed exchange rates be achieved?

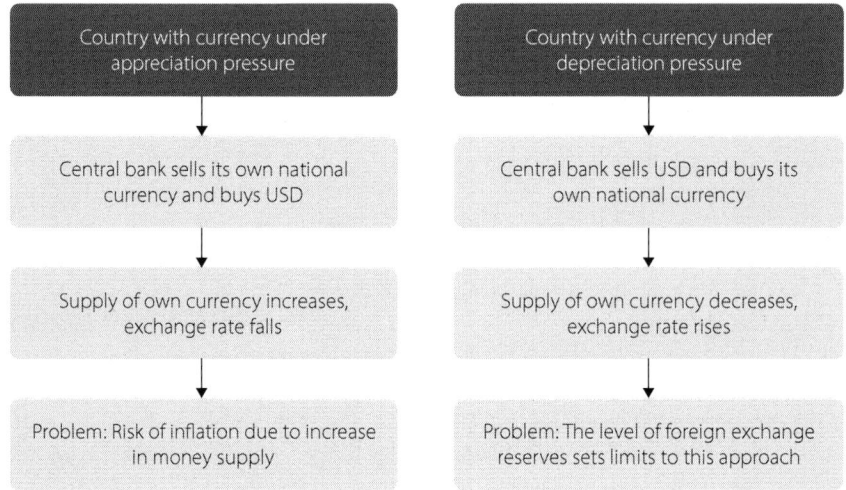

Fig. 19: Foreign exchange market interventions in the Bretton Woods system

The economic mechanisms on which the Bretton Woods system was based are explained step-by-step below. The focus is on the question of how a politically desired fixing of exchange rates is possible on free foreign exchange markets with convertible currencies.

Here is an example: The central rate (or parity) between the US dollar and the Deutschmark in the post-war period was 1 $ = 4.20 DM (or 1 DM = 0.2381 $). At the end of the 1950s, Americans increasingly demanded Deutschmarks because Germany manufactured attractive products and/or because it was an attractive investment location for them. Therefore, Americans needed Deutschmarks to import German products or to buy assets in Germany (real estate, shares, etc.). This increased demand exerted appreciation pressure on the Deutschmark exchange rate. In order to be able to buy the attractive products or assets from Germany, the Americans would have been prepared to pay 0.25 (instead of 0.2381) dollars for one Deutschmark, for example. The Deutschmark would therefore have been appreciated and the dollar depreciated. The new exchange rate would then have been 1 $ = 4 DM. In the Bretton Woods system, it was now the Bundesbank's task to prevent this. It had to offer Deutschmarks on the foreign exchange market at a fixed exchange rate of only 1 DM = 0.2381 $ and thus satisfy the increased American demand for Deutschmarks. The increased supply of Deutschmarks – due to the Bundesbank's interventions – kept the exchange rate at 1 DM = 0.2381 $ or 1 $ = 4.20 DM.

Fig. 20: Core elements of a fixed exchange rate system

	Description	Bretton Woods system
Parity central rate	Politically desired fixed exchange rate between two currencies	Dollar exchange rates for the currencies of the participating countries
Bandwidth	Range in which the exchange rate may deviate upwards and downwards from parity	+/– 1 %
Obligation to intervene	Asymmetric: obligation limited to one of the two countries to secure the fixed exchange rate by buying and selling the two currencies Symmetric: obligation of both countries to secure the fixed exchange rate by buying and selling the two currencies	Asymmetric: no intervention obligation for the Federal Reserve, but only for the respective central bank of the IMF member country
Rules for parity adjustment	Conditions under which the parity can be changed (adjustable peg)	Multilateral (in coordination with the IMF and the other member countries)
Assistance system	Support for countries that have to defend the exchange rate of a currency threatened with devaluation by selling foreign currency and are confronted with the finite nature of their foreign exchange reserves; usually provided in the form of loans	IMF loans possible, conditionality (e.g., implementation of structural policy measures as a condition)

If, as in this example, only one of the two central banks involved is obliged to intervene, it is an asymmetric fixed exchange rate system. The Bretton Woods system was explicitly asymmetric. Only the other central bank, not the Federal Reserve, was obliged to intervene if the exchange rate of a currency moved too far (= beyond the bandwidth[8] of +1 %/-1 %) from its parity.

In our example, the Bundesbank can theoretically intervene indefinitely because, as a central bank, it can produce the needed number of Deutschmarks required for

---

8   The example above is based on a point fixation of 1 $ = 4.20 DM. In reality, however, the aforementioned deviation of one percent upwards or downwards was possible.

its interventions itself. As a result, the Bundesbank's dollar holdings increase, but so does the number of Deutschmarks in circulation. The latter can lead to inflation. This is a form of so-called 'imported inflation.'

It is more difficult to fix an exchange rate if the currency in question is under devaluation pressure. For example, this would be the case if many French people wanted to buy American goods and assets. This would increase the supply of French francs and the demand for dollars on the foreign exchange market, which, ceteris paribus, would cause the price of the franc, i. e., its exchange rate, to fall below the value fixed within the framework of the Bretton Woods system. To prevent this from happening, the Banque de France was obliged to satisfy the additional demand for dollars. It had to sell US dollars in exchange for French francs. However, it could only do this as long as it had the corresponding dollar holdings – i. e., currency reserves. This variant of exchange rate fixing is therefore not possible indefinitely.

2.2.3 The EEC currencies in the Bretton Woods system

As Figure 21 shows, the exchange rate fixing in the Bretton Woods system was successful for the EEC members at first glance. Between 1958 and 1970, there were only isolated changes to the central rate. In 1961, the Dutch guilder and the German mark were revalued, in 1969 the French franc was devalued and the German mark was revalued once again. These exchange rate adjustments were highly controversial in domestic politics and only came about after lengthy discussions.

Fig. 21: Fixed exchange rates of EEC currencies in the Bretton Woods system (currency units per US dollar)

	German mark	French Franc	Dutch guilder	Belgian Franc	Italian Lira
1958	4,20	4,9371	3,80	50	625
1961	4,0	4,9371	3,62	50	625

This will be illustrated using the example of the two DM revaluations and the devaluation of the French franc. In the course of the 'economic miracle', the German mark had become an attractive investment currency by the late 1950s, which led to considerable upward pressure on its value. This was because the increasing demand for German assets was accompanied by increasing demand for the DM. The Bundesbank could respond to this in two ways: Firstly, with foreign exchange market interventions, in this case: with dollar purchases. This would increase the supply on the market for Deutschmarks as well as the demand for dollars and thus counteract the revaluation pressure. Secondly, the Bundesbank could attempt to dampen German interest rates and thus make interest-bearing assets relatively unattractive for foreigners in particular. Both policy options had a potentially expansive and price-driving effect and were therefore associated with inflationary risks.

Business associations and, surprisingly, the Bundesbank also opposed the revaluation of the DM in 1961. The business associations feared negative effects on the price competitiveness of German exports. A revaluation of the DM meant that foreign importers would have to pay more units of their own currency per DM. At a given DM price for German products, they would therefore also have to spend more units of their own currency. At the time, the Bundesbank did not consider parity adjustments to be a suitable foreign economic policy instrument – even though it naturally recognized the intervention obligations resulting from the undervaluation of the Deutschmark and the associated risk of inflation. Instead, the German central bankers advocated increasing the competitiveness of those countries from which capital flowed into Germany. If these countries had more attractive export products and investment assets, the problem would be less pressing or non-existent, they argued.

The devaluation of the franc and the revaluation of the Deutschmark also only took place in 1969, some time after the underlying problems (France's lack of competitiveness, Germany's foreign trade surpluses) had become manifest for the first time. In Germany, the trade associations again resisted the revaluation. In France, devaluation was perceived as a loss of face. In November 1968, the two governments therefore initially attempted to restore balanced current accounts with a combination of capital controls and import promotion: Regulatory requirements made it unattractive for German banks to accept foreign investment money, for example; this was intended to reduce the inflow of foreign capital. At the same time, changes to tax law came into force that made imports to Germany cheaper and exports more expensive. As a result, demand for the Deutschmark fell and with it the pressure to revalue, albeit only temporarily.

These two examples show how important fixed exchange rates were in the thinking of the time. They were associated with monetary stability, while flexible exchange rates were blamed for the instability before the Second World War. At the time, few people could imagine a stable development of international trade without a fixed exchange rate system. This applied not least to the members of the EEC, whose economies had grown ever closer together since the signing of the Treaty of Rome. In addition, the price system of the common agricultural policy – one of the most important policy areas of the EEC – was urgently dependent on reliable exchange rate relations in order to function. Governments therefore tended to delay exchange rate adjustments as long as possible.

2.2.4   The trilemma of monetary policy

We have already seen that in the long term, fixing exchange rates can lead to inflation in the trade surplus country and fail in the deficit trade country due to a lack of foreign exchange reserves.[9] In addition, the domestic money supply in circulation can fall in the deficit country, which can be accompanied by inflationary and recessionary tendencies.

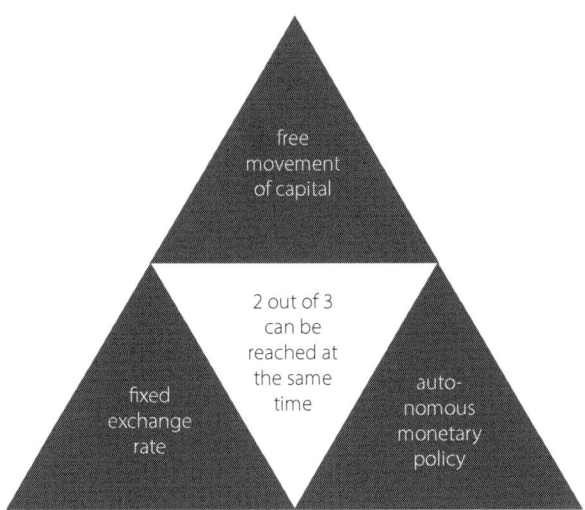

Fig. 22: The trilemma of monetary policy

This leads us to a phenomenon known as the 'trilemma of monetary policy' (or, 'impossible trinity'): of the three objectives of fixed exchange rates, free movement of capital and autonomous monetary policy, only two can ever be achieved simultaneously (▶ Fig. 22). In the Bretton Woods era, this meant that the participating states had to decide whether they wanted to combine the fixed exchange rates in force with free cross-border capital movements or an autonomous national monetary policy.

How can restricting the free movement of capital help countries to both fix their exchange rate and continue to control the amount of money in circulation? The starting point for this is the capital market-related part of the supply of and demand for domestic currency. Countries with currencies under appreciation pressure increase the supply and reduce the demand for their currency, while countries with currencies under devaluation pressure act in the opposite way. To this end, governments and central banks take regulatory measures with the aim of making financial transactions that lead to the purchase or sale of domestic currency either attractive or unattractive. Figure 23 provides an overview.

---

9   Surplus countries have a persistent current account surplus. The demand for their export goods drives the demand for their currencies and tends to put them under appreciation pressure. The reverse is true for deficit countries.

2.2 Western Europe's currencies in the Bretton Woods era

Fig. 23: Restrictions on capital movements

On the one hand, foreign exchange market interventions and capital controls are questionable in terms of regulatory policy because they represent direct state intervention in the workings of market forces on the foreign exchange and capital markets. On the other hand, they tend to be effective in the short term. We have already shown this with regard to foreign exchange market interventions. Restrictions on capital movements only have a limited effect in the medium and long term because financial market players find ways to circumvent them relatively quickly. As financial markets became increasingly mechanized, liberalized and internationalized after the Second World War, governments and central banks found it increasingly difficult to influence cross-border capital flows in their favor.

If a fixed exchange rate is to be sustainable in the long term, there is therefore no way around the participating countries aligning their economic policies. The inflation rate plays a special role here. The assumption is that a rising inflation rate will make all products (here: cars) more expensive in the medium term and on average due to higher prices of intermediate products and rising wages. Fixed exchange rate systems can hardly survive significantly diverging inflation rates in the long-term. If one country has a higher inflation rate than another, the country with the higher inflation rate loses competitiveness because its products become more expensive more quickly than those of the partner country. Figure 24 illustrates this relationship. We assume a fixed exchange rate between the US dollar and the German mark of 1:4. The American inflation rate is 5 %, the German 2 %. In the initial situation, an American car costs 1,000 $ (or 4,000 DM for German buyers) and a German car 4,000 DM (or 1,000 $ for American buyers). The price competitiveness of the American and German car industries is therefore initially the same.

Fig. 24: Diverging inflation rates and competitiveness

	American car		German car	
	Price in $	converted to DM	Price in DM	converted to $
Initial situation	1,000 $	4,000 DM	4,000 DM	1,000 $
1 year later	1,050 $	4,200 DM	4,080 DM	1,020 $

The different inflation rates mean that a German car is now cheaper than an American car for prospective buyers in both the US ($ 1,020 instead of $ 1,050) and Germany (DM 4,080 instead of DM 4,200). Although the nominal exchange rate (defined as the exchange rate of the two currencies on the foreign exchange market) remains unchanged (namely at 1:4), the relative prices of products for consumers in the two countries have changed. This is measured by the real exchange rate. It combines price and exchange rate changes. In this case, America has appreciated in real terms and Germany has depreciated in real terms.

If German consumers now turn away from American cars and American consumers turn to German cars, the demand for dollars falls and the demand for Deutschmarks rises. The Deutschmark comes under appreciation pressure.

If inflation rates diverge in the long term (if neither foreign exchange market interventions nor capital movement restrictions can be sustained in the long term), the solution must be that either the American inflation rate falls or the German inflation rate rises. In an asymmetric system such as the Bretton Woods system, where only the Bundesbank was obliged to intervene, Germany would have had to adapt to America, for example in the form of a less stability-oriented economic policy. In terms of different policy areas, this could have meant:

- Monetary policy:
  The Bundesbank pursues a laxer monetary policy (in the form of comparatively low interest rates) than would actually have been appropriate from a domestic economic point of view so that the German inflation rate approaches the (initially higher) American inflation rate. Comparatively lower interest rates in Germany would also have reduced the inflow of foreign capital and thus the appreciation pressure on the Deutschmark.

- Fiscal policy:
  The German government pursues a more expansive fiscal policy than would actually have been appropriate from a domestic economic perspective. This creates inflationary pressure due to the additional demand and also increases demand for imported products. The latter reduces the appreciation pressure on the DM.
- Structural policy:
  Inflation can also rise in the medium and long term if the structures of the economy are changed in the direction of less competition or if competition-oriented structural reforms fail to materialize. Privatization, breaking up monopolies and oligopolies, opening up markets to foreign competition, restricting the power of trade unions, reducing bureaucracy, lowering taxes and social security contributions, investing in infrastructure and building up human capital – these so-called structural policy measures have a dampening effect on companies' price-setting behavior. If such measures are not implemented, or only half-heartedly, the inflation rate will be higher.

One of the reasons for the failure of the Bretton Woods system is that the governments of the participating countries were not prepared to make such adjustments to their own economic policy. A fixed exchange rate system requires domestic economic goals (here for the example of Germany: a low inflation rate) to take a back seat to external economic goals, which was not viable at the time.

2.2.5 From the mid-1960s onwards: Problems and collapse

From the mid-1960s, doubts grew as to whether the Bretton Woods system was really suitable for ensuring the desired predictability of international economic exchange relations. The prerequisite for a fixed exchange rate system to fulfill its task is, on the one hand, that the system is flexible enough to react to short-term shocks (with the help of foreign exchange market interventions, monetary and economic policy measures at national level and, if necessary, capital controls) and long-term changes in the basic framework (with the help of parity adjustments). On the other hand, the fundamental need for flexibility must not result in a hectic back and forth of interventions, national policy measures, capital controls and parity adjustments, because this would not only complicate the planning of companies and private households, but would also undermine the urgently needed confidence in the long-term viability of the fixed exchange rate system. In order to build and maintain this confidence, we need, firstly, a functioning intervention and support system. Required are, secondly, macro policies that converge in the long term. Thirdly, a parity adjustment procedure that is credible but does not undermine the idea of the fixed exchange rate system is needed.

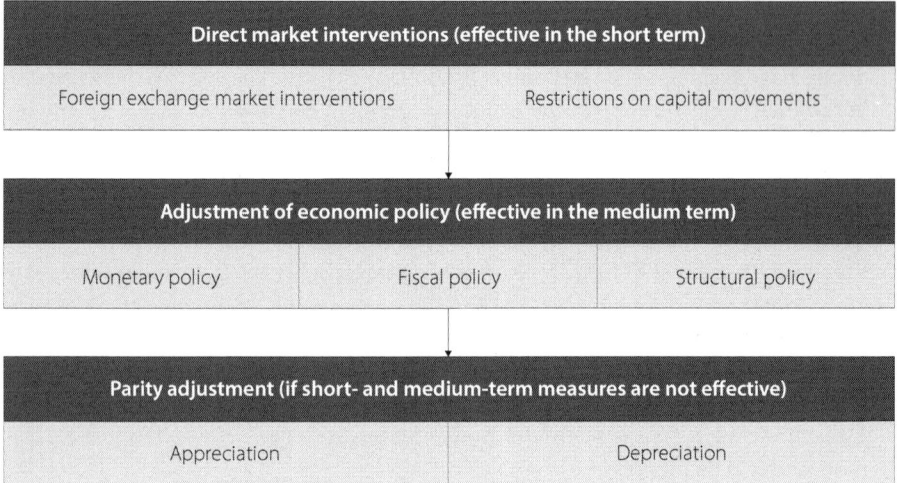

Fig. 25: Dealing with tensions in a system of fixed exchange rates

Fixed exchange rate systems therefore have an adjustment problem and a confidence problem. They must remain adaptable, but must not lose the confidence of market participants. Exactly these conditions were increasingly no longer met or could no longer be met by more and more countries in the Bretton Woods system – foremost among them the USA – from the mid-1960s onwards. The US played a central role as the guarantor of the gold-dollar standard. An increasingly inflationary policy was pursued there, as a result of which American goods and assets became less attractive. Demand for these goods fell, both from the US itself and from the rest of the world. There was an oversupply of US dollars on the international currency markets, which the central banks outside the US had to buy up in order to prevent the dollar from depreciating or their respective currencies from appreciating. This is where the so-called 'n-1 problem' came into play. In a fixed exchange rate system with n participating currencies, all participating countries except one (hence 'n-1') must subordinate their economic and monetary policy to the requirements of the fixed exchange rate system. Country n can set the direction that the others must follow. In the Bretton Woods system, the US was country n. Its economic policy had consequences for the supply of and demand for US dollars, to which all other Bretton Woods countries had to react.

In this specific case, this had two effects:

1. The central banks of the surplus countries accumulated increasingly large dollar reserves, which at some point (at the fixed price of $ 35 per ounce) threatened to exceed the Federal Reserve's gold reserves. If the world's central banks had presented their dollar reserves according to the conditions of the system to the Fed and demanded one ounce of gold for every 35 dollars, the system would have collapsed due to the USA's inability to fulfill its obligations. Neither party wanted

that. The central banks concerned kept the system alive by not exchanging dollars for gold but by allowing dollar reserves to grow.
2. In the surplus countries, the domestic money supply increased due to the intervention requirement and thus the risk of inflation. Countries with lower competitiveness and current account deficits (i. e., the deficit countries) could not or did not want to devalue their currencies but tried to defend the fixed exchange rates by selling dollars in Exchange for their currency. The alternative would have been for the surplus countries to pursue an inflationary and for the deficit countries to pursue a deflationary monetary and fiscal policy in order to approach the level of the American inflation rate 'from below' or 'from above,' as it were. This would have aligned their competitiveness with that of the US economy and reduced the appreciation and depreciation pressure on their currencies. A large part of the interventions and parity adjustments could thus have been avoided. However, both the surplus and deficit countries were less and less willing to bear the consequences of this policy (inflation and overheating or recession and higher unemployment).

The basic problem of a system of fixed exchange rates became increasingly clear: it cannot permanently withstand diverging inflation rates as a result of diverging national economic policies (which in turn result from diverging stability policy ideas). This is because the cost increases for companies and thus the competitiveness of the participating countries diverges with the inflation rates. This has an impact on exports and imports, which puts pressure on fixed exchange rates.

As a reaction, there were repeated adjustments to the dollar exchange rates of EEC member states until the end of the 1960s, as already described. Yet the parity adjustments could not prevent the system from collapsing. In 1969, the gold convertibility of the dollar was severely restricted and completely abandoned by US President Nixon in a TV address on August 15, 1971 ('Nixon Shock'). Nixon also announced a series of protectionist measures to reduce the US current account deficit. The other countries in the system also intervened in foreign trade and also worked with capital controls in order to survive this volatile phase as unscathed as possible. Between 1971 and 1973, there were still fixed exchange rates against the dollar on paper, but these were not maintained. In 1973, the major industrialized nations switched to a system of flexible exchange rates. The age of fiat money (= money that is neither directly nor indirectly backed by precious metals) and (largely) free currency markets had begun.

2.3 The 1970s: the Werner plan and the 'European Currency Snake'

2.3.1 The Werner plan: Creating an EC monetary union by 1980?

By the end of the 1960s, the European Community had achieved two central goals of the Treaty of Rome: a customs union and a common agricultural policy. At the same time, the decline of the Bretton Woods system was accelerating. In search of a new impetus for the integration process and concerned about monetary stability in Europe, the heads of state and government set up a commission of experts on the monetary future of the Community in 1969. Under the chairmanship of Luxembourg's Prime Minister Pierre Werner, the group drew up the so-called 'Werner Plan.' which proposed the establishment of an economic and monetary union in three steps by 1980.

The Werner plan considered the following key points to be essential for the implementation of an economic and monetary union:

- Exchange rate fluctuations within the Community were to become a thing of the past. To this end, the parities between the EEC currencies were to be irrevocably fixed. Whether the national currencies were to be completely abandoned in favor of a new common currency remained unclear.
- There was to be complete freedom of capital movements. Neither current account nor capital account-based transactions were to be subject to any kind of exchange control or capital controls.
- A European monetary institution was to decide on monetary policy in the Community. The plan left open how this new institution would be structured in concrete terms. The only thing that was clear was that there would have to be some kind of community central banking system along the lines of the (decentrally organized) US Federal Reserve.
- However, the authors of the plan were convinced that a central body should be given far-reaching economic policy powers. This new decision-making body would have been politically accountable to the European Parliament. The capital market policies of the member states were to be standardized and the key parameters of the public budgets as well as the main features of regional and structural policy were to be defined at Community level. Regular and systematic consultation of the collective bargaining parties was also planned at the central level.

The aim was to create a Community "within which goods and services, people and capital will circulate freely and without competitive distortions, without thereby giving rise to structural or regional disequilibrium."[10] The measures envisaged to achieve this ambitious goal can be systematized as follows:

---

10 Werner, P.: Report to the Council and the Commission, on the realisation by stages of economic and monetary union in the Community, supplement to EC bulletin 11, Oct 8, 1970, p.9.

- Stage 1: Intensive consultations and ever-increasing coordination of national economic policies (including monetary policy); narrowing of the bandwidths around the parities between European currencies (within the Bretton Woods system that still existed at the time the Werner Plan was published), while at the same time establishing a system of assistance in currency policy; dismantling of restrictions on capital movements.
- Stage 2: Establishment of European institutions to which the coordination of national economic and monetary policies is gradually transferred. Establishment of a European reserve fund, to which the national currency reserves and responsibility for foreign exchange market interventions should be gradually transferred; further reduction of restrictions on capital movements.
- Stage 3: Takeover of central decision-making powers in economic and monetary policy by European institutions; completely free movement of capital.

When discussing the Werner Plan, there was broad agreement on the ultimate goal, namely a European economic and monetary union, but not on how to get there. The Werner Plan is characterized by a parallelism of two necessary developments: the establishment of European institutional structures in monetary policy on the one hand, and the harmonization of national economic policies, business cycles and economic structures on the other. This approach was intended to reconcile two fundamentally different views of the monetary integration process (▶ Fig. 26).

Fig. 26: The two divergent approaches to European monetary integration

'Monetarists'	'Economists'
France, Luxembourg, Belgium, [Italy[11]]	Germany, Netherlands, [Italy[8]]
Key message: Common monetary institutions lead to the convergence of national economies.	Key message: The convergence of national economies is a prerequisite for the establishment of common monetary institutions.
Central planning approach characterized by skepticism towards market processes ("planification')	Evolutionary approach characterized by skepticism towards the central control of economic processes (ordoliberalism)
'locomotive theory'	'coronation theory'
top-down integration	bottom-up integration

The 'monetarists' (not to be confused with the followers of Milton Friedman and his monetary policy concept) were particularly keen on standardizing monetary institutions. They advocated narrower bandwidths between the European currencies within the Bretton Woods system, coordinated dollar interventions by the central banks of the EC member states and the creation of a foreign reserve equalization fund. The

---

11   Italy could not be clearly assigned to either camp.

latter was initially intended to coordinate and later standardize intervention policies within the Community. The aim was a closer monetary link between the Europeans (i.e., internally) combined with as uniform an approach as possible towards the US and the IMF (i.e., externally). According to the monetarist view, this would have led to the harmonization of business cycles and economic structures. The monetarist approach is characterized by trust in the central planning activities of the state, as expressed in French 'planification.' In an interim report by the Werner Commission, this sounds as follows: "In addition to the technical advantages associated with the creation of the fund, this institution is also of undeniable interest from a political and psychological point of view. In this way, the intentions expressed at the Hague Conference will be realized by providing the Community with an effective instrument for the balanced development of economic and monetary union."[12]

The 'economists' proposed the opposite sequence. Their approach was evolutionary and reflected skepticism towards the central control of economic processes. For them, economic integration had to precede monetary integration. The orientation of national economic policies must lead to a common stability policy. The convergence of economic policies would then ultimately result in a convergence of economic cycles and economic structures, which would almost automatically lead to a limitation of exchange rate fluctuations between European currencies. Fixing exchange rates too early and too rigidly (in the sense of very narrow bandwidths) would, by way of contrast, inevitably cause stability problems because surplus countries would be forced to pursue an expansionary monetary and fiscal policy and deficit countries a restrictive one. This would lead to undesirable inflation in the surplus countries and undesirable unemployment and a lack of foreign exchange reserves in the deficit countries. The interim report of the Werner Commission thus states: "The other members of the group believe that neither an institutional narrowing of the fluctuation margins nor the creation of an exchange equalization fund is desirable in the first phase. In their view, significant measures in the field of Community monetary policy can only be considered when, through real progress in the harmonization of economic policies, certain conditions have been created that ensure the equilibrium of the Community economy as a whole."[13]

The conflict between monetarists and economists was not really resolved. The two camps were only able to agree on compromise formulas and a step-by-step approach. Attempts were made to avoid controversial points by using vague formulations. This was reflected in the fact that the Werner Plan was not legally based on an amendment to the EEC Treaty but on two summit declarations (= declarations by the heads of state and government) and two resolutions by the Council of Ministers.

---

12 Cf. Werner, P. (1970a): Zwischenbericht an Rat und Kommission über die stufenweise Verwirklichung der Wirtschafts- und Währungsunion der Gemeinschaft, Luxemburg, 20. Mai 1970, Dokument 9.504/II/70-D, p. 14. [Translation by the authors]

13 Cf. Werner, P. (1970a): Zwischenbericht an Rat und Kommission über die stufenweise Verwirklichung der Wirtschafts- und Währungsunion der Gemeinschaft, Luxemburg, 20. Mai 1970, Dokument 9.504/II/70-D, p. 14.p. 15. [Translation by the authors]

These were expressions of will rather than legally enforceable decisions on decisive steps towards integration. This 'integrationist' view also shows that the concept was built on a rather thin foundation – too thin for the global economic turbulence of the early 1970s, which was reflected in the failure of the Bretton Woods system and the stagflation in the wake of the first oil crisis, among other things.

Pierre Werner and the other Commission members could not have foreseen these difficulties. They had drawn up the plan at the end of a long period of growth. Despite all the discussions about revaluation and devaluation and the widespread fear of imported inflation, particularly in Germany, the 1950s and 1960s were a period of prosperity and internal and external monetary stability that was unique by historical standards. When the Werner Commission was established in 1969, the Bretton Woods system, despite all signs of fatigue, was still fundamentally functional. Compared to the following decade, unemployment figures and inflation rates were low and exchange rate fluctuations were small. In addition, capital controls were still widespread. Political decisions with harsh domestic economic and political consequences in the form of rising unemployment or inflation hardly had to be made. Against this backdrop, the Werner Report saw structural divergences between the participants in a monetary union rather than inflation and periods of economic weakness as the main problem. Above all, however, it was based on the implicit premise that there would continue to be an international monetary system like that of Bretton Woods with a strong anchor currency, a gold peg and fixed exchange rates. After 1973, however, the Europeans were on their own in this respect. There were flexible exchange rates between fiat currencies. Of the measures envisaged by the Werner Plan for the three stages leading up to a European economic and monetary union, only those relating to exchange rate policy therefore had any lasting effect, as it was in the area of exchange rate policy that the problems were most pressing (▶ Ch. 3.2).

Moreover, the monetary order was unable to make a real contribution to the standardization of economic policy. On the contrary, the economic policies of the European states diverged to an unprecedented extent in the 1970s. The national reactions to the economic crises in the middle of the decade could not have been more different. There was one simple reason for this: the national governments and central banks were not prepared to subordinate their respective domestic economic and political interests to the foreign trade and European policy objective of fixed exchange rates. In the economically turbulent 1970s (end of the Bretton Woods system, oil crisis, stagflation, rising unemployment), governments found it particularly difficult to meet the requirements of the 'trilemma of monetary policy.' The Werner Plan actually demanded their own price levels to be kept as stable as possible in order to maintain the agreed currency relations. However, a monetary, fiscal and structural policy in line with stability required sacrifices (particularly in the form of rising unemployment figures), which governments were increasingly unwilling to make. Attempts to save the day with the help of capital controls not only failed regularly, but also violated the goal of the Werner Plan to establish a monetary union with an integrated capital market by 1980. As early as 1973, the Commission stated in its "Review of stage one" that the conditions for a further deepening of monetary integration had not been met. As the member states were neither prepared to transfer economic policy competences to EC institutions (which might have to be newly created) nor to coordinate their economic and financial policies, they could not enter the second stage of the Werner Plan.

2.3.2 The 'European Currency Snake'

The EPU, the Bretton Woods system and the EEC were intended to achieve the goal of closer trade links between the participating countries in different ways. These efforts were generally crowned with success. However, with closer integration, the flow of foreign exchange between the countries increased and current account-related foreign exchange flows became increasingly difficult to distinguish from capital account-related flows. This made fixed exchange rates increasingly important (at least within the EEC), but it also made a fixed exchange rate system more difficult to implement. As the volume of cross-border flows of goods and capital increased, so did the supply of and demand for the currencies involved. In this environment, the central banks had to deploy ever larger sums to defend the fixed exchange rates by means of foreign exchange market interventions. In addition, the need to intervene increased with economic volatility and the associated divergences between Western European countries. In this sense, the 1970s turned out to be a perfect storm. This is made clear by the EC's exchange rate policy efforts between 1971 and 1979. The will of the member states to at least make progress in terms of exchange rate policy (even if the Werner Plan could not be implemented) encountered enormous economic and political difficulties.

Nevertheless, the period of the 'European Currency Snake' represents an important step in the history of Western Europe's monetary emancipation. The EEC countries broke away from the gold-dollar standard of the Bretton Woods system and began to establish European monetary policy institutions. This process took place in three stages:

1. Until 1971, the Bretton Woods system guaranteed fixed exchange rates. The EEC members intervened by buying and selling dollars in order to defend the parities with the dollar. The fixed dollar parities resulted in fixed exchange rates between the EEC currencies.
2. The year 1971 was characterized by considerable turbulence on the foreign exchange markets. In spring, some countries, including the Federal Republic of Germany, stopped intervening and switched to flexible exchange rates. With the Washington Agreement ('Smithsonian Agreement') of December 1971, the Bretton Woods participants made a new attempt to return to fixed exchange rates. At the same time, the EEC countries took up preparatory work from March 1971 and, in April 1972, established the 'European Currency Snake'. They mutually committed themselves to fixed exchange rates between the EC currencies with a bandwidth of +/- 2.25 %. If this limit was reached, both participating central banks were obliged

to intervene. At the same time, the respective dollar parities had to be defended (through interventions in US dollars). The European Currency Snake owes its nickname 'snake in the tunnel' to the graphical representation of the corresponding exchange rate movements over time. This new 'European Currency Snake' was initially only an agreement within the Bretton Woods system, which continued to exist (at least pro forma). With it, the EC nonetheless took a decisive step towards the Europeanization of monetary policy.

A credit-based support system was created so that central banks with currencies at risk of devaluation could credibly fulfill their intervention obligations. The central banks of the surplus countries made their currency available to the central banks of the deficit countries in the short term. A new 'European Monetary Cooperation Fund' offset the claims and liabilities from the central bank loans. If the Werner Plan had been fully implemented, the currency reserves of the EEC central banks and the responsibility for foreign exchange market interventions would have been transferred to this fund. It could thus have formed the basis for a European central banking system.

3. In March 1973, the dollar came under heavy pressure. A veritable wave of dollars flowed into Germany in particular, causing enormous appreciation pressure on the German mark. The Bundesbank would have had to intervene to an unprecedented extent, which would have inflated the DM money supply with potentially very damaging consequences for price stability. As a result, the fixed exchange rates of the Bretton Woods system were finally abandoned. However, the EEC currencies were to continue to have fixed exchange rates with each other. To defend them, both central banks involved had to intervene in the respective common currencies. This configuration was referred to as 'group floating.' The EC currencies had fixed exchange rates with each other and at the same time the value of each individual currency fluctuated ('floated') against the dollar.

The 'snake' regulated European monetary relations for almost seven years – on the whole more badly than well. It was unable to develop into a stable order. Initially launched in April 1972 with the original six member states of the Community, the EMU was expanded in the same year (on May 1) to include the EC accession candidates Great Britain, Ireland and Denmark. Norway also joined shortly afterwards.

Just a few weeks later, however, it became apparent that the agreed set of rules did not provide a stable basis for an internally and externally coordinated monetary policy among the participants. In June 1972, the pound sterling and the Irish punt left the system, followed by the Danish krona in June – although the latter returned in October. At the beginning of 1973, the Italian lira left the system (for good). A little later, in March 1973, the Swedish krona joined, leaving again in August 1977. The 'founding member,' the French franc, left the 'snake' in 1974, rejoined in 1975 and then left for good in 1976. Only the German mark, the Belgian franc and the Dutch guilder were members throughout. At the same time, there were numerous revaluations and devaluations, i.e., adjustments to the parities. In the end (1978), there was a 'Deutschmark bloc' (Deutschmark, Belgian franc, Dutch guilder, Danish krone) and four floating currencies (French franc, British pound, Irish pound, Italian lira). The actual aim of a system of fixed exchange rates, namely the predictability of currency relations, had clearly been missed.

Fig. 27: Comparison of how exchange rate systems work

Bretton Woods system	'European Currency Snake'
unilateral commitment to intervene	bilateral intervention commitment
(until 1971) convertibility of dollar into gold	fiat money
US not obliged to take balance of payments policy measures	all member countries obliged to take balance of payments policy measures
asymmetric	symmetric
multilateral	multilateral

2.4 The European Monetary System (EMS)

2.4.1 Objectives, functioning and development over time

Fig. 28: The European Monetary System over time

In 1976, France – the second largest economy in the EC – declared its withdrawal from the 'currency snake.' This made it clear that the European Currency Snake would never be able to fulfill its task of establishing stable currency relations in Western Europe. The original goal of establishing an economic and monetary union by 1980 on the basis of the Werner Plan had already been declared a failure by the Marjolin Report[14] in 1975. The question of how to proceed with monetary policy was once again open. For three reasons, flexible exchange rates were not a realistic option for the EC: First, the interconnection of its economies was too close; second, the dependence of the common agricultural policy on fixed exchange rates was too strong and, third, the global experience with fluctuating exchange rates after the end of the Bretton Woods system had been too negative. A revitalization of the 'snake' was also ruled out. It had functioned so poorly that a credible restart did not appear feasible to either the public or 'the markets.' In addition, France would have had to rejoin. This would have entailed a considerable reputational setback for the Grande Nation.

At the same time, however, the French government was also interested in fixed exchange rates. In addition to their advantages for foreign trade within the EC and agricultural policy, fixed exchange rates were possibly also associated with a certain disciplining effect on the economic policy debate within the country: the responsible politicians hoped to be able to better defend a stability-oriented policy (namely with reference to foreign trade requirements within the framework of European monetary integration). Thus, in the late 1970s, the course of events led to the establishment of a new fixed exchange rate system for the EC. The discussion about this followed the familiar lines of argument of 'monetarists' and 'economists:' While Germany (and the Bundesbank in particular) was aware of the danger of an inflationary community and advocated a cautious approach, France wanted to take relatively far-reaching steps towards integration – not least with the aim of preventing Germany from dominating European economic policy.

In 1978, President Giscard d'Estaing and Chancellor Schmidt presented a proposal for a 'European Monetary System' (EMS) to the public. Unlike the ambitious Werner Plan, their concept was geared towards the short-term feasibility and medium-term survival chances of a system of fixed exchange rates (called the 'exchange rate mechanism' in the EMS). Possible steps in the future remained the subject of non-binding declarations of intent. For example, a European Monetary Fund (EMF) with the newly created 'ECU' (European Currency Unit) as a reserve currency was to be created within two years. The EMF would have taken over the national central banks' currency reserves and responsibility for foreign exchange market interventions. This would have created the nucleus of a future economic and monetary union. The goal, formulated without being legally binding, was the gradual establishment of a supranational institution with exchange rate and (in the long term) monetary policy powers. Noth-

---

14 Marjolin, Robert: Report of the Study Group "Economic and Monetary Union 1980", Brussels, March 8, 1975, http://aei.pitt.edu/1009/1/monetary_study_group_1980.pdf

ing came of it. Throughout its existence, the European Monetary System was nothing more than a system of fixed exchange rates.

The exchange rate mechanism (ERM) focused on the ECU as a basket currency.[15] Its value was calculated based on the sum of the market rates of the participating currencies according to a certain weighting. For example, the Deutschmark value of the ECU was calculated by adding up the current DM values of all participating currencies according to the defined weighting. Central rates were set between all EC currencies and the ECU. A bilateral central rate could then be calculated for each ECU currency pair from these ECU central rates. The representation of all bilateral central rates in a matrix resulted in the so-called 'parity grid.'

If the bandwidth of +/- 2.25 % around the bilateral parity between two currencies was exceeded, the two central banks concerned were obliged to intervene with an unlimited volume. A sophisticated credit system was intended to enable the central banks of countries with currencies under devaluation pressure to meet their intervention obligations despite limited foreign exchange reserves. If a bilateral parity could not be defended, a change had to be applied for, which all member states had to agree to.

When the EMS was launched in 1979, the UK was the only one of the nine EC countries at the time, that did not participate in the exchange rate mechanism. Italy and Ireland took advantage of an exemption and operated within a fluctuation margin of +/- 6 %The first four years were turbulent. The high and in some cases considerably fluctuating inflation rates before and after the second oil price shock in 1979/80 and the initially explicitly non-stability-oriented economic and financial policy of the new French President Mitterand required nothing less than 23 central rate adjustments between 1979 and 1983. From 1984 onwards, the EMS sailed in calmer waters. France switched to a 'hard franc' policy ('franc fort'), the global 'Great Moderation' began with falling inflation rates worldwide and the Bundesbank slowly developed into the dominant central bank in the system, with more and more member states adapting to its stability policy. From 1987 to 1992, there were no more central rate changes, and the UK (in 1990) and the two new EC members Spain (in 1989) and Portugal (in 1992) joined the exchange rate mechanism.[16]

Then, at the apparent peak of its success, the system entered a serious crisis in 1992/93. The Danish rejection of the Maastricht Treaty in a referendum on June 2, 1992 is generally regarded as a possible trigger for the turbulence. Confidence in the further progress of European monetary integration was shaken. Nervousness increased further as opinion polls predicted a close outcome for the French referendum on September 20 of the same year. The Italian lira and the British pound came under

---

15 The functioning of the EMS can only be outlined here. For a detailed introduction, see Ungerer, H. (1983): The European Monetary System – The Experience 1979-1982, International Monetary Fund, Washington, D.C., 1983

16 With the exception of Great Britain (member of the exchange rate mechanism from 1990 to 1992) and Italy (interruption of membership from 1992 to 1996), all founding states were members until the introduction of the euro in 1999.

such strong devaluation pressure that both countries had to leave the ERM. In addition, the Spanish peseta, the Portuguese escudo and the Irish punt were devalued. The ERM continued to exist after the crisis until December 31, 1998 (i.e., until the introduction of the euro), albeit with a significantly wider bandwidth of +/- 15 % from August 1993 onwards. As a two-year membership of the ERM (without a central rate adjustment) was one of the Maastricht criteria for euro aspirants, Italy rejoined at the end of 1996, as did two of the three countries that joined the EU in 1995, namely Austria and Finland. The third country, Sweden, did not want to join. Thus, on December 31, 1998, only two of the 15 EU countries (Greece and Sweden) remained outside. On January 1, 1999, the 'Exchange Rate Mechanism II' (ERM II) replaced the previous regulations of the EMS. It is intended to bind the EU members that have not yet joined the eurozone to the currency union in terms of monetary policy. Until today, Sweden is not a member of ERM II.

2.4.2 Analyzing the EMS from the perspective of economic history (1): Was it a success story?

The EMS has been the subject of economic criticism from the outset and remains so to this day. One question that is debated is whether it has brought about the exchange rate stability that the EC countries urgently needed.

The results here are mixed. For as we have seen, unlike in the European Currency Snake before it, the participation of the EC countries (later: EU countries) in the EMS was comprehensive and characterized by relatively great continuity. However, this superficially positive balance sheet belies the turbulence to which the system was exposed in the two decades of its existence. After the difficult early years with numerous central rate changes, a phase of relative stability began in 1983; the divergence in inflation rates decreased. Two possible causes were identified for this development. On the one hand, it is possible that membership of the exchange rate mechanism brought about a convergence and a stronger focus on stability in national economic policies. On the other hand, the EMS could also have benefited from a favorable macroeconomic environment. This is because inflation rates in the western world converged at a comparatively low level during the 1980s ('Great Moderation'). The question is therefore whether the impact of the EMS resulted in a convergence of inflation rates or whether the convergence of inflation rates was a prerequisite for the survival of the EMS.

In any case, the phase of relative stability found its end with the crisis of 1992/93, after which the bandwidths were increased to +/- 15 %, allowing such wide-ranging exchange rate movements that it was hardly possible to speak of a system of fixed exchange rates.

It is not surprising that the crisis of 1992/93 is of particular interest to economic historians. A great deal of space is devoted to researching the causes of the crisis. What could shake the EMS to such an extent after it had apparently functioned well since 1983, i.e., for almost a decade? One answer to this question is that the exchange rate mechanism may indeed only have 'apparently' worked well. The absence of any parity changes between 1987 and 1992 was therefore no proof of its functionality; rather, the European Monetary System proved to be (politically) dysfunctional in the sense that parity changes did not take place, which should actually have happened. Alternatively, the later crisis countries could have pursued a more stability-oriented policy during these years. After all, the inflation differentials compared to Germany had narrowed, but not disappeared. Once again it became clear that a fixed exchange rate system cannot cope with permanently diverging inflation rates.

The pent-up problems came to light when Germany experienced the unification boom after 1990, while much of the rest of Europe fell into recession from 1991 onwards. The Bundesbank resolutely fought the inflation resulting from the economic boom. German interest rates rose sharply in absolute terms and in comparison to those of the other EMS countries. The resulting influx of capital into the German capital market triggered appreciation pressure on the Deutschmark and depreciation pressure on the pound, the escudo, the peseta, the lira and the French franc, among others. Intervention on an unprecedented scale would have been necessary to successfully defend the central rates. In the countries with currencies at risk of devaluation, a debate arose as to whether the disadvantages in the form of an intensified recession and even higher unemployment were worth tightening monetary policy in order to defend the exchange rate.

These discussions aroused the interest of capital market players who did not consider the political will to defend exchange rates to be particularly strong. Through targeted speculation, they created additional pressure on exchange rates (not least that of the pound), which triggered even more far-reaching (and therefore even more unpopular) economic policy countermeasures. The speculative attacks turned out to be at least partly self-fulfilling prophecies. They exposed the problems of the fixed exchange rate system and thus exacerbated them. It became apparent that the interests of national decision-makers in the countries particularly affected (Germany, the UK, Italy and France) were dominated by domestic factors, not exchange rate policy. This led to destabilizing speculation against individual currencies, which made it even more difficult for governments and central banks to cautiously weigh up the various options (intervention, central rate adjustment, change in economic policy, leaving the system) calmly.

2.4.3 Analyzing the EMS from the perspective of economic history (2): Was it a Deutschmark bloc with the Bundesbank as its central bank?

Economic history research is not only interested in the cause of the 1992/93 crisis but also in the question of whether the EMS was really a symmetrical system. After all, it had been announced as such in 1979. In the course of the 1980s, however, the EMS developed into an asymmetrical system with the Deutschmark as the reserve currency and the Bundesbank as the central bank. German monetary policy set the direction that the rest of the EC followed.

The subordination of the other participants to the leading role of the Bundesbank was only partly involuntary. The thesis of a partly voluntary asymmetry is supported by the assumption that the traditionally less stability-oriented countries were able to import monetary policy credibility by participating in the EMS. This resulted from the economic policy constraints associated with membership of a fixed exchange rate system. If a government did not want to constantly suffer the loss of face associated with devaluations, it had to pursue a stability-oriented monetary policy because defending the exchange rate caused foreign exchange reserves to dwindle and led to indebtedness in the system. These constraints strengthened its position vis-à-vis 'the capital market,' but also vis-à-vis its own population, to whom economic policy burdens could be explained with reference to the EMS.

Whether devaluations under pressure on the exchange rate would really have been a lasting solution is – beyond the political problem of the associated loss of face – also economically questionable. In the simplest case, devaluation leads to a reduction in the price of the country's own exports for foreign buyers and an increase in the price of imported goods for domestic buyers. Exports rise, imports fall and the current account balance returns to equilibrium. At the new, lower exchange rate, supply and demand for the currency in question are now balanced again and the new central rate corresponds to the market rate. So much for the simple textbook theory. In reality, the country whose currency is devalued is at risk of falling into a devaluation-inflation spiral. In the event of a devaluation, the extensive trade integration in the EC would have provided suitable framework conditions for the demand for the export goods of the devaluing country to react very strongly to the lower exchange rate (which was entirely desirable), but this would have caused the prices of the goods in question to rise. At the same time, a lower exchange rate means that imported goods become more expensive for domestic consumers. In terms of balancing the current account, this is also actually desirable. However, if there are no domestic substitutes for these imported goods and demand for them is inelastic, as can be the case with energy, for example, then domestic import expenditure will hardly fall or may even rise. This is the result of barely decreasing quantities if prices rise at the same time. The rising prices of imported goods – also for domestic export companies that work with imported primary products – together with the increased demand from foreigners for the country's export goods can trigger a surge in inflation and a loss of real income at home. If the trade unions are able to push through higher wages in response to this, inflation will become entrenched and the competitiveness of the export industry, which initially increased as a result of the devaluation, will fall again as a result of higher labor costs. The result would be a current account deficit and thus new devaluation pressure.

The only alternative to devaluation was to align with the economic policy of the anchor currency country, Germany. In this way, the other EMS members hoped to be able to indirectly influence cross-border payment flows in order to keep the exchange rate stable. The fact that the Deutschmark became the anchor currency and the Bundesbank the lead central bank was of course also due to the size and economic importance of Germany within the European Community. As described above, the other EMS countries tried to participate in the anti-inflation reputation that the Bundesbank had previously built up. They saw this as an opportunity to reduce the political costs of their disinflationary policy. There was a gradual consensus in the former high-inflation countries of Southern Europe that such a disinflation policy (i. e., a reduction in the previously very high inflation rates) was necessary due to the detrimental economic and social effects of the considerable inflation in the 1970s and early 1980s.

In addition to such politically motivated subordination to a central bank, fundamental economic considerations also showed that the EMS would not be a symmetrical exchange rate system in the long term. The so-called 'n-1 problem' (▶ Ch. 2.2.5) also exists in a system geared towards multilateralism and symmetry. In the EMS it was also the case that one central bank could set the direction and the others had to adapt. This was typically the central bank of a country whose currency was under pressure to appreciate due to export surpluses and capital inflows. In contrast to a country with a currency at risk of devaluation, the surplus country could intervene practically limitless without having to borrow from the partner central bank. Capital controls could still be introduced to reduce or eliminate inflationary pressure due to a rising domestic money supply as a result of the interventions.

In the context of the EMS, it later emerged that the German government had given the Bundesbank an informal assurance that its obligation to intervene would cease if price stability in Germany was threatened. In 1986/87, for example, considerable Bundesbank intervention might have been necessary, but the Bundesbank successfully urged the Federal Government to push through a change in parity in Brussels. The Bundesbank has also been criticized to this day for failing to live up to the responsibility arising from its power in the early 1990s and for thus triggering the EMS crisis. At that time, it had ruthlessly prioritized the fight against inflation in Germany and paid no attention to the effects its restrictive monetary policy stance had on the partner countries and thus on the EMS.

All in all, the economic and political arguments presented here suggest that the EMS was an asymmetrical system in practice and, like its predecessor, the European Currency Snake, failed to achieve the goal of a genuine Europeanization of monetary policy. A multilateral, symmetrical solution to the exchange rate problem was not found.

2.4.4 Analyzing the EMS from the perspective of economic history (3): Was it a precursor to the monetary union?

Despite the clearly far-reaching ambitions that were evident at its foundation, the EMS was no more than a fixed exchange rate system, and an asymmetrical one at that. Although it lasted until 1992/93 and probably also contributed to a greater focus on stability in the member states, this does not change the fact that, as in the 1970s, a 'hard currency bloc' with Germany and the Netherlands at its core and a group of 'soft currency countries' (Italy, Spain, Portugal) continued to be opposing each other. Some currencies were under constant pressure to appreciate, while the others were under permanent pressure to depreciate. The European Monetary System is therefore, particularly with regard to its development from 1990 onwards, another example of the fact that a system of fixed exchange rates requires participants to share economic policy ideas. Sooner or later, the member states will have to decide in a specific situation whether to fight inflation (accepting recession and higher unemployment) on the one hand or unemployment (accepting higher inflation) on the other. Both the apparent success of the EMS before and its actual failure with the crisis of 1992/93 can serve as an explanation for the impetus with which Delors, Kohl, Mitterrand and the other heads of state and government pushed ahead with the project of a common currency:

- The apparent success of the EMS from 1987 to 1992 once again impressively demonstrated to Europeans what they had long known anyway: a united Europe needs predictable currency relations. This was all the more true after the initiation of the single market program with the Single European Act (1986, ▶ Ch. 3.1). The complete liberalization of capital movements in the EC (among other goals), which was aimed for in 1990, is also one of the causes of the EMS crisis. It became clear that a system of fixed exchange rates with gradual flexibility could no longer be defended without accompanying controls of capital movements.
- The actual failure of the 1992/93 crisis sent out contradictory signals. Economically and politically, the convergence of the EC countries was clearly not yet great enough. The structures of the national economies were still so different that asymmetric shocks could lead to considerable tensions on the foreign exchange markets, which in turn forced the national decision-makers to weigh up domestic and foreign trade factors against each other. The 'soft currency countries' of the South and France also had to answer the prestige question of whether they wanted to continue to operate under the monetary policy leadership of the Bundesbank. In this mixed situation, what the economic historian Barry Eichengreen summed up as follows came to bear: "Limited measures cannot succeed in a world with unlimited capital mobility."[17] The only unlimited measures available were the complete floating of exchange rates or their irrevocable fixing within the framework of a monetary union. The complete floating of exchange rates was no longer an option in the Europe of the single market, in which the 'four freedoms' were realized from 1993. This left only the path to a monetary union.

---

17   Eichengreen, B. (2008): Globalizing capital – The history of the international monetary system, Princeton University Press, 2nd. ed., Princeton 2008

3 Paving the way: Delors Report, Maastricht Treaty, Stability and Growth Pact (1989–1998)

3.1 The Delors report

Jacques Delors was born in 1925. The economist held various positions in the French administration, politics and the central bank and was also active as a university lecturer. He was President of the European Commission from 1985 to 1995. In this office, Delors implemented the single market program based on the 'Single European Act' and paved the way for the monetary union with his 'Delors Report.' This makes him one of the most influential European politicians ever. Delors died in 2023 in his native city of Paris. [Photo: European Communities 1993/EC 1993]

Around the same time as the gradual stabilization of the European Monetary System (EMS) took place from 1983, European integration as a whole picked up speed again. In 1985, the Commission presented a strategy paper ('White Paper') on the completion of the single market, which was defined as an area without internal borders with free movement of people, goods, services and capital ('four freedoms'). The goal to create such a single market by 1993 became a binding task for the Community institutions (in particular the Commission) and the then twelve EC Member states with the 'Single European Act.'

This 'Single European Act' came into force on July 1, 1987, i.e., thirty years after the signing of the Treaty of Rome and just under twenty years after the completion of the customs union. For the first time in decades, tangible progress towards integration was being made in the form of fundamental changes to the EEC Treaty with ambitious goals. These treaty changes affected the competences of the EC as well as its decision-making processes. Monetary integration was also an issue – although the term 'economic and monetary union' was mentioned but not specified.

However, as would soon become apparent, the Single European Act triggered a new dynamic, not least in terms of monetary integration. It contained an extensive catalog of almost three hundred measures to implement the 'Four Freedoms.' Obstacles caused by national product norms, food standards and tax laws were to be abolished, as were controls on persons and goods at intra-Community borders, market access restrictions in individual sectors (e. g., financial services, transportation, energy supply) and state monopolies (e. g., postal services, telecommunications, railroads). In order to facilitate the necessary political steps, the Single European Act abolished the previous unanimity principle in the Council. Now, all decisions relevant to the single market would only require a qualified majority.

This also concerned a directive which aimed at the complete liberalization of capital movements in the Community and provided for the lifting of all restrictions on cross-border capital flows in the EC from 1 July 1990. Following the deliberations on the trilemma of monetary policy in section 2.2.4, EMS members among the EC countries would no longer be able to preserve their remaining room for maneuver in economic and, in particular, monetary policy by intervening in cross-border capital movements. This was true at least as long as they wanted to maintain the fixed EMS exchange rates.

It is therefore not surprising that in 1987/88, with a view to the single market and in particular the free movement of capital, several initiatives were undertaken in the direction of deepening monetary cooperation in Europe. Most prominent among them were the 'Balladur Memorandum,' the 'Padoa-Schioppa Report' and the 'Genscher Memorandum.' On the one hand, the specific aim was to overcome the asymmetry of the EMS, which was particularly strongly perceived in France (▶ Ch. 2.4.3). Also, the free movement of goods and services was to be made independent of exchange rate fluctuations once and for all. On the other hand, there was also the strategic goal of developing the EC beyond the undeniable advantages of the Single European Act. The ultimate goal was to develop it into a true union with far-reaching competencies not only in economic and monetary policy, but also in domestic, foreign and defense policy. Thus, the idea of a monetary union was put back on the agenda when the European Council met in Hanover in the summer of 1988. Without extensive discussions, the heads of state and government commissioned a working group headed by Commission President Jacques Delors with the task of examining the possibilities and limits of monetary integration beyond the EMS. In addition to Delors, this working group consisted of three independent experts, the eleven central bank governors and a representative of the Luxembourg Ministry of Finance.[18]

In April 1989, the experts released their final report, titled the 'Delors Report,' which unexpectedly endorsed an economic and monetary union. They saw the following as constitutive features of an economic union

- the single market with the 'Four Freedoms'
- a uniform competition policy to ensure a level playing field for all market participants
- the coordination of national fiscal policies (e. g., through binding rules for the budgets of the member states)

---

18 Luxembourg and Belgium had formed a monetary union for decades. Luxembourg therefore did not have its own central bank.

- a structural and regional policy to enable the weaker parts of the EC to catch up with the rest

According to the Delors Report, a monetary union in turn requires

- the unlimited and irreversible convertibility of currencies
- complete freedom of capital movements and the integration of national banking and financial markets
- the elimination of bandwidths and irrevocable fixing of exchange rates

An economic and monetary union defined in this way was to be achieved in three stages:

- Stage 1: National economic and monetary policies were to be better coordinated within the existing institutional framework (including, for example, the complete liberalization of capital movements on 1 July 1990).
- Stage 2: Community institutions for EC economic and monetary policy were to be created and gradually given powers.
- Stage 3: Full transfer to the Community institutions of all powers that would be relevant to the functioning of economic and monetary union

The Delors Report shared both the same definition of the ultimate goal of monetary union as the Werner Plan (▶ Ch. 2.3.1), which had been drawn up two decades earlier, and the strategy of how to approach this goal in three stages. In two areas, however, the two concepts differed considerably: first, the Werner Plan considered an economic policy decision-making body at Community level to be necessary; it was to steer European economic and financial policy and be accountable to the European Parliament. Second, it left the institutional anchoring of the common monetary policy open as it merely referred, without further details, to a body "analogous to the Federal Reserve Board."

Exactly the opposite is true for the Delors Report (and later for the Maastricht Treaty): its tenor remained cautious with regard to European coordination – and even more so control – of economic and financial policy; at the same time, it clearly favored an independent, federally structured European System of Central Banks (ESCB) committed to price stability.

The ESCB was thus clearly planned along the lines of the German Bundesbank – which did not at all correspond with French ideas of how economic policy should be shaped. In France, monetary policy was traditionally considered to be part of the executive branch of government. French politicians were also used to actively intervene in the economic process through fiscal policy, regulation and large state-owned companies. The lack of a European 'economic government' (French: gouvernement économique) in the Delors concept intensified French unease, as this 'economic government' could have represented a counterweight to the independent central banking system. The Delors Commission's unanimous support for the German central bank model may have stemmed from the belief that monetary union required Germany's backing. As the largest member state, Germany traditionally supported its central bank and favored a stability-oriented monetary policy.

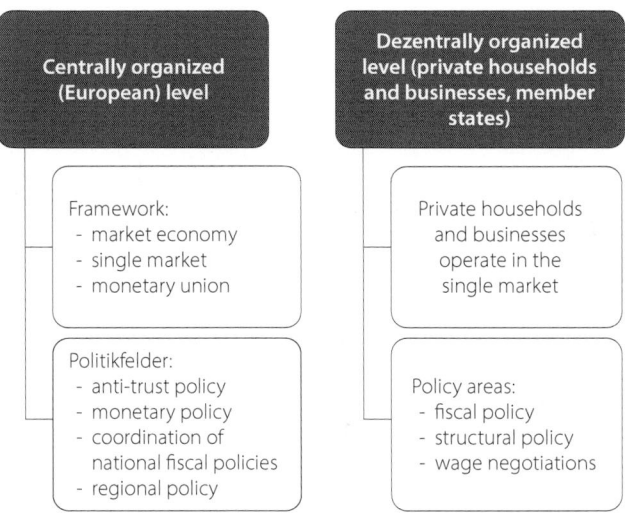

Fig. 29: 'Double decentralization' of the monetary union according to the Delors report

The Delors plan is characterized by two parallel forms of decentralization (▶ Fig. 29):

- Economic decisions should (in case of doubt) not be made centrally by the state, but by private households and companies. The EC safeguarded this fundamental decision in favor of the market economy by guaranteeing private property, individual freedom of choice, the protection of free competition and compliance with the principles of the rule of law. At the same time, 'Brussels' was to contribute to the coordination of national fiscal policies and work with regional policy measures to ensure that poorer parts of the Community were not left behind. On this basis, the emerging single market and the future European monetary order provided the framework within which private households and businesses could interact in a decentralized manner.
- The regulatory structure was thus determined at Community level. However, it is also necessary for the state to pursue process policies (i.e., to intervene in the course and structure of the economy). This task was assigned to the member states. These were to ensure that their economies were able to meet the requirements of the single market and the single currency. The mechanisms for wage setting were also to be regulated at national level.

The Delors Report thus combines the need for a central, European framework for the operations of companies, private households and national governments with the quintessence of the principle of subsidiarity, which holds that decentralized decision-making is generally superior to central regulation. This results in a special setup: there should be a common currency and a strong central bank, but no political union. The new European currency would therefore not be assigned to a (national) state, but to a market organized by a group of states. The title of an EC Commission study from the early 1990s ("One Market, One Money"[19]) puts it in a nutshell. This particular arrangement is the result of the two different motives behind the establishment of the Delors Group. One motive was to overcome German hegemony in the EMS, as France in particular wanted to break the power of the Bundesbank by Europeanizing monetary policy. At the same time, however, the proposals had to be enforceable, i.e., they had to take into account Germany's defensive stance towards a politicized central bank and a European economic government. These tactical and power-political considerations were accompanied by a second, pro-European strategic motive. Quite a few advocates of the single currency considered it a pacemaker on the way to a real (political) union. Apart from national interests, politicians like Delors also had integration policy motives. For them, Europe was a historic project that would bring Europeans together forever. Thus, when Delors stated in early 1989: "You cannot fall in love with the single market"[20], he also had the emotional significance of the (future) euro for European integration as a whole in mind. Although the single market was enormously important, it was primarily an economic and technocratic project. Europeans were to not only accept Europe, but to fall in love with it. And the euro was to be an object of this love.

3.2 Economic foundations of the discussion in the 1990s

3.2.1 The theory of optimum currency areas

Whereas the economic reasonableness of the single market was never seriously questioned, the opposite holds true for the idea of a monetary union: following the publication of the Delors Report, economists began an intensive debate on the pros and cons of a common currency in Europe. Numerous contributions to the debate referred to the Optimum Currency Area Theory (OCA), which had developed since the 1960s on the basis of a fundamental contribution by Robert Mundell.[21]

---

19 European Commission (1990): One market, one money – An evaluation of the potential benefits and costs of forming an economic and monetary union, European Economy, Vol. 44, October 1990, https://ec.europa.eu/economy_finance/publications/pages/publication7454_en.pdf
20 Delors, Jacques: Address given to the European Parliament, January 17th, 1989, https://www.cvce.eu/content/publication/2003/8/22/b9c06b95-db97-4774-a700-e8aea5172233/publishable_en.pdf
21 Cf. Mundell, R. (1961): A theory of optimum currency areas, in: American Economic Review, Vol. 51 (4/1961), pp. 657–665.

The theory of optimal currency areas is intended to answer one simple question: When is it worthwhile for a country to give up its own currency and join another currency area or to establish a new currency area with other countries? The answer to this question is as simple as the question: such a step is worthwhile if the benefits for the specific country are greater than the costs. It is, however, less easy to identify and quantify these benefits and costs.

Chapter 1 of this book has shown that international trade requires an international means of payment. Network effects are at work here. The more buyers want to use a means of payment, the more sellers will accept it. And the more sellers accept a means of payment, the more buyers will use it. This seems to suggest that the entire world should commit to one and the same means of payment. But things are not quite that simple. This is due to asymmetric shocks. These are relatively sudden price and/or volume developments that have different geographical effects (= asymmetric). Contrary to common parlance, shocks do not necessarily have to be negative, but can also be positive.

Fig. 30: Examples of asymmetric shocks

	Example of asymmetric price development	**Example of asymmetric volume development**
Positive shock	Oil and gas prices fall when new deposits are discovered • Positive for countries whose energy consumption relies heavily on fossil fuels	Demand for rare earths soars due to e-mobility and digitalization • Positive for countries that mine and export rare earths
Negative shock	CO_2 price rises sharply due to climate policy measures • Negative for countries with energy-intensive industrial production	Embargoes against oil and natural gas producing countries significantly reduce volumes • Negative for sanctioned countries • Negative for countries whose energy consumption relies heavily on fossil fuels

Here is an example: Imagine two countries which differ in the type of products they export. The first country mainly exports agricultural products, while the second exports cars. If – for whatever reason – there is a global slump in the demand for cars, this will trigger a recession with rising unemployment in the second country, but will leave the first country largely unscathed. If the two countries each have their own currency, the second country can strengthen its domestic economy with an expansive monetary policy in the hope that an exchange rate devaluation will also boost exports. Likewise, if there is a sharp rise in demand for cars. If the additional demand triggers a boom in the second country and causes high rates of price increases, the country can respond with higher interest rates to dampen domestic demand. In turn, this could lead to a fall in demand for the country's export goods and a fall in the price of imported goods in the event of an exchange rate appreciation. As a result, the boom would be weakened, as would inflation.

These options do not exist if the second country is a member of a monetary union and can no longer pursue an independent interest and exchange rate policy. This is not only of theoretical interest. Inflation and unemployment can have a massive impact on the welfare of citizens, and in extreme cases there is a risk of serious social upheaval. If the government lacks the leverage of a monetary and exchange rate policy and it is therefore unable to solve the problems in such a situation, not only the government, but the political system as a whole will lose the support of its citizens in a worst-case scenario.

This serious disadvantage of giving up one's own currency is offset by a number of advantages:

- Costs will fall for consumers and producers alike if there are no longer any exchange fees for payments for cross-border trade.
- Planning security increases for both importers and exporters, and the costs of exchange rate risk management are eliminated if agents only have to carry out their calculations in one currency.
- The greater planning security and the elimination of exchange rate risk also benefit multinational companies that have production sites in several member states of the currency union.
- A single currency enables consumers to compare the prices of domestic and foreign products. This strengthens competition.
- Provided that both the investor and the investment asset are based in the currency union, capital market investors no longer need to take exchange rate risks into account when making investment decisions. Interest rates on government and corporate bonds will fall ceteris paribus.

All in all, it can be expected that the single currency will make the goods and capital markets work better. Economic resources can be put to better use and growth will increase.

The theory of optimal currency areas has not only worked out the costs and benefits of a common currency, but also the conditions under which these advantages come into play and outweigh the disadvantages.

- Trade integration:
  The elimination of exchange rates within a single currency area reduces transaction costs for consumers, producers, importers, and exporters, while enhancing planning certainty. This effect is amplified in economies characterized by a high volume of cross-border trade.
- Homogeneity and degree of diversification of the economies involved:
  In the example above, the collapse in global demand for cars caused an asymmetric shock. The situation would be different if both countries [1] primarily produced

either both cars or both agricultural products (i.e., if they were homogeneous in the sense that either only cars or only agricultural products were produced in this monetary union) or [2] specialized in both sectors simultaneously (i.e., diversified). In the first case, the collapse in demand for cars would either affect both countries simultaneously or neither of them. If both countries were car exporters and thus faced with a decline in demand, the common central bank in a monetary union could effectively counter this symmetrical shock with an expansionary monetary policy. In the second case, the car industry in both countries would not be dominant to the degree that the global slump in demand could drag one or both countries into a serious crisis.
- Wage flexibility:
In our example, the slump in demand on the car market would reduce the labor demand of car manufacturers. If wages are flexible, they are likely to fall. Falling wages in turn increase the competitiveness of the export industry, which makes its products more attractive on the global market and the country as a whole more attractive for investment. Foreign demand for domestic goods and capital goods would increase and at least partially compensate for the negative effects of the asymmetric shock.
- Openness of national capital markets within the monetary union:
If there is a recession in a country in the monetary union due to an asymmetric shock, the prices of assets such as securities, company shareholdings and real estate fall. This makes them a worthwhile object for investors from other parts of the currency union – in our example, from the country that mainly exports agricultural products. The capital flowing into the 'car country' stabilizes asset prices and thus consumption and facilitates investment. This process can develop its stabilizing effect all the better the easier it is to make cross-border investments, i.e., the more open the capital markets of the member states are to each other.
- Cross-border diversification of capital investments in the monetary union:
If private households, companies and banks from all countries in the monetary union have distributed their capital investments evenly across all countries in the monetary union, the effect of an asymmetric shock is spread across the entire monetary union. In our example, this would mean that private households, companies and banks in the two countries have divided their capital investments equally between the agricultural and automotive sectors and therefore each receive part of their income from these sectors. The asymmetric shock now causes income from investments in the automotive industry to fall, whereas income from investments in the agricultural sector is not affected. This means that income in the agricultural country is lower and income in the automotive country is higher than it would be without cross-border capital investments. The effects of the asymmetric shock are mitigated in the country that is affected in the first place and are partially borne by the other country. The asymmetric shock becomes (partially) a symmetric shock.

- Financial transfers:
A negative asymmetric shock can also be mitigated by public transfer payments to the government of the affected country. There are different forms of transfer payments. For example, if the monetary union has a central budget, less money would be paid into the budget from the 'car country' due to the economic weakness, but at the same time the monetary union would continue to spend money in the country, for example to build a cross-border transport or energy infrastructure. This would constitute an implicit financial equalization scheme because this expenditure would be partly financed by the 'agricultural country.' The same would happen if there was a central unemployment insurance system. Fewer contributions would then flow into the unemployment insurance system from the affected member state, while unemployment benefit payments would increase there. In the member state not affected by a shock, it would be the other way around. Another possibility would be to implement explicit financial equalization. In our case, part of the tax revenue of the 'agricultural country' would then flow into the 'car country' in order to stabilize its national budget (and thus the national demand for goods and services).
- Homogeneity of economic policy preferences:
A monetary union can only function without tension if the member states have similar visions regarding their monetary policy priorities. Otherwise, conflicts over the central bank's course threaten to arise on a regular basis.

Fig. 31: Overview of the theory of optimum currency areas

Advantages and disadvantages of giving up a country's own (national) currency
Advantages: lower costs, greater planning security, greater market transparency Disadvantages: Abandonment of independent interest rate and exchange rate policy in the event of asymmetric shocks
Framework conditions that bring the advantages of a monetary union to bear or limit its disadvantages
The more pronounced the trade integration between the partner countries, the more advantageous the monetary union. • Disadvantages can be limited through the following factors: • A high degree of homogeneity and diversification of the economies involved • Pronounced wage flexibility • Openness of national capital markets • Cross-border diversification of capital investments • The existence of financial transfers • Homogeneity of economic policy preferences
Alternative approach: Endogeneity of the optimality conditions
The monetary union, by its very existence, establishes the conditions necessary for its effective functioning.

3.2.2 Endogeneity of the functional conditions of a monetary union?

The findings of the traditional theory of optimal currency areas were supplemented by a new line of argument in the 1990s: according to this theory, the conditions for the functioning of a monetary union can arise of their own accord; they can be endogenous, i.e., arise from the process of monetary integration. In other words: through its very existence, the monetary union brings about the necessary economic and political convergence of its members.

In economic terms, it is to be expected that the monetary union will promote trade integration. This means that the longer the monetary union exists, the greater the benefit from the elimination of exchange rates becomes. At the same time, the increasingly intensive interdependence ensures that economic structures and business cycles converge. If the car manufacturers in one country in our example have outsourced parts of their production to the other country and this country sources its food from there because a common currency has increased planning security, then a slump in global demand for cars will also have a negative impact on the 'agricultural country:' the parts production now based there will decline just as much as the export of food to the 'car country' – the initial asymmetric shock has (partially) become a symmetric one.

Financial processes reinforce such mechanisms. It is to be expected that the capital markets of the member states of a monetary union will become more open to each other with the elimination of exchange rate risk and that capital investments will be diversified across borders. In addition to the advantages of financial integration described above, it can also promote the harmonization of economic structures. Ideally, capital will flow from the richer countries of the monetary union to those with a need to catch up if a higher return on the capital invested can be expected there. The use of this inflowing capital for the modernization of their economies then helps the economically weaker countries to service their foreign liabilities resulting from the capital inflow later on.

The existence of the monetary union itself can also improve the functioning of political institutions. This applies to both the European and the member state level. At European level, it is to be expected that the participants in the monetary union will constantly adapt to new challenges and improve the institutions of the common currency. Competitive pressure is forcing the member states to make their labor and product markets more flexible now that they can no longer react to asymmetric developments with their own monetary policy measures. This not only makes it easier for them to cope with country-specific shocks, as described above, but also leads to higher growth potential for the national economies.

Paul Krugman's economic theory of geography provides substantial counterarguments to the debate on the possible endogeneity of functional conditions. According to this theory, the integration of economic areas does not necessarily lead to a diversification of economic structures. On the contrary, it is also conceivable that individual sectors concentrate in certain parts of the monetary union in order to exploit economies of scale. Due to historical circumstances, the production of different sectors is not evenly distributed geographically, but is characterized by clusters. For example, where companies in one sector set up a long time ago, suppliers have followed them and training facilities have been established in the surrounding area. This has created regional know-how centers that cannot easily be replicated elsewhere. The dismantling of trade barriers and the abolition of exchange rates mean that more and more companies are settling in or near the long-established production and knowledge clusters. For a monetary union, this could mean that there is no geographical diversification but, on the contrary, a specialization of economic structures. As a result, asymmetric shocks would become more likely.

Chapter 5.3 will show that the financial integration of the eurozone in particular did not improve its functioning, but on the contrary paved the way for the euro sovereign debt crisis from 2010 onwards.

3.2.3   The political economy perspective

The juxtaposition of the older and newer theory of optimal currency areas reflects the traditional opposition of 'economistic' and 'monetarist' attitudes towards European monetary integration (▶ Ch. 2.3.1). The statement of the older theory that certain conditions must be met for a monetary union to succeed supports the argument of the proponents of the 'economist' viewpoint; in contrast, the 'monetarists' can refer to the assumption of the newer theory that a monetary union automatically creates the conditions for its success once it has been established.

Nobody could even begin to predict which side would be right after the publication of the Delors Report, when the discussion about a common currency was gaining momentum in politics, academia and the public. The benefits and costs of a monetary union were too difficult to determine and the mechanisms behind the possible endogeneity of its operating conditions were too complex. Ultimately, every political decision – especially in the supranational sphere – is the result of a multitude of influencing factors; and the contributions of economic theory are generally not the most important among these.

Against this backdrop, the economic theory of politics (public choice theory) contributed political-economic aspects to the discussion. These are based on the assumption that politicians are rational self-interest maximizers and make their decisions accordingly. In the 1990s, this led to two questions: [1] What was the self-interest of the acting persons (i.e., primarily the heads of state and government of the initially twelve and, after the 1995 enlargement round, 15 EC or EU members? [2] What decisions would their self-interest maximization lead to – both before the introduction of a common currency and (if it came to that) afterwards?

The public choice theory initially answers the first question with the re-election orientation of politicians. Accordingly, the heads of state and government had to be able to communicate everything they decided on in terms of European monetary integration to their respective voters 'back home.' In addition to the interest to remain in office, securing themselves a 'place in the history books' can also be a driving force for politicians. And last but not least, it is also possible that politicians maximize their self-interest altruistically, by doing what they firmly believe to be in the interests of the country or even an entire continent – possibly even at the cost of lower chances of re-election and regardless of the retrospective judgment of the historians' guild.

Which of these motives prevailed in individual cases would influence the answer to question [2]. The negotiations of a group of self-interested heads of state and government had to result in a compromise that would ideally give the new money a good future.

3.2.4 Monetary policy and public debt in a currency union

The two fiscal criteria were the focus of attention throughout the 1990s and remain to be so to this day – through the constant criticism of the Stability and Growth Pact (▶ Ch. 3.4). The reason why government budgets are so important in the political debate is the risk of fiscal dominance. This refers to a situation in which the central bank sets aside its actual objective (ensuring price stability) in favor of the government's fiscal policy interests. Fiscal dominance can occur in nation states that have their own currency, but it poses a particular challenge in a monetary union.

Democratic processes are often characterized by the 'deficit bias.' In order to be able to offer their voters both relatively low taxes and relatively high state benefits before the election, governments finance their budgets in part through borrowing when in doubt, i. e., they accept government deficits. At the same time, after the election they generally lack the strength to sufficiently reduce the resulting debt – even in good times when tax revenues are booming. As a result, the national debt threatens to rise incessantly over the years and decades. In principle, fiscal dominance can now occur if the level of public debt has gotten so out of hand that the government – this is the rarer case – either no longer has access to the capital market at all, i. e., can no longer borrow there; in another and more common case, borrowing is only possible at ever higher interest rates. This is because if a country's fiscal policy is not sustainable, i. e., if it leads to constantly increasing debt as described above, the confidence of (potential) lenders in its solvency decreases. In return, they demand a higher risk premium in the form of an interest surcharge. The government will then only be able to take out new loans or refinance old ones at higher interest expenses. This reduces the governments scope of fiscal policy action. 'The markets' (in the sense of international investors who also invest their capital in government bonds) have 'punished' the government's unsustainable actions. The additional money that now has to be spent on interest payments is then no longer available to politicians. The only way to continue financing government activity is to increase taxes and cut spending. In extreme cases, these measures could cause the economy to collapse and provoke a national crisis.

In such a situation, the central bank could feel compelled to alleviate the state's fiscal distress by taking monetary policy measures. At an early stage of the government's budget problems, this could simply mean not raising or even lowering interest rates, although a higher interest rate level would be appropriate in view of price stability. This would at least provide the finance minister with relief in terms of interest payments. If the state's financial crisis is already more advanced, the central bank can finance the state budget directly, either through direct lending or the purchase of government bonds. On the one hand, this would increase the money supply beyond a level that is compatible with stability and, on the other, it would shake public confidence in the central bank's will to combat inflation. Inflation expectations would increase and, along with them and the increased money supply, inflation would soon follow.

In a monetary union, this mechanism is exacerbated by two factors: Spillover effects and de facto foreign currency debt. Spillovers require the coordination of national fiscal policies in a monetary union. Here are a few examples: An expansive fiscal policy in one country also increases demand in the neighboring country via import demand because its export industry benefits accordingly. A contractionary fiscal policy can also curb demand in the neighboring country via the same channel. If, for example, taxes are reduced/increased to stimulate/restrain economic activity in a member state, this measure increases/reduces the demand for consumer goods from private households living there. As private households also consume consumer goods from other member states, the tax policy measure of the national government in one member state also has an impact on consumer goods sales in the other member states. This can result in undesirable incentives. If, for example, all member states of a monetary union are in recession, each government could hope to benefit from the spillovers of expansionary fiscal policy in neighboring countries and therefore hold back with its own efforts. Overall, the fiscal policy response to the recession could then be too weak. Spillovers can also cause problems if one part of the monetary union is experiencing a boom while the other is suffering from a recession. If the boom countries pursue a restrictive fiscal policy, they also reduce demand in the recession countries and exacerbate the problems there. Conversely, if the recession countries pursue an expansive fiscal policy, they further fuel the economy in the boom countries.

However, in a monetary union, the central bank is dependent on all member states to pursue a fiscal policy that conforms to stability. This is not only due to the risk of falling under fiscal dominance, but also due to the additional inflationary pressure that can emanate from an excessively loose fiscal policy. In a boom phase, for example, it is advisable to increase taxes and/or reduce government spending in order to curb the demand for goods and services and thus the upward pressure in prices. The political costs of this policy in the form of dissatisfied voters are borne by the respective government alone, while the stabilizing effect, as we have seen, also extends to the other participating states. As a result, the consolidation of public budgets in the member states could turn out to be lower than necessary in terms of stability policy because the political costs appear too high for each individual government and it therefore hopes that the neighboring governments will lead the way.

Finally, it is also conceivable that national fiscal policies are in fact coordinated with each other but that they are at odds with the direction of European monetary policy. In the event of a supply shock, for example, the central bank could pursue a restrictive monetary policy in order to counter the inflation risks resulting from the shock. If, at the same time, national governments initiate fiscal support programs for private households and companies, this has the potential to drive up prices and counteract the restrictive monetary policy. Consider the following example: a geopolitical crisis leads to a massive increase in the price of fossil fuels. This increases the inflation rate. The central bank must react to this with a restrictive monetary policy to prevent inflation from becoming entrenched. At the same time, the member states of the monetary union decide to provide massive financial support to private households and companies so that they can better cope with rising energy prices. The restrictive monetary policy of the central bank is therefore countered by an expansive and inflation-promoting fiscal policy on the part of governments. Uniform fiscal policy can therefore also have negative consequences in a common currency area.

In addition, public debt in a monetary union is de facto debt in a foreign currency. In this context, 'foreign' is to be understood in the following sense: Each individual member state alone has no control over monetary policy, as this is decided upon by a supranational institution. The described alleviation of the government's fiscal emergency by means of a compliant monetary policy can therefore not take place. For government bondholders, the (nominal) risk of loss then increases because the government cannot maintain its solvency by accessing the central bank. As a result, government bond yields in every member state of the monetary union would be higher, ceteris paribus, than in a hypothetical comparable situation with national currencies.

The lack of independent national central banks means that fiscal dominance at the level of the individual member states is actually ruled out. After all, there is no longer a national central bank that would ultimately rush to the aid of 'its' government. However, the close political and economic interdependence within the monetary union can force the single central bank to act in favor of individual national governments. This is particularly the case when large member states are in financial difficulties and the possibility of national bankruptcy can no longer be ruled out. It would then possibly either pursue a looser monetary policy than would actually be necessary with a view to price stability, or even switch to the targeted purchase of government bonds from individual or all member states – in other words, finance their government deficits with money. The common central bank would do this not least with the aim of preventing a crisis of confidence that could spread to the entire monetary union.

As market participants (private households, companies, capital market investors) are aware of the extensive interactions between fiscal and monetary policy and of the problem of fiscal dominance, they only trust the central bank to combat inflation decisively if the possibility of influencing monetary policy for fiscal policy reasons is ruled out as far as possible. The relevant articles of the Maastricht Treaty and the secondary legislation based on them continue to matter to European politicians (and to some extent the courts) to this day.

3.3 The Maastricht Treaty

3.3.1 The ECB as a 'European Bundesbank'?

The global political upheaval in the fall of 1989 initially pushed the Delors Report published in the spring of that year into the background of European public attention. This was particularly true for Germany, which was tasked with implementing its own monetary union in the wake of the fall of the Berlin Wall and the reunification process. In the second half of 1990, the debate on European monetary integration then picked up speed again. French policymakers reiterated their call for the establishment of a European 'economic government,' advocating that the European Central Bank (ECB) should assign equal importance to fostering economic growth and employment alongside maintaining price stability. In contrast, the German Bundesbank responded to the Delors Report from a macroeconomic perspective, emphasizing the imperative of safeguarding against inflation within a prospective monetary union. Again and again, its representatives pointed to what they considered to be serious political, institutional and economic differences between the EC member states. They therefore called for the harmonization of economic structures and the completion of the political union before the introduction of a common currency. They warned against a European system of financial equalization, called for strict rules for national budgetary policies and demanded that the ESCB should have sole responsibility for foreign exchange market interventions. In addition, the future European Central Bank was to be given a say in external monetary policy. Otherwise, they argued, exchange rate policy decisions might eventually be made, for example in relation to the US dollar or the yen, with resulting intervention obligations, which could undermine the central bank's monetary policy autonomy.

The Maastricht agreement by the heads of state and government on the "Treaty on European Union" in December 1991 surprised many observers at the time and still raises questions today. Skepticism about the project was widespread in Germany and the other traditionally more stability-oriented countries as well as in France and the former weak currency countries. Thus, Germans were afraid the fight against inflation might no longer be the top priority – as with the Bundesbank – and worried that the future money could become a 'soft currency.' Many French and southern Europeans, however, were afraid of the opposite, namely a Europe that would be too 'German' in terms of monetary and fiscal policy, i.e., too restrictive and rule-oriented. Some were thus frightened by the prospect of losing the Bundesbank, whereas others were afraid of a future ECB that could turn out to be a new, even more powerful 'European Bundesbank.'

Why did 'Maastricht' nevertheless become possible? Answering this question is the task of historians, not economists. The findings of the theory of optimal currency areas (▶ Ch. 3.2.1) certainly only played a minor role in the decision-making process. This is due to the fact that the economic advantages and disadvantages of a monetary union cannot even be estimated, let alone seriously quantified. If you then add to this the basic idea that the conditions for the success of monetary integration could be endogenous (▶ Ch. 3.2.2), it is no longer possible to form a clear, economically sound opinion. The vote of the heads of state and government in favor of an economic and monetary union can therefore only be understood in the political context of the time. Germany's integration into Europe is very likely to have played a role, especially after reunification. Chancellor Helmut Kohl may also have had a certain self-commitment of his country in mind. However, his dictum that the "German and European unity are two sides of the same coin" only reflects part of the truth. After all, the Delors Report was published when no one even dared to dream of the fall of the Iron Curtain; moreover, the 'taming' of the economic hegemon had already been a goal of the EMS. However, German unification is likely to have significantly accelerated the process of European monetary integration. The fact that France and the southern European EC countries had been modeling their economic policy on Germany since the mid-1980s certainly made it easier for them to accept a European central bank modeled on the Bundesbank. They were certainly guided by the reasonable hope that they would be able to have a say in the monetary policy of this future 'European Bundesbank' and thus make it a little less 'German.'

'Maastricht' adopted the key elements of the Delors report. Most important was the transfer of monetary policy to a new supranational organization, the European Central Bank, or more precisely the Eurosystem, in which the ECB to be founded would work together with the existing national central banks.

The Eurosystem was conceived as a federal system and was to be independent and committed to the primary goal of price stability. At the time of the Maastricht conference, the idea of central bank independence had by no means become an established practice in most countries, but it had been in the academic analysis of monetary policy. Independent central banks were believed to be the most likely to overcome the time inconsistency problem. This means that a political promise can be credible at the time it is made; however, it is possible to conceive of circumstances under which this promise cannot realistically be expected to be kept. For example, if the responsibility for monetary policy was in the hands of the government, the government could credibly promise at the beginning of the election period to use monetary policy instruments solely for the purpose of combatting inflation. Shortly before the next election, however, its interest in winning this election might be so great that it would expand its monetary policy regardless of inflation in order to increase economic growth and thus its chances of re-election. However, such surprise inflation would only have a one-off and short-term growth-promoting effect. If this approach was repeated, it would lead to higher inflation but lower growth rates in the long term.

To prevent this from happening, the decision-makers of the ESCB should be able to carry out their work independent of re-election and other interests. This independence has different dimensions:

- Institutional dimension:
  The Treaty on European Union clearly stipulates that "...neither the ECB, nor a national central bank, nor any member of their decision-making bodies shall seek or take instructions from Union institutions, bodies, offices or agencies, from any government of a Member State or from any other body." And: "The Union institutions, bodies, offices or agencies and the governments of the Member states undertake to respect this principle and not to seek to influence the members of the decision-making bodies of the ECB or of the national central banks in the performance of their tasks." The national central banks must also be independent; as their representatives have the majority of votes in the Governing Council, the most important decision-making body, the institutional independence of the ESCB also has a vertical or federal component.
- Personal dimension:
  The Council appoints the members of the Executive Board of the ECB for a term of office of eight years and without the possibility of reappointment. They can only be dismissed if they are charged with very serious misconduct or if a member of the Executive Board is no longer able to perform their duties for health reasons. The member states must lay down similar rules for the governors of the national central banks. On the one hand, these rules are to prevent decision-makers from simply comply with governments in order to be reappointed after their term of office has expired. On the other hand, governments should not be able to remove members of the Executive Board or governors of national central banks from office if their monetary policy runs counter to the interests of governments.
- Financial dimension:
  The ESCB finances itself through the proceeds of its activities and is therefore not dependent on the goodwill of state donors (government, parliament).
- Instrumental dimension:
  No specific instruments are prescribed to the ECB; it "...shall be completely independent in the performance of their duties..." In particular, the ESCB may not be used for the so-called 'monetization' of government debt: Neither the ECB nor the national central banks are allowed to grant loans to government entities or to buy debt instruments from them directly. This rule is intended to prevent government debt – and therefore government spending – from being financed 'by the printing press' (i.e., with newly created central bank money). If that happened, its monetary policy would no longer pursue its primary objective.

The members of the ECB Executive Board and the national central bank governors are appointed by the European Council or the governments of the member states, and thus by democratically legitimized bodies; during their term, however, they are free from political influence and can hardly be challenged legally. Such far-reaching independence of appointed, but not elected technocrats requires special justification in a constitutional democracy. Three conditions must be met:

- The fulfillment of this task is of outstanding importance for society as a whole.
  This applies to the primary mandate of the ESCB, namely to ensure price stability. In a market economy, prices are to inform market participants in countless markets about the scarcity of supply and the strength of demand and thereby direct resources to where their use promises the greatest benefit for producers and consumers. Inflation significantly impairs these functions of prices. There is therefore a positive correlation between low, stable inflation rates and long-term growth. If inflation gets out of control, there is a risk of sudden ups and downs in economic development in a long phase of weak growth. Inflation also has distribution effects, which many citizens dislike. For example, richer people with a relatively low consumption rate and high income from real assets (real estate, shares, company investments) are generally better able to protect themselves against inflation than poorer people, who live on wage or transfer payments and have to spend (almost) all of their income on rent and everyday goods.
- The degree of the achievement of the ECB's targets must be measurable and the central bank must be able to have a determining influence on it.
  The extent to which the goal of price stability is achieved can be measured using the consumer price index and the inflation rate according to internationally recognized scientific standards. The central bank has suitable instruments at its disposal to control the inflation rate in the medium and long term.
- The central bank is accountable for its activities to the democratic bodies and the public.
  The ECB must report on its activities to the European Parliament, the Council and the Commission once a year. The President of the ECB and, if applicable, other members of the Executive Board are also obliged to answer the questions by European Parliament's Economic and Monetary Affairs Committee on a quarterly basis. In addition to these mandatory information obligations, the Eurosystem publishes the minutes of Governing Council meetings, but does not publish individual opinions or the voting behavior of individual members of the Governing Council. The aim is to Europeanize or 'denationalize' the debate. After the Governing Council meetings, the President answers journalists' questions at a press conference.

The commitment to ensure price stability, the decentralized structure, the ban on lending to public institutions and the independence from directives explain why the ECB has been described as a central bank 'modeled after the Bundesbank' – because these were all essential features of the German central bank. As a reminder, this set-up was considered necessary in order to win over the German population, which was both inflation-averse and loyal to the Bundesbank. At the same time, however, there were also significant differences between the ECB and the Bundesbank: For example, the ECB's stricter accountability obligations (which the Bundesbank did not have to the same extent) and the higher level of legal anchoring of rights and obligations. Whereas the Bundesbank Act could be amended by the legislator with a simple majority, the Treaty on European Union with the accompanying Protocol on the European Central Bank is part of European primary law. Therefore, it can only be amended unanimously, i. e., with the consent of all member states. As described above, core elements of central bank independence now have constitutional status in all EU countries.

In a sense, the ECB has thus arguably become more independent than the Bundesbank ever was. However, this did not necessarily mean that the ECB would find it easier to achieve the primary goal of price stability. This is due to the special position of the central bank in a monetary union whose Maastricht blueprint follows the recommendations of the Delors Report and places fiscal policy in the hands of the member states.

Monetary and fiscal policy therefore take place at different levels. This can be an advantage because the member states no longer have access to the money creation of 'their' respective national central banks. At the same time, the central bank does not have to face a powerful central government, which might try to influence it. Each national government must accept the monetary framework implemented by the higher authority and the loss of an independent interest and exchange rate policy. The national governments are on their own here, as the Maastricht Treaty stipulates that neither the member states nor the EU as a whole are liable for the liabilities of the participating countries of the monetary union or of their federal subdivisions (so-called 'no bailout clause'). There is also no financial equalization scheme nor a significant budget at the European level. Finally, there was to be no 'European finance minister' or 'European economic government.' All these provisions would have contradicted the above-mentioned 'double decentralization principle' of the Delors Plan and would probably not have been politically feasible. For many countries, handing over fiscal policy powers 'to Brussels' would have meant giving up too much sovereignty. The external control of national fiscal policies was therefore in the hands of the countries' creditors, i.e., the capital market investors who held government bonds. The rules were based on the assumption that markets would discipline national finance ministers: if a country's fiscal policy threatened to leave the path of sustainability, 'the markets' would sanction this type of behavior by demanding yield premiums (i. e., higher interest rate demands to compensate for the increased risk of insolvency) and thus force this country's politicians to adopt a more stability-oriented budget management.

There were also fears that a centralized European budget or a redistribution mechanism would not improve the functioning of the monetary union, but rather worsen it. The reason for this concern were the negative incentive effects (moral hazard) on the part of national governments that could have emanated from any kind of fiscal support. Specifically, there were concerns that the member states could forego their own economic and fiscal policy efforts and instead rely on cash payments from other member states or from Brussels. Without the pressure to consolidate, for example, there would be no pressure to carry out privatizations and subsidy cuts. There was a general concern that the state sector and the social system might be bloated. The argument was that structural reforms might not be carried out because countries would be able to maintain a certain level of prosperity without such reforms due to the support 'from Europe.' At the same time, in an environment with attractive jobs in the public sector and a high (implicit) minimum wage as well as relatively generous social benefits, the trade unions could push through high wage demands. All of these factors would impair competitiveness.

The central bank, as the only truly effective economic policy institution at Community level, was therefore to be faced with a dozen or more member states which would act autonomously. Because their actions and interactions were hardly foreseeable and might impact the common monetary policy, the authors of the Maastricht Treaty considered it necessary to define conditions that would have to be met to participate in the monetary union: the convergence criteria were developed. These criteria were to ensure that only suitable countries would participate in the monetary union. Institutions aimed at coordinating national economic policies were, however, not created.

3.3.2 The convergence criteria

The convergence criteria breathe the spirit of the experiences that (Western) Europeans gained in the 1970s and 1980s in an environment of high and fluctuating inflation rates with two fixed exchange rate systems ("currency snake" ▶ Ch. 2.3.2 and EMS ▶ Ch. 2.4). They resulted from the realization that fixed exchange rates – and thus ultimately also a monetary union – cannot withstand permanently diverging inflation rates and economic policies in the participating countries (▶ Ch. 2.2.5). Against this background, the convergence criteria test the will and the ability of national governments and central banks to meet the requirements of a monetary union. It is noticeable that the criteria only cover monetary, exchange rate and fiscal policy. Convergence of the real economic structures (e. g., GDP per capita, employment rate) and the institutional framework (labor market flexibility, wage policy procedures, social systems) in the potential member states of the future monetary union was not the focus of interest. There may be various reasons for this. For example, such factors were not primarily seen as the cause of the failure of the 'currency snake' and the difficulties of the EMS in 1992/93. Apart from that, they were relatively difficult to quantify – if not through GDP per capita. In addition, more and more observers assumed that the optimality conditions were endogenous, i.e., they expected that real economic structures would quasi-automatically converge. Ultimately, the member states would also probably have regarded any focus on fields such as social policy or labor market structures as an encroachment on their own competencies and would therefore have rejected any specifications made on the European level.

The following convergence criteria were defined:

- Inflation criterion:
  The inflation rate must not be higher than 1.5 percentage points above the inflation rate of the three countries with the most stable prices.
- Interest rate criterion:
  The long-term nominal interest rate must not be higher than two percentage points above the corresponding values in the three countries with the most stable prices.
- Exchange rate criterion:
  The country must have participated in the exchange rate mechanism of the EMS for at least two years without any problems.
- Deficit criterion:
  The net new government debt must not exceed 3 % of gross domestic product.
- Debt criterion:
  Total government debt must not exceed 60 % of gross domestic product.

Countries that meet the inflation criterion are expected to be able to pursue the policy of monetary stability required in a monetary union. In order to counter the risk of fiscal dominance of monetary policy (▶ Ch. 3.2.4), only countries with sustainable public finances should be able to participate in the monetary union. This is the purpose of the two fiscal criteria among the convergence criteria outlined above. The interest rate and exchange rate criteria complement the other three criteria: They are intended to assess how capital market participants judge the fiscal and monetary soundness of the currency union candidates. Key determinants of the long-term nominal interest rate are a country's credit rating and inflation expectations. With low long-term interest rates, the capital market rewards the fact that an issuer of government bonds has its finances under control and pursues an economic policy aimed at price stability. If the exchange rate criterion is met, international investors do not expect the currency in question to depreciate, which in turn suggests that this country's economic policy is sustainable.

The two fiscal criteria in particular were already highly controversial in the 1990s. In addition to the fundamental question of whether such a restriction of national fiscal policies could be sensible and justified, many critics were bothered by the rigid figures of 3 % and 60 %, respectively. On the one hand, it was argued that these figures were set arbitrarily and therefore faced a credibility problem from the very beginning. Implausible targets, in turn, would only be followed reluctantly and would be hard to enforce. On the other hand, one could argue that simple rules such as the deficit and debt criteria were particularly enduring in the political process because they were easy to understand and their violation could be easily recognized. If rules are more flexible and complex, they invite circumvention, which can then hardly be detected due to the lack of transparency associated with flexibility and differentiation.

Irrespective of this dispute, which has not yet been resolved, the determination of the specific figures of 3 % and 60 % lies in the darkness of history. As far as the debt criterion is concerned, it is often assumed that 60 % appeared to be achievable, particularly for the two large countries France and Germany. There are different explanations for the 3 % deficit limit. In their book *The Economics of European Integration*, Richard Baldwin and Charles Wyplosz attribute it to the debt rule that prevailed in Germany at the time.[22] According to this 'Golden Rule,' net new government debt was not allowed to exceed the level of public investment. The latter, in turn, averaged around 3 % of gross domestic product in Germany over the long term. This figure was then introduced by Germany into the negotiations on the convergence criteria and accepted by the other member states. According to another hypothesis, the figure goes back to a French proposal dating back to 1981. According to this theory, the then newly elected President Francois Mitterand needed a justification for not being able to fulfill all election promises immediately. The Ministry of Finance officials tasked with finding this justification decided to limit new borrowing to 3 % without any theoretical basis. This figure seemed strict enough to ward off overly ambitious demands, but given the revenue and expenditure situation at the time, it did not require overly strict savings targets. A decade later, this figure was then brought into the discussions over the framework conditions for the monetary union, where it was met with approval.[23]

The two criteria were then brought into a seemingly rational relationship: with a nominal growth of 5 % and an inflation rate of 2 %, a net new borrowing of 3 %, based on a debt level of 60 %, was precisely the level of borrowing that would keep government debt constant at the same 60 %.[24] This economic linking was devised in hindsight and suggested that the two figures had a theoretical underpinning; yet it was based on an unrealistic growth assumption and therefore quickly proved to be untenable.

3.4 The Stability and Growth Pact

As part of the preparations for the monetary union, there was a debate about how the fiscal soundness of the EU countries could be ensured even after the introduction of the single currency. This was because the Maastricht convergence criteria initially only applied to the accession to the monetary union, whereas the specific rules for the period afterwards still had to be defined. Germany's Finance Minis-

---

22 Baldwin, R./Wyplosz, C. (2023): The Economics of European Integration, 7th edition, McGraw Hill 2023, p. 378.
23 Cf. Schubert, C. (2013): Wie das Maastricht-Kriterium im Louvre entstand, Frankfurter Allgemeine Zeitung vom 25.9.2013, p. 10, and Anon. (2012): The secret of 3 % finally revealed, voxeurop, https://voxeurop.eu/en/the-secret-of-3-finally-revealed/
24 Cf. voxeurop.eu/en/the-secret-of-3-finally-revealed. Cf. Sachverständigenrat zur Begutachtung der gesamtwirtschaftlichen Entwicklung (1994): Jahresgutachten 1994/95, Drucksache des Deutschen Bundestages 13/26 vom 21.11.1994, Randnummer 183, p. 155.

ter Theo Waigel played a leading role in this process. At the time, the debt policy of the states was seen as a major threat to a stability-oriented monetary policy, which could threaten the central bank with fiscal dominance (▶ Ch. 3.2.4). From 1995 onwards, Waigel therefore resolutely advocated a 'stability pact' for EU member states. Clear rules (particularly with regard to new government debt) as well as sanctions if those rules were violated were to ensure sustainable public finances in the long term. France, which was skeptical or even opposed to Waigel's concept, argued that national governments should be given as much leeway as possible in terms of fiscal policy. They should continue to be able to use state revenue and expenditure to actively shape economic policy. The negotiations resulted in a compromise. Although there was a pact, Waigel had to accept changes to his plan. The change of name to 'Stability and Growth Pact,' which was pushed through by the French, was a rather cosmetic measure. However, the fact that automatic sanctions for breaches of the rules were abandoned was crucial. Instead, the Council was now to decide on the enforcement of sanctions by majority vote.

The Stability and Growth Pact finally came into force on July 1, 1998. In principle, it also applies to EU countries that are not members of the eurozone, and it has two parts:

- A preventive arm:
  The aim here is to avoid breaches of the fiscal criteria from the outset. The Commission monitors the budget situation of the member states, particularly with regard to new government debt. In the medium term, the budgets of the member states should be balanced. To this end, the governments must submit a stability program that shows the medium-term path to a balanced budget. The Commission examines the stability programs and can demand corrections. At this point in the procedure, member states can be obliged to make an interest-bearing deposit if they break the rules. This deposit is only repaid if they meet the requirements regarding the medium-term budget.
- A corrective arm:
  In addition to the medium-term budget balance, the 3 % target has to be observed – except in case of a severe economic downturn or an exceptional event beyond the control of the member state. Otherwise, net borrowing of more than 3 % of gross domestic product leads to the initiation of an excessive deficit procedure. This is to be recommended by the Commission to the Council, which then initiates the procedure if it determines that an excessive deficit exists. Then, sanctions are possible. They range from the conversion of the above-mentioned interest-bearing deposit into a non-interest-bearing deposit to a fine of 0.2 % of the national gross domestic product, which can be further increased if the recommendations are not followed. The sanctions are to be decided by the Council.

Neither party could really be satisfied with the compromise. Those in favor of a strict stability pact considered it a problem that the Council had to decide on the imposition of sanctions. The problem was that the heads of state and government were to decide whether and to what extent one of their colleagues (or rather the country they represented) would be punished for fiscal misconduct – knowing full well that each of them could soon find themselves 'on the dock.' This politicized the implementation of the rules. The individual procedural steps of the pact would become part of the negotiating mass of the Brussels political establishment – a phenomenon that was promptly labeled by critics as "sinners judging sinners," highlighting perceived hypocrisy in the enforcement of the regulation. However, the advocates of the greatest possible political flexibility in the procedure opposed such a view. They argued that automatic sanctions of member states would constitute a too far-reaching intervention in their budgetary autonomy and thus constitute an infringement of democratic self-determination.

The question was also raised as to the extent to which financial penalties made sense in this context. After all, it was argued that such penalties increased the problems of the sanctioned countries in two ways. On the one hand, these countries were involved in the proceedings precisely because their deficits or debt levels were too high. The fines to be transferred to Brussels only made their financial situation worse. On the other hand, the implementation of the rules would enforce an austerity policy that would prove to be counterproductive. Also, the acute budget problems of the "sinners" would typically come to light in a phase of low or even negative GDP growth rates. If they were now forced to increase taxes and reduce spending in order to avoid the sanctions of the excessive deficit procedure, this would further worsen the economic situation and thus the budget situation. The attempt to "save their way out" of a crisis, so to speak, was tantamount to squaring the circle. Irrespective of their concrete implementation and possible sanctions, the requirements made it difficult for EU countries to react appropriately to the situation in a recession. Countercyclical fiscal policy was difficult if the government deficit was subject to a rigid limit even in a recession.

The supporters of the pact countered this with what the European Council had stated in 1997 in a resolution on the Stability and Growth Pact: "Adherence to the objective of sound budgetary positions close to balance or in surplus will allow all Member states to deal with normal cyclical fluctuations while keeping the government deficit within the reference value of 3 % of GDP." This statement confirms that the medium-term goal of government fiscal policy, which is to be achieved over the economic cycle, must be a balanced budget. In the event of a recession, the permissible deficit of 3 % of gross domestic product provides sufficient leeway for counter-cyclical revenue and expenditure management. In practice, however, the 3 % deficit quickly developed into the actual target for both good and bad times. According to the advocates of the Stability and Growth Pact, the pro-cyclical fiscal policy during the crisis was therefore not due to the 3 % deficit criterion, but to excessively lax budget management during upswings and booms.

3 Paving the way

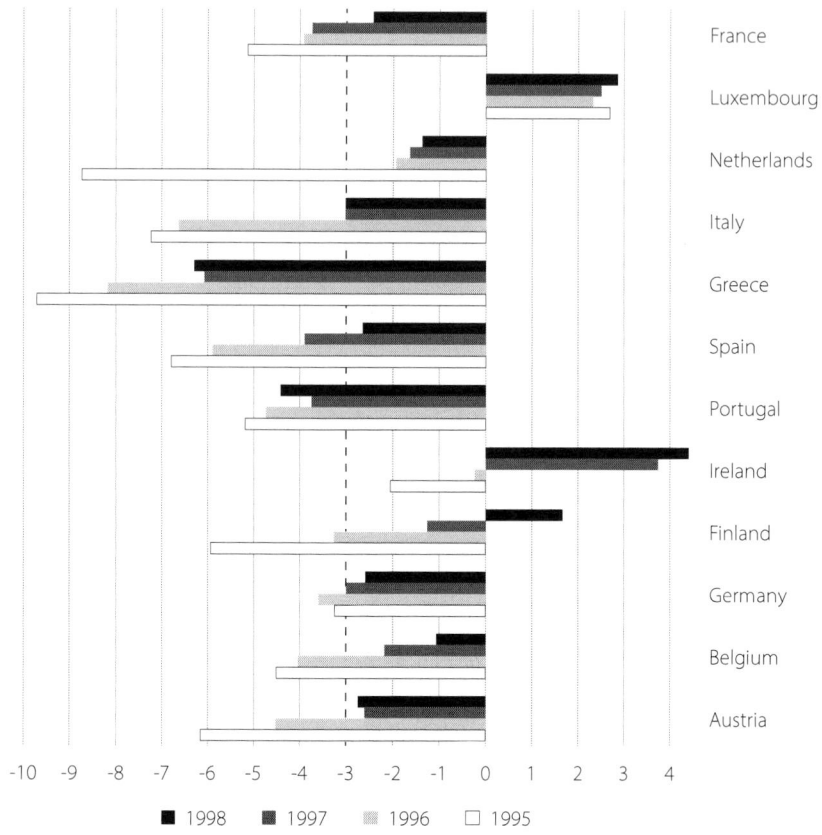

Fig. 32: Public deficit as % of GDP in the starting formation of monetary union member countries (plus Greece, which joined in 2001; data: ECB)

3.5   Decisive steps on the road to monetary union

After ratification by the twelve member states, the "Treaty on European Union" came into force on November 1, 1993. This meant that almost two years had passed since the Maastricht Conference. During this time, the project not only survived the EMS crisis, but also one referendum in France and two in Denmark. The second referendum had become necessary because the Danes had initially rejected the Maastricht Treaty. They were then granted an opt-out from the monetary union, which secured their approval in the second attempt. Such an opt-out had been a condition for the British to sign the treaty from the outset. With their vote in favor of establishing the European Union, the other ten member states also accepted the obligation to introduce the single currency as soon as they would meet the convergence criteria. Although there was no referendum in Germany, various plaintiffs lodged a constitutional complaint with the Federal Constitutional Court against the ratification of the treaty by the Bundestag. In their 'Maastricht ruling,' the judges declared the Maastricht Treaty to be in line with Germany's Basic Law. However, they also stated that the democratic influence of the citizens of the Federal Republic of Germany on European decision-making must be preserved and that the future monetary union must be designed as a stability union.

With the start of the second stage of the monetary union, the European Monetary Institute, which was based in Frankfurt, began its work in 1994. It was responsible for the closer coordination of national monetary policies and, in particular, preparatory work for the future European monetary policy. During this period, the member states were required to create the legal framework for their possible accession. To achieve this goal, they were to anchor the independence of their respective central banks in constitutional law and to rule out monetary financing of the national budget.

The phased plan agreed in Maastricht then provided for the third stage – i.e., the actual monetary union – to begin between January 1, 1997 at the earliest and January 1, 1999 at the latest. A start before 1999 would have required the Council of Ministers to determine that a majority of the (since 1995) fifteen member states fulfilled the accession conditions. If necessary, the mandatory entry into the monetary union in 1999 was also to take place with a minority of member states. This stipulation was a concession to the 'monetarists,' including France in particular. Member countries were, on the other hand, compelled to fulfill the convergence conditions, which was a requirement based on 'economistic' reasoning. It was soon apparent that neither the inflation, nor the exchange rate or interest rate criteria would be the decisive hurdle. The 'Great Moderation,' which had been in effect since the mid-1980s, caused inflation rates to fall worldwide. This was also noticeable in Europe. The inflation rates of the former 'weak currency countries' in southern Europe fell sustainably, approaching those of the 'hard currency countries.' The exchange rate criterion had already been considerably softened through the widening of the bandwidth after the EMS crisis. But even if this had not been the case, exchange rates would have converged from the mid-1990s onwards. Because inflation and exchange rate expectations are decisive determinants of the long-term nominal interest rate, these rates also converged. This positive development resulted from three factors: In addition to the 'Great Moderation' mentioned above, there was actual material progress towards a stability-oriented (monetary) policy as well as the expectation that a future European Central Bank would ensure the stability of the monetary framework. Just what was the 'mixing ratio' of the three determinants that brought about the convergence of inflation rates, exchange rates and interest rates remains the subject of economic history debates to this day.

3 Paving the way

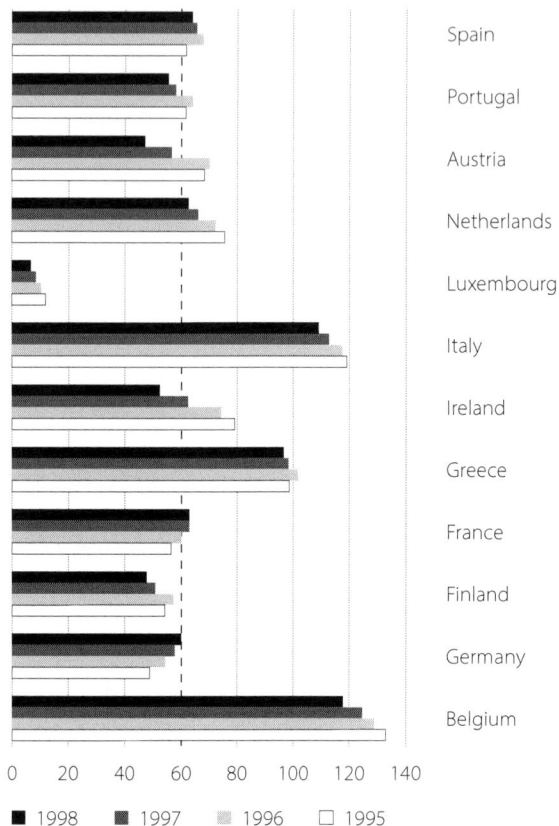

Fig. 33: General government debt as % of GDP in the starting formation of monetary union member countries (plus Greece, which joined in 2001; data: ECB)

Regarding borrowing and debt levels, the situation was different. Many member states found it very difficult to comply with the two fiscal criteria. The deficit criterion (3 % of GDP ▶ Fig. 32) was, however, easier to influence in the short term than the debt criterion (60 % of GDP ▶ Fig. 33). Belgium and Italy in particular were far from the required 60 %. They had to rely on the passage that membership of the monetary union was still possible if the value was sufficiently close to the target figure. In their fiscal policy efforts, the euro aspirants benefited from a generally more favorable economic trend after the severe recession at the beginning of the decade. In addition, a stronger dollar from 1995 onwards boosted exports, and low oil prices also contributed to favorable external economic conditions in 1997 and 1998. Finally, the convergence of long-term interest rates at a historically low level also eased the burden on national budgets. Nevertheless, some EU countries sought refuge in one-off measures and ad hoc actions, some of which took on the character of 'accounting tricks' in the eyes of the public. In addition to spending cuts and tax increases, these included the (partial) privatization of state-owned companies (e. g., in Germany or France) or the early booking of tax revenues that would not have accrued until 1999 (in Italy). In Germany, Finance Minister Theo Waigel also brought a revaluation of the Bundesbank's gold reserves into play. However, the project failed because both the Frankfurt monetary authorities and the public opposed the measure.

While such one-off measures met with unanimous criticism, the fiscal policy efforts of the euro aspirants were judged differently overall. The optimistic interpretation was that the expectation of the coming monetary union would change the behavior of the players, as governments, unions and employers as well as the population in the member states had recognized that new rules of the game would apply once the monetary union was established. Politicians and companies would have to face greater competitive pressure on the single market due to increased price transparency. At the same time, national monetary and exchange rate policies would no longer serve as a balancing mechanism. Against this backdrop, a consensus had emerged that structural reforms were necessary at both state and company level. In addition to a stability-oriented fiscal policy, the reforms included making the labor and goods markets more flexible, reducing social policy to the essentials and aligning companies with the European single market. The optimists therefore assumed there would be a fundamental change in behavior towards a market-oriented economic policy.

This was contrasted by a rather pessimistic perspective, according to which the fiscal policy tour de force in the years leading up to the introduction of the euro was merely tactically motivated. According to this view, there had been no change in economic policy preferences on the part of the countries, as they had merely wanted to leap over the hurdle ahead of them. Therefore, the homogeneity of economic policy preferences as a functional condition for an optimal currency area did not exist. One important player who repeatedly voiced this concern was the German Bundesbank. In countless speeches and publications, its representatives emphasized that a monetary union needed more than convergence conditions, fiscal policy rules and an independent central bank. At the end of 1991, shortly after the Maastricht Conference, Bundesbank President Schlesinger in the Handelsblatt had called for a "'culture of stability' in public and politics" like the one that had developed in Germany after two hyperinflations. He went on to write: "Politics and society must promote a focus on stability and actively support it" because "we must not forget that the central bank cannot ensure stable prices on its own, even if a good monetary policy is the essential building block."[25] Without a stability-oriented fiscal policy, competition-oriented structural framework conditions for companies' activities and, last but not least, suitable mechanisms that help employers and trade unions to come together in a productivity-oriented wage policy, it would hardly be possible to combat inflation successfully in the long term. According to this line of argument, the desire for stability should not just be written on paper in the Maastricht Treaty, but must be put into practice by politicians and the population in everyday economic life.

---

25 Schlesinger, H.: "Eine europäische Währung muss genauso stabil sein wie die D-Mark ", in Handelsblatt of December 31, 1991, p. 9.

Fig. 34: Approval of the euro in the EU countries (%; spring 1998; data: Eurobarometer 49)

Meanwhile, the heads of state and government pressed ahead with preparations for the third stage. They endorsed German Finance Minister Waigel's proposal to call the new currency the 'euro.' Also, in a diplomatic move to win over the still euro-skeptic Germans, they chose Frankfurt as the seat of the European Central Bank because that was the city of the Bundesbank and its predecessor institution, the "Bank deutscher Länder," which had provided stable money for half a century. The implicit signal was that the future euro would be just as strong as the Deutschmark. On May 2, 1998, the Council finally determined that 13 of the 15 EU countries met the convergence criteria. Greece proved to be not (yet) ready for the monetary union. Denmark and Great Britain made use of the opt-out clause granted to them in the Maastricht Treaty. Sweden deliberately did not participate in the exchange rate mechanism and thus voluntarily failed to meet the exchange rate criterion which brought about a de facto opt-out. Sweden, Denmark and the UK chose not to join the monetary union, which reflects the skepticism of these countries' citizens. Here, more citizens were against the euro than in favor of it. Everywhere else, approval prevailed, even though only just over half of the population was in favor of the single currency in Germany, Portugal, Finland and Austria. Among the eleven countries that started on January 1,

1999, on average a two-thirds majority was in favor of the project. In Italy, the level of support for the euro was the highest (▶ Fig. 34).

Fig. 35: Membership of the eurozone

The euro was launched on January 1, 1999 with eleven countries, i.e., a relatively large number of participants (▶ Fig. 35). This fact was the result of a complicated political situation. The 'economists' were unable to push through their insistence on a strict interpretation of the convergence criteria. France did not want a monetary union that was too small and in which Germany would be too strong, as this would have meant a continuation of the EMS dominated by the Bundesbank under different auspices (▶ Ch. 2.4.3). Belgium and Italy in particular were at the center of the debate. In the 1950s, they had been among the six members of the Coal and Steel Community and signatories of the Treaty of Rome. The two countries also had close economic ties with Germany and France. At the same time, however, their debt level was over 100 % of GDP and thus far from the 60 % limit. Those in favor of Belgium and Italy joining the euro as soon as possible cited a passage in the treaties according to which it was sufficient for the debt level to approach the target figure recognizably. Clearly, it is a success criterion for decisions at European level if they are not formulated too precisely but instead remain open to interpretation, thus reflecting the positions of many member states at the same time. Both the conditions for joining the monetary union and the Stability and Growth Pact are exemplary in this respect. Overall, the 1990s show once again that progress in European integration is only ever possible as the result of a finely balanced system of compromises (▶ Fig. 36). The extent to which the underlying decisions shape the continent's economic and political situation or merely reflect it often remains unclear at the time the decisions are made. It is only in the longer term that the determining factors become apparent.

In addition to determining the group of participants as of January 1, 1999, other important decisions had to be made, not least the appointment of the six-member Executive Board of the European Central Bank. A fierce dispute over the appointment of the president ended with a compromise to accommodate France's strong claim to the top post: Wim Duisenberg from the Netherlands was to become the first president. At the same time however, Duisenberg announced that he would step down after four years, i. e., half of his term of office, in favor of a French successor. This compromise, like the previous dispute, faced fierce public criticism: The fact that the ECB, which would still have to earn its monetary policy credibility, had already been caught in the crosshairs of the member states' political interests before it was even founded, was seen by many as a bad omen for the euro. In contrast to the position of President, who was to become the first Chief Economist proved to be an uncontroversial issue. This position was filled with the former Würzburg economics professor Otmar Issing, who had previously held the same post at the German Bundesbank. Christian Noyer from France became Vice President, and the other members of the Executive Board came from Finland (Sirkka Hämäläinen), Spain (Eugenio Domingo Solans) and Italy (Tommaso Padoa Schioppa). Since then, the three major eurozone countries Germany, France and Italy have always been represented on the ECB Executive Board.

Fig. 36: The euro as a compromise between contending economic concepts

How has the German position (which tends to be 'economistic') been reflected?	How has the French position (which tends to be 'monetarist') been reflected?
ECB based on the Bundesbank model ECB headquarters in Frankfurt	No political union before economic and monetary union
Euro only for suitable countries (convergence criteria)	Start by 1/1/1999 at the latest; no strict interpretation of convergence criteria; therefore, relatively many participants at the beginning
Stability pact with fiscal criteria becomes part of the regulatory framework	Growth as a goal was to be at least conceptually reflected in the name of the Pact; Pact does not provide automatic sanctions
Wim Duisenberg, Otmar Issing on first ECB executive board	Duisenberg voluntarily steps down after four years in favor of a Frenchman

3.6   The ECB formulates its strategy

The European Central Bank began its work on July 1, 1998. For the first six months, this work consisted of carrying out one of the biggest experiments in the history of money. Initially, the six members of the Executive Board only had the limited experience of the European Monetary Institute and a few hundred employees at their disposal. The national central banks, on the other hand, were able to look back on a history dating back to the 19th century and also had altogether a five-digit number of employees.

3.6 The ECB formulates its strategy

Wim Duisenberg (1935–2005) was a Dutch economist who worked at the International Monetary Fund, the Dutch Central Bank and as a minister and member of parliament before becoming President of the Dutch Central Bank after a stint at Rabobank. Before taking up the post of President of the European Central Bank in 1998, Duisenberg headed the European Monetary Institute, the ECB's predecessor institution. Duisenberg made his position available in 2003 to a successor from France, Jean-Claude Trichet, as agreed before his appointment in 1998. [Photo: European Central Bank]

The ECB now had to achieve two objectives within a limited timeframe and with very limited resources. The first was to build its reputation. The most important resource for a central bank is the trust of the public that it will fulfill its task (in this case: to ensure price stability). As a completely new institution, the ECB also had to start from scratch in this respect. It was also necessary to prepare internally for the assumption of monetary policy responsibility on January 1, 1999. In order to turn eleven national monetary policies into one European policy, the ECB needed an operational concept of how to achieve price stability for the entire (future) eurozone. This means that the ECB needed a toolbox.

Otmar Issing (born 1936) was professor of economics (with a focus on money and international economic relations) at the Universities of Erlangen-Nuremberg (1967–1973) and Würzburg (from 1973). In this function he was a member of the German Council of Economic Experts from 1988 to 1990. He became Chief Economist at the German Bundesbank (1990–1998) before moving to the European Central Bank in the same capacity. Issing, who is regarded as the intellectual father of the two-pillar strategy, stepped down from the ECB Executive Board after the end of his eight-year term of office. Since then, he has been involved in a variety of activities, including at the Center for Financial Studies at Goethe University Frankfurt, where he served as President from 2006 to 2022. [Photo: O. Issing]

As a basis for achieving both goals, the ECB needed to develop and communicate a monetary policy strategy. The latter is a binding statement on how the central bank intends to generate and process the information required to form its opinion as well as on how it intends to arrive at its monetary policy decisions on this informational basis. In short: the central bank announces the fundamental way in which it intends to fulfill its mandate.

Unlike other central banks, the ECB had to define its strategic direction without really knowing its field of action, the future eurozone. By December 31, 1998, there would be eleven national currency areas, each with its own economic structures, financial system and monetary policy traditions. The only experience extant was that the involved national banks had gained with respect to how their instruments worked for their respective currency areas. In addition, any historical data was also available almost exclusively at the level of the future member states of the monetary union. The ECB could therefore not rely on historical data to determine how the eurozone would develop economically. Neither could the ECB work on the basis of adding up the key macroeconomic indicators, as the economies of the member states differed considerably in terms of their fundamental structure and economic policy institutions. This lack of a suitable data basis also made it very difficult to analytically describe the actual situation on an aggregated level, i. e., for the eurozone level.

In addition, the new entity was very likely to be a 'moving target.' This means that the founding of the eurozone itself could have changed the economic area in unknown directions. For example, it was completely unclear how all eleven national economies together would react to the European monetary policy that came into effect on January 1, 1999. The banks and capital market players in the member states had no experience with a single cross-border interest rate that was implemented through the same and, in some cases, new monetary policy instruments. The elimination of exchange rate risk could increase competition on the national financial markets, and was, at the same time, expected to deepen them. It was also conceivable that the improved comparability of prices would impact competitive structures on the product markets. And, last but not least, former hyperinflationary countries would experience unprecedented price stability.

The great uncertainty in the fall of 1998 made it even more important to formulate a consistent strategy. The aim was to manage and stabilize public expectations regarding the ECB's approach. On October 13, 1998, the Governing Council of the ECB made a groundbreaking decision regarding three core elements: a concrete quantitative definition of the objective of price stability, the alignment of monetary policy with a reference value for money supply growth and the assessment of future price developments using a broad catalog of indicators.

The Maastricht Treaty only specified that the ECB's primary objective was to be price stability, but it left open what this meant in particular. The ECB closed this gap by defining price stability as an annual change in the Harmonized Index of Consumer Prices of less than 2%. This target was not to be achieved at any point in time, but rather in the medium term. The medium-term focus is partly due to the fact that monetary policy measures usually begin to take effect with a time lag of several months. Also, inflation rates above the target level can be temporary and caused by factors that cannot be influenced by the central bank. This is particularly significant in the case of external shocks. Such shocks can force a central bank to decide whether or not to temporarily postpone its primary goal of price level stability in favor of secondary goals such as growth and labor market development. An example for such a development is a crisis in the Middle East that briefly pushes up the price of oil and gas and thus inflation. Once the crisis is overcome, the inflation rate falls again. In such a situation, a central bank should act with a steady hand because, firstly, it cannot influence oil and gas prices with its instruments anyway. Secondly, it takes time for restrictive monetary policy measures to take effect; therefore, it is not unlikely for the geopolitical situation in the Middle East to have changed again before monetary policy measures have any effect. Against this backdrop, for a central bank to react too hastily to external shocks could bring about unpredictable consequences for real economic development. In addition to emphasizing the medium-term orientation of its monetary policy, the ECB placed particular emphasis on the fact that the 2 % target should apply to the entire eurozone. National inflation rates have to this day never been the focus of the ECB. It wants to pursue a European monetary policy that turns a blind eye to the interests of the member states.

The two other elements of the decision the Governing Council of the ECB made on October 13, 1998 are the bank's orientation towards a reference value for the money supply and a broad-based analysis of possible inflation determinants. These elements reflect the discussion about monetary policy strategies at the time. There were two contending approaches, namely monetary targeting and direct inflation targeting.

Monetary targeting means that the central bank uses its monetary policy instruments to influence the percentage change of an 'intermediate monetary target,' which is a money supply variable. This approach is based on the assumption that there is a predictable relationship between the selected monetary aggregate and the price level or between the percentage change in this monetary aggregate and the inflation rate. With inflation targeting, the central bank sets a target figure for the inflation rate and controls it. The most important point of reference for its monetary policy actions are inflation expectations as an intermediate target, as they influence wage negotiations between the parties to collective agreements as well as the pricing behavior of companies – and therefore the actual future inflation rate. As soon as inflation expectations are above the target inflation rate, the central bank tightens the monetary reins. Otherwise, it reacts by easing its course.

The extent to which monetary targeting or inflation targeting were to determine the ECB's actions was hotly debated. One of the arguments in favor of monetary targeting was that the intermediate monetary variable could be influenced directly with monetary policy instruments. A disadvantage was, however, its unclear connection with the price level. Inflation targeting, on the other hand, is easy to communicate, but the actual links between monetary policy, inflation expectations and the inflation rate are a 'black box.'

The unclear outlook for the period after January 1, 1999 prompted the ECB to commit itself to a 'two-pillar strategy.' This refers to the ECB's announcement, as described above, that it would base its monetary policy on both a reference value for the growth of the money supply ('monetary analysis') and a broad-based analysis of price developments in the eurozone ('economic analysis'). The fact that the bank took this middle course between the opposite approaches (monetary targeting vs. inflation targeting) was essentially due to the eurozone's status as a 'moving target.'

Monetary targeting had been a central component of the Bundesbank's communication since the mid-1970s. By announcing a reference value for the growth of the money supply, the ECB was on the one hand following the tradition of the German central bank's successful stability policy, hoping to benefit from its credibility in the fight against inflation. On the other hand, many economists expressed strong doubts about the existence of a more or less direct, predictable correlation between money supply growth and inflation in the future eurozone. The ECB therefore did not pursue a strategy of monetary targeting in the sense that it regarded the money supply variable as the only intermediate target of its monetary policy and aimed for a concrete percentage change in the money supply. Instead, it formulated a reference value for the percentage growth of the money supply. If the actual money supply growth was higher, this could signal price risks, but that did not mean that the ECB would automatically tighten its monetary policy. The reference value for the development of the money supply was therefore more of an information basis for monetary policy than a real intermediate target to be achieved. In addition, the 'monetary analysis' was to also include a detailed consideration of the lending behavior of commercial banks. Bank loans were a mainstay of investment financing at the time (as they still are today). The financing conditions of the real economy (in terms of the quantitative level of the credit volume, but also interest rates and collateral requirements) therefore provide an indication of the future economic situation and growth prospects of an economy. This part of the 'monetary analysis' therefore also primarily plays the role of an information basis for monetary policy, albeit an important one.

Just as the first pillar of its strategy does not constitute full monetary management, the second pillar does not mean that the ECB pursues a strategy of direct inflation targeting. Although publishing an inflation forecast and keeping a constant eye on the inflation expectations of market participants and the public is also the basis of inflation targeting, its implementation in the narrower sense would have required the central bank to be given a specific target for inflation. Much like the Bundesbank, whose statutory objective was to "safeguard the currency," the ECB only has an abstract target, namely to "ensure price stability." Moreover, inflation expectations are not intended to be an intermediate target of ECB monetary policy but they are, like money supply growth, only one (albeit important) piece of information among many on which the central bank wanted to base its assessment of the risks to price stability. Finally, in the statement of October 13, 1998, the ECB did not state (as it should have done in the case of direct inflation control) that it would publish a specific inflation forecast, but rather a "a broadly-based assessment of the outlook for future price developments."

4 Honeymoon: The euro before the financial crisis (1999–2007)

4.1 The ECB stands the test – and adapts its strategy

January 1, 1999 brought a 'regime shift' to Europe's monetary system, which in turn also affected the global monetary system. In general, the term is used if a system undergoes a fundamental structural change, which is the case here. In fact, it is not exaggerated to speak of a historic change. This is because for the first time in history, so many (i.e., eleven) independent states gave up their monetary sovereignty on the basis of a voluntary agreement under international law, ceding it to a common supranational institution. From that day on, 300 million people in eleven countries paid with the euro, although the majority was not even aware of this change at the time because euro cash was not to be introduced until three years later. The banknotes and coins of the previous currencies were thus still in circulation until the beginning of 2002. At the same time, all transactions between commercial banks and with the European Central Bank were already being settled in euros, and receivables and liabilities in the national currencies had already been converted into euros at a fixed rate. The national notes and coins, which were still valid until December 31, 2001, were therefore de facto already euro cash. For example, anyone spending one Deutschmark on a product actually paid 51 cents for it (at a conversion rate of € 1 = DM 1.95583) even before 2002.

The regime shift meant that all eyes were on the ECB from the end of 1998. The bank had to build up the necessary trust to guide the emerging eurozone safely through this transition phase. The eurozone economy was a moving target for the ECB as market participants would react to any new information the bank published on the currency union itself and change their behavior accordingly. As a result, the monetary union itself would change in the course of an ECB analysis. This was particularly true at the beginning, when information about the new entity was still scarce. In uncertain terrain, ECB President Wim Duisenberg and his colleagues had to ensure stable inflation expectations with a consistent monetary policy and comprehensible communication. To this end, the ECB had formulated its monetary policy strategy in November 1998 (▶ Ch. 3.6) and developed a set of monetary policy instruments based on preparatory work by the European Monetary Institute.

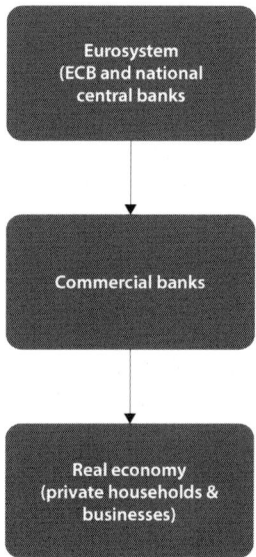

Fig. 37: Two-tier banking system in the euro area

For a basic understanding of monetary policy, it is first necessary to gain an overview of the banking system in the European Monetary Union. A distinction must first be made between the central bank and the commercial banks. In the following, the terms central bank and European Central Bank (ECB) are used synonymously, although in many cases the 'Eurosystem' refers to a combination of ECB and national central banks (NCB, in Germany: Deutsche Bundesbank). The terms banks, commercial banks and credit institutions – Germany has a special 'three-pillar structure' of private banks, savings banks and cooperative banks – are also used synonymously. This means that the banking system has two tiers, namely the central bank and commercial banks. Whereas the former only deals with commercial banks, but not with private households and companies, the latter is solely responsible for supplying financial services to private households and companies (▶ Fig. 38).

Fig. 38: Forms of money

Created by...		Used by...
...the central bank (central bank money)		
	Reserves (liquidity, account balances of commercial banks at the central bank)	...the commercial banks
	Cash (bank notes and coins)	...the commercial banks, private households und businesses
...the commercial banks: commercial bank money (deposits)		...private households and businesses

In a nutshell, monetary policy means that the central bank determines the conditions under which the commercial banking sector is supplied with liquidity. This liquidity consists of the 'reserves,' i.e., balances held by commercial banks at the central bank. Together with cash, the reserves form the so-called central bank money. The commercial banks need the reserves for two reasons:

- They can have the reserves paid out in banknotes and coins to satisfy their customers' cash requirements.
- They use the reserves to process transfers from their customers to other commercial banks.

In addition, commercial banks are obliged to hold reserves amounting to 1 % of their short-term liabilities (including not least their customers' current account balances) as a minimum reserve.[26] Deposits held by commercial banks at the ECB in excess of the minimum reserve requirement are referred to as excess reserves.

Figure 38 provides an overview of the forms of money. It starts with reserves, without which commercial banks cannot operate. In daily transactions, commercial banks lend each other liquidity, i.e., reserves. Commercial banks that have more reserves in their account at the central bank than they currently need make their surplus liquidity available on loan to those commercial banks that are currently suffering from a shortage of reserves. The interest rate at which these interbank loans are settled is called the money market rate. As the central bank is the only institution that can create reserves, it can control the money market rate. If it makes the reserves available at less favorable conditions and thus increases the money market rate, commercial bank loans to private households and companies generally also become more expensive. In turn, if the central bank makes the reserves available at more favorable conditions and thus lowers the money market rate, commercial bank loans become cheaper. The rise or fall of interest rates results in commercial banks granting fewer or, respectively, more loans. Lending by commercial banks to the real economy, in turn, creates current account balances, i.e., so-called commercial bank money. Private households and companies dispose of their current account balances by bank transfer, direct debit or credit card. Alternatively, they can have current account balances paid out in cash. Figure 39 provides an overview.

The technical handling of how reserves are provided results from the monetary policy instruments:[27]

- The weekly main refinancing operations are the core. Here, banks can receive liquidity for seven days against the provision of collateral or securities. The ECB defines which assets (usually securities and credit claims) it accepts as 'eligible

---

26 Before January 18, 2012, the minimum reserve rate was 2 %.
27 The overview here explains the basic mechanisms of European monetary policy prior to the financial and sovereign debt crisis that began in 2008.

collateral' and under what conditions that is the case in its 'collateral framework.' It is important to note that the ECB only provides liquidity if a commercial bank has eligible collateral. The interest rate for the main refinancing operations is the key policy rate.
- It is flanked by the interest rate of the marginal lending facility and that of the deposit facility. The marginal lending facility allows commercial banks to borrow liquidity at very short notice, while they can 'park' surplus liquidity in the deposit facility at short notice. The money market rate, measured in the eurozone as EONIA (Euro Overnight Index Average), normally moves within this corridor. This is why this way of conducting monetary policy is also referred to as a 'corridor system.'
- Longer-term refinancing operations (LTROs) and structural operations are only used in special situations. Longer-term refinancing operations are used to provide reserves for three months; structural operations are carried out if the ECB wishes to provide or withdraw liquidity in individual cases in such a specific manner that this is not possible with the broad-based main refinancing operations.

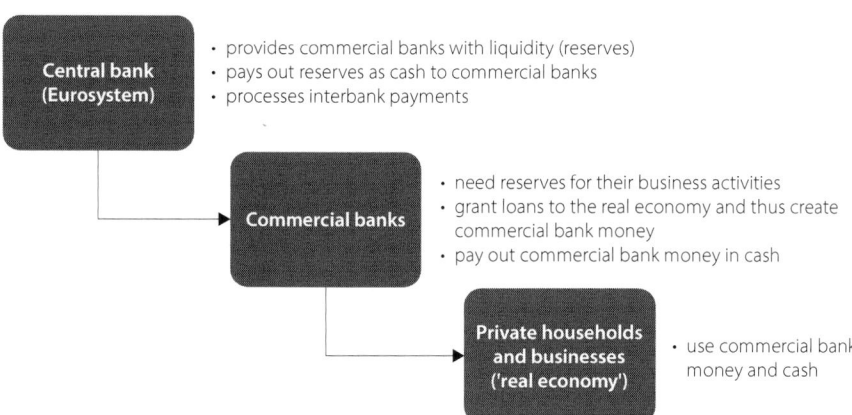

Fig. 39: The relationship between the central bank, the commercial banks and the real economy

Controlling the money market rate is, however, not the central bank's ultimate goal. Rather, it aims to create a monetary framework in which commercial banks lend and create money to the point that aggregate demand is compatible with the central bank's primary objective of price stability. The path from money market rates to aggregate demand is referred to as the transmission process. Changes in the money market rate influence long-term interest rates in the real economy as well as asset prices, the exchange rate and, not least, inflation expectations. These factors ultimately also affect the domestic price level.

The European Central Bank pursued its monetary policy on this conceptual basis from January 1, 1999. Its monetary policy was a success (and a surprising one at that, in the eyes of quite a few observers). The ECB built up a reputation for stability policy and quickly established the credibility of the 2 % target. As a result, the bank was not forced to pursue an activist policy, but was in fact able to act with a steady hand. This was remarkable given the circumstances: Firstly, as described above, the introduction of the euro represented a structural break, which meant that all players (including those in charge of the eurozone) had to act in an environment of unprecedented uncertainty. Secondly, the eurozone faced considerable adversity in the first two years of its existence: Thus, the oil price rose sharply, the euro depreciated significantly and the New Economy bubble first approached its peak and then burst. Against this backdrop, gross domestic product and price levels in the eurozone developed better than many had expected (▶ Fig. 40).

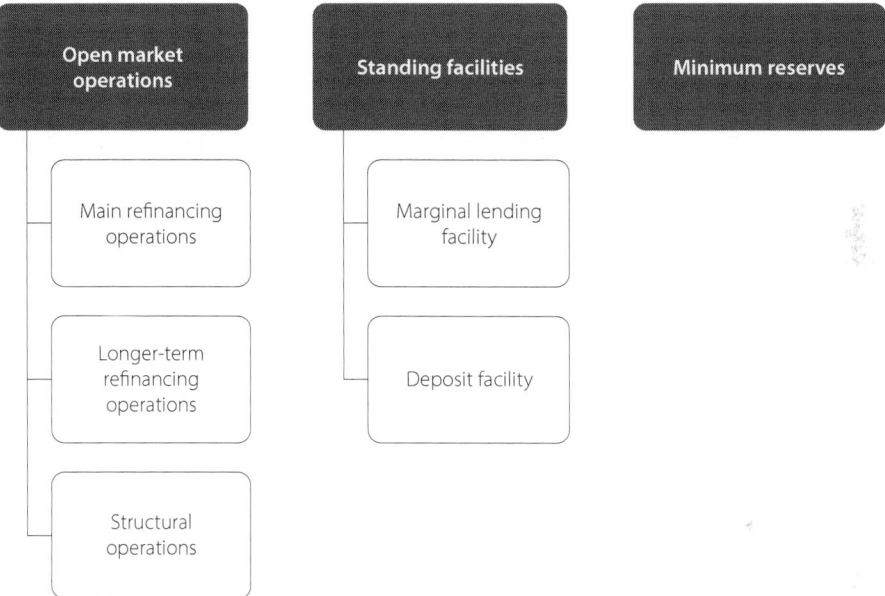

Fig. 40: The ECB's monetary policy instruments

It should be noted, however, that it is easy to lose track of broader developments that take place when the primary focus is on the eurozone average of inflation and growth. The ECB therefore had to trust that its interest rate policy was appropriate not only for abstract aggregates, but for the currency union as a whole – i.e., for all its member states ('one size fits all'). It faced, at the same time, the risk that its monetary policy might not really suit any or – if at all – suit only very few eurozone countries ('one size fits none'). One problem in this context was the fact that economic development diverged. While Germany fell into recession after 2001, Portugal, Ireland, Greece and Spain, among others, experienced a boom. They imported the monetary policy credibility of the ECB and subsequently benefited from historically low interest rates, which boosted consumption, government spending and (construction) investment. Though the inflation rate for the eurozone as a whole was relatively constant with just over 2 % on average from 2000 to 2007, there were considerable differences beneath the surface of the euro area average: For example, while the German inflation rate was below 1 % in 2002, the inflation rate in Ireland, Portugal and Spain exceeded 4 %.

On January 1, 2002, the ECB put the first series of euro banknotes (▶ Fig. 41) into circulation in denominations of € 5, € 10, € 20, € 50, € 100, € 200 and € 500. The theme of the banknote motifs was "ages and stylistic eras in Europe." Windows or gates are depicted on the front and bridges on the reverse. These windows, gates and bridges represent the classical style (€ 5), Romanesque style (€ 10), Gothic style (€ 20), Renaissance style (€ 50), Baroque and Rococo style (€ 100) as well iron and glass architecture (€ 200) and contemporary architecture (€ 500) styles. All of the motifs show fictitious buildings.

Fig. 41: First banknote series 2002 [Photo: Deutsche Bundesbank]

The approach is different regarding the coin design: Each of the eight denominations (1, 2, 5, 10, 20 and 50 cents or 1 and 2 euros) has a uniform European side, which shows the continent either together with Asia and Africa (1, 2 and 5 cents) or only Europe (10 cents and higher). Also, each member state can design its own national side. In addition to this basic set of coins with a fixed national design, each country can issue two € 2 commemorative coins per year with a specially designed national side. These commemorative coins are legal tender like all other euro banknotes and coins. Issuing coins is the task of the member states, but the ECB must approve how many coins are issued.

Yet the monetary policy debate was not primarily about these divergences, but about the risk of deflation, despite the constant (albeit slight) overshooting of the inflation target from 2000 onwards. The deflation debate had begun at the end of the 1990s, when inflation rates had converged to a low level across Europe and had fallen below 1 % in several countries (not least in Germany). At the time, it was argued that the ECB's definition of price stability as an inflation rate below 2 % did not sufficiently protect the eurozone against slipping into a deflationary downward spiral due to measurement errors. The argument was that the official inflation rate overestimates the actual price increase that reaches people's wallets by up to one percentage point because it is difficult to measure changes in quality (quality effect) and the tendency of consumers to find alternatives for products that have become more expensive (substitution effect). Inflation measurement based on a fixed basket of goods can only deal with these phenomena to a limited extent. As a result, this means that if the official inflation rate is, e.g., reported as amounting to 0.4 %, prices in fact may have fallen by 0.6 %. Therefore, the argument is that when the ECB sets the inflation target, it should strive to keep a safety margin from the 0% mark in order to avoid an unintentional slide into deflationary territory.

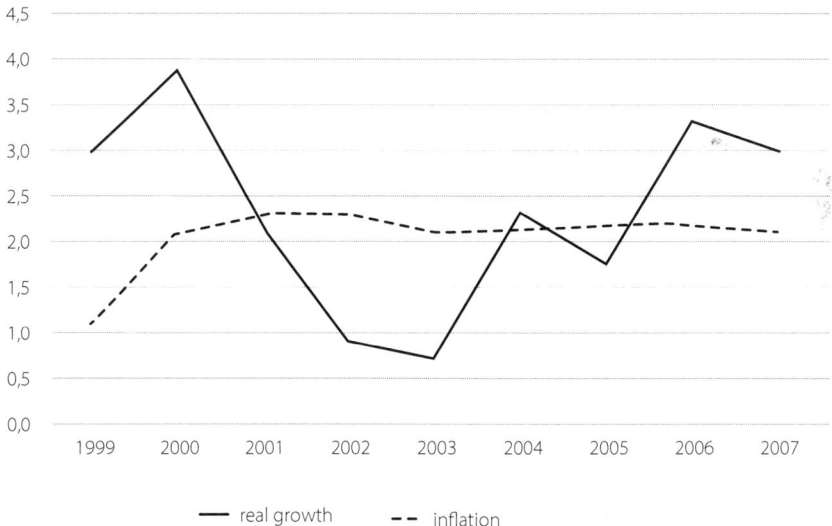

Fig. 42: Real growth and inflation in the eurozone 1999–2007 (% year-over-year, data: ECB/IMF)

In addition to the reasons outlined above and with regard to the particular challenges of a monetary union, critics also presented two other arguments against an inflation rate target that is too low:

- The Samuelson-Balassa argument:
  According to this argument, economies in the catch-up process that are opening up to other countries tend to have higher inflation rates than those that are already more developed. This also applies to the countries on the periphery of the eurozone (initially in particular Portugal, Ireland, Greece and Spain and later Malta, Cyprus and the Baltic countries, among others). Companies engaged in the sector of cross-border tradable goods face intensive competitive pressure due to foreign competition. They are thereby forced to increase their productivity, which is reflected in rising wages. If the wage increase in the tradable goods sector roughly corresponds to the increase in productivity, the situation will not initially result in any price pressure. Depending on the wage policy framework, however, the wage settlements of companies that produce tradable goods may be transferred to sectors that are not subject to international competition. In many cases, this applies to sectors in which productivity increases are only possible to a limited extent (e. g., private or public services, construction industry). Sooner or later, wage increases in these sectors feed into price setting and then lead to inflation in the economy as a whole. The divergence of inflation rates in a monetary union means that inflation is higher than the average in some countries and lower in others. If the ECB has an inflation target of between 0 % and 2 % and the actual inflation rate is 1.5 %, for example, the national inflation rates from which this average value is derived can for example vary between -0.5 % and 4.5 %. The inflation rate could therefore slip into deflationary territory in countries with strongly below-average inflation.
- Real adjustment with nominal rigidities:
  A further rationale for permitting moderate inflation in a monetary union is to facilitate adjustments in relative competitiveness. If the export products of a member state are not competitive in terms of price, this country can no longer improve its competitiveness by nominally devaluing its own currency. Instead, the country must now devalue in real terms, i. e., manufacture its products at a lower cost than its foreign competitors. One step in this direction could be wage cuts, for example. Yet nominal wage cuts are generally almost impossible to implement. Thus, if the inflation rate is positive and the nominal wage level remains the same or at least rises less quickly than the price level, companies will be less affected by wage costs in real terms – i. e., inflation-adjusted – and their competitiveness will increase. This effect cannot take place with an inflation rate of zero.

The discussion about the pros and cons of an upwardly adjusted inflation target was accompanied by increasing doubts about the predictive value of growth of monetary aggregates. In the first years of the monetary union, there was no significant correlation between money supply and price trends. Nevertheless, most observers agreed that phases of sustained inflation or falling (disinflation) or even negative inflation rates (deflation) had to result from a money supply growth that was too strong or too weak, respectively. In addition to these conceptual difficulties, there were also uncertainties regarding economic development. The inflation rate was low until the middle/end of 2001, but rising energy and food prices caused prices to rise by up to more than three percent. At the same time, the bursting new economy bubble and the terrorist attacks of September 11, 2001 resulted in weak growth, falling inflation expectations and restrained credit development. Whereas the credit volume increased in the upswing and decreased in the downturn, money supply growth appeared to be increasingly erratic.

In this situation, leading representatives of the Eurosystem found it increasingly difficult to communicate monetary policy credibly on the basis of the November 1998 strategy. As a result, the ECB adjusted its strategy in two respects:[28]

- The definition of price level stability was changed. The inflation rate compatible with the primary mandate was no longer defined as "below 2 %" but as "below, but close to 2 %." What did not change was that this value was to be achieved in the medium term. When asked what "close to" meant, leading representatives of the ECB indicated that they favored an inflation rate of 1.7 % to 1.9 %.
- The two pillars (economic and monetary analysis) were no longer on an equal footing. Instead, the monetary pillar was now to take on a more informational character and to complement the economic pillar. In other words, the growth of monetary aggregates was no longer an intermediate monetary policy objective, but served informational purposes. In addition, other financial aggregates were increasingly included in the analysis, not least in order to identify undesirable developments on the asset markets. Accordingly, the ECB stated: "In this respect, the monetary analysis mainly serves as a means of cross-checking, from a medium to long-term perspective, the short to medium-term indications coming from economic analysis."

4.2 Greece, the Stability and Growth Pact, and international imbalances – dark clouds on the horizon?

While the ECB was apparently successful in its monetary policy, putting it on a new conceptual footing in 2003, there were developments in these years that paved the way for the major euro crisis from 2010 onwards. The first was Greece's accession on January 1, 2001. Its critics had pointed to the high level of national debt and questioned the competitiveness of the Greek economy. They claimed that without the possibility of nominal devaluation, the country was threatened by a structural crisis

---

28 ECB (2003): The ECB's monetary policy strategy, Frankfurt, 8.5.2003, https://www.ecb.europa.eu/press/pr/date/2003/html/pr030508_2.en.html

with high unemployment. Also, the state and companies were not sufficiently prepared for competition in the monetary union. Those in favor of Greece joining argued primarily on political grounds: the cradle of democracy could not be permanently excluded from the eurozone. Moreover, the country was so small that it could not pose a threat to the monetary union as a whole.

In the two following years, the Stability and Growth Pact was subjected to its first test – and failed. In 2002, the budget deficits of Germany and France were 3.8 % and 3.2 % respectively and thus (in the case of Germany significantly) above the maximum value of 3 %. The German government declared that the summer floods in eastern Germany constituted an exceptional event that was beyond its control and that significantly impaired the state's financial situation. German officials claimed that given this situation and based on the current rules, no excessive deficit procedure should be initiated. The Commission could not follow this argument. In view of the unfavorable budget forecasts for the following years, it recommended that the Council initiate an excessive deficit procedure. The Council followed this recommendation. However, in the fall of 2003 at the latest, it became clear that neither the German nor the French government were willing to follow the Commission's fiscal policy recommendations, which it had addressed to the two 'sinners' as part of the excessive deficit procedure. Germany and France should have been sanctioned, but the Council suspended the procedure by qualified majority vote. This meant that what many critics of the Stability and Growth Pact as adopted in 1997 had anticipated and warned against (▶ Ch. 3.4) had come true: without automatic sanctions, the Pact would remain a 'toothless tiger.' The politicization of the procedure by the Council as the authoritative body meant that "sinners would judge sinners," who would show mercy in case of doubt. Many viewed it as a serious blow to the credibility of the rules that Germany and France – the two core countries – were the first to violate the very regulations they had helped negotiate only a few years earlier. The absence of any consequences for their actions further intensified concerns about the integrity of the framework.

The events of 2002 and 2003 led to a renewed discussion about whether the deficit criterion as such was useful. The argument was that it forced governments to reduce expenditure and increase revenue in a phase of economic weakness, i.e., to pursue a pro-cyclical fiscal policy. In defense of the 3 % threshold, it was argued that counter-cyclical management of government revenue and expenditure was indeed possible. After all, the national governments had committed themselves in 1997 to achieving a balanced or even surplus budget in the medium term. Based on such a 'black zero' in the normal economic situation, the 3 % deficit limit would have offered sufficient fiscal leeway to react appropriately to a downturn. In 2005, agreement was finally reached on the first reform of the Stability and Growth Pact. The medium-term budget target was specified. From then on, the member states had to show in their stability programs how they intended to bring the structural budget balance to zero or keep it at zero in the medium term. Under certain conditions, a structural budget deficit of up to 1 % of GDP was to be tolerated. The structural budget balance is a hypothetical figure that reflects the difference between government revenue and expenditure in a state of normal utilization of economic resources, i.e., when the respective country is neither in a downturn nor in an upswing. At the same time, the Commission was given greater discretion in assessing deficits and could, for example, take the economic situation of the respective country into account when deciding whether or not it would recommend the initiation of an excessive deficit procedure. In addition, more flexibility was granted regarding the time given to a country that had to reduce its excessive deficit. Yet the fundamental problem of "sinners judging sinners" was not tackled. Sanctions for infringements still had to be decided upon by a majority in the Council.

The admission of Greece and the special treatment of Germany and France are political decisions that, in hindsight, are partly responsible for the problems of the eurozone from 2010 onwards. In the early years of the monetary union, there were also economic developments in the later crisis countries Portugal, Ireland, Greece and Spain ('GIPS') that already hinted at future problems. Although they were described by some observers, they were not the subject of a broad political debate. These include, firstly, the growth differences in the monetary union. Between 1996 and 2005, the average real GDP growth rate of the four GIPS countries was continuously two to three percentage points higher than that of Germany. The same applied to the inflation rate. While these phenomena could already be observed several years before the introduction of the euro, the current account balances only began to diverge after the introduction of the euro. Until 2000, Germany had a slightly negative current account balance, which turned into a large surplus in the following years. The current account balances of Greece, Ireland, Portugal and Spain remained – like the German one –, slightly negative until the end of the 1990s, but then deteriorated considerably, reaching a negative record value with an average deficit of 10 % of GDP (▶ Ch. 5.2.1).

5 Crisis years: The monetary union on the brink of collapse (2008–2015)

5.1 From the global financial crisis to the European sovereign debt crisis

In 2007, the situation on the US real estate market deteriorated increasingly. After years of strong growth, house prices initially stagnated and then began to fall, particularly in former boom regions like California. The upswing, underpinned by massive mortgage lending, seemed to have been an excess and the word spread of "the bursting of the bubble." Credit institutions specializing in real estate financing were the first to run into difficulties. As real estate loans had very frequently been bundled into packages as mortgage-backed securities (MBS) and then resold, the holders of such securities, including many banks, now faced large write-downs. Regardless of the extent to which individual banks were involved in the real estate lending business or had invested in MBS, there was a general crisis of confidence on the interbank market, and American credit institutions stopped lending money to each other. As a consequence, the Federal Reserve had to step in and provide substantial liquidity as lender of last resort in order to stabilize the US banking system.

Many European observers initially considered these events to be a primarily American problem. However, it soon became clear that Europe could be affected through various channels. The banking crisis in the US first impacted the US economy itself, and the future expectations of both investors and consumers became gloomier. As a result, US demand for European export goods fell noticeably. In addition, the difficulties of the American economy gradually led to general uncertainty in European countries as well. As a result, economic risks were reassessed and investment projects were critically scrutinized. Last but not least, it soon became apparent that European banks had also invested heavily in securitized US real estate loans. When the European banking market faced liquidity problems for the first time in August 2007, the ECB acted as lender of last resort and provided massive amounts of liquidity. In the months that followed, the financial markets in Europe were thrown into turmoil, and more and more commercial banks had to be rescued through either capital injections by the state or through takeovers by other banks. The banking crisis reached its peak in September 2008, when the long-established American investment bank Lehman Brothers became insolvent.

These developments had an impact on the real economy in Europe. As banks reduced lending as a precautionary measure, a so-called 'credit crunch' emerged. From that point on, banking and economic problems started to mutually reinforce each other: Thus, when growth in the eurozone declined significantly, this led to loan defaults at the banks. The increasingly hesitant lending by banks in the course of the crisis in turn weakened investment and consumption, i.e., economic development. This resulted in the worst economic crisis for most of Europe since World War II. Due to the close interdependence between the EU member states, none of them were able to escape the massive downward trend. This in turn put European banks under even greater pressure across the board. Countries with banks that had invested heavily in US MBS were particularly affected by the banking problems, including Germany with IKB and Sachsen LB. At the same time, however, it also became clear that Spain and Ireland in particular faced similar problems as the US commercial banks there also came under pressure in the wake of a credit-financed real estate boom. The difficulties of the European banking sector finally became systemic when the banks stopped lending money to each other, and the interbank market collapsed.

Initially, the serious economic problems did not impair the creditworthiness of the euro countries. The global financial crisis had not yet led to a European sovereign debt crisis. This was soon to change, as, on the one hand, the massive economic slump in 2009 caused a rapid fall in tax revenues and an equally rapid rise in social spending, resulting in considerable budget deficits. On the other hand, many governments were forced to stabilize their banking markets. First and foremost, this applied to the Irish government, which had to rescue Anglo Irish Bank at the beginning of 2009 after it lost the confidence of potential lenders and was therefore no longer able to refinance its loans to property developers. The sum that the Irish state had to raise for the rescue was enormous: It amounted to around 30 % of gross domestic product. The national bank bailouts had become necessary because the ECB, while supplying the entire banking market with liquidity, did not step in as lender of last resort for individual institutions. The collapse of Lehman Brothers underscored that even smaller financial institutions can be systemically significant due to their extensive interconnections within the global financial system. Consequently, the disorderly insolvency of such banks must be avoided, as it can severely undermine public confidence in the banking sector as a whole. As a consequence, even banks that were not „too big to fail" were directly or indirectly protected by the taxpayer. The banks were considered so important to the structure of the economy that stabilizing the sector became a top political priority. States employed a variety of measures to achieve this aim. For example, they nationalized individual banks (partially or completely), publicly guaranteed bank deposits or even supported – in extreme cases – the liquidation of banks that were no longer viable, using taxpayers' money.

The extensive measures taken by governments burdened public budgets, which were already strained due to the crisis, and induced capital market players to scrutinize the countries' solvency. When in late 2009 the newly elected Greek government was forced to admit that the budget figures for 2009 and 2010 had been far too optimistic and that the corresponding figures had been repeatedly embellished in the past, sovereign debtors lost confidence on the financial markets. In addition to Greece and Ireland, other countries now came under scrutiny, including Portugal and

Spain in particular. In early 2010, Greece was no longer able to refinance its maturing government bonds. In other words, the European sovereign debt crisis had begun.

The causes of the crisis that the eurozone had to contend with from 2010 onwards are more diverse than the term 'euro sovereign debt crisis' would suggest. Although the euro crisis was a sovereign debt crisis, it was also a current account crisis, a banking crisis and, last but not least, a crisis of private debt. There are overall three (interconnected) factors that caused the outbreak of the crisis:

- In the years leading up to the crisis, the crisis countries Portugal, Ireland, Greece and Spain had built up massive current account deficits that were largely financed by capital inflows from the core of the eurozone (especially Germany and France). This mechanism is presented in detail in section 5.2.1.
- A considerable part of these capital inflows took the form of, first, interbank loans that banks from the core countries had granted to banks in the later crisis countries, and, second, the purchase of Greek and Portuguese government bonds in particular by banks in the core countries. The banks in the core countries were thus involved in the crisis countries; at the same time, the banks in Spain and Ireland in particular had set off a credit-financed real estate boom. The euro crisis was therefore a banking crisis in a twofold sense of the word. This is discussed in section 5.2.2.
- Sovereign debt was only in Portugal and Greece, the root of the problem. However, the fiscal situation of the member states as well as the core countries became a crucial point of the crisis via the so-called sovereign-bank nexus. The euro crisis as a sovereign debt crisis is examined in section 5.2.3.

5.2 Dimensions of the euro crisis

5.2.1 The euro crisis as a current account crisis

The euro crisis revealed that the discussion in the early 1990s about the economic prerequisites for the success of a monetary union (▶ Ch. 3.2) had, at least to a large extent, overlooked the causes of the subsequent problems. Rather than asymmetric shocks, the problem was long-term structural differences and short-term asynchronous economic cycles, which made the severe crisis possible. The endogeneity of the functional conditions of a monetary union that many had hoped for before its introduction had failed to materialize, and the cross-border capital flows had not promoted diversification, but rather the accumulation of risks.

The former 'weak currency countries' of Southern Europe had entered the monetary union with an extraordinary boom. For Greece, Ireland, Portugal and Spain (later known as the 'GIPS' or 'periphery' countries), joining the eurozone (or, even before that point, the mere expectation that they would join) meant importing a certain degree of credibility with regard to an anti-inflationary monetary policy stance. The prospect that exchange rates would be eliminated and that an independent central bank would be responsible for monetary policy resulted in historically low interest rates. Although Ireland had already become a so-called 'Celtic Tiger' by the early 1990s, its economy developed in many respects similarly to that of Greece, Portugal and Spain: Namely, domestic demand in the future crisis countries rose sharply, even though the main areas of growth were distributed differently. In Spain and Ireland, construction investment played a particularly important role, while in Portugal and not least in Greece, government spending increased noticeably. Private consumption was an important pillar of the economy in all four economies. As a result, over a decade real economic growth in the GIPS countries was two to three percentage points higher than in Germany (▶ Fig. 43).

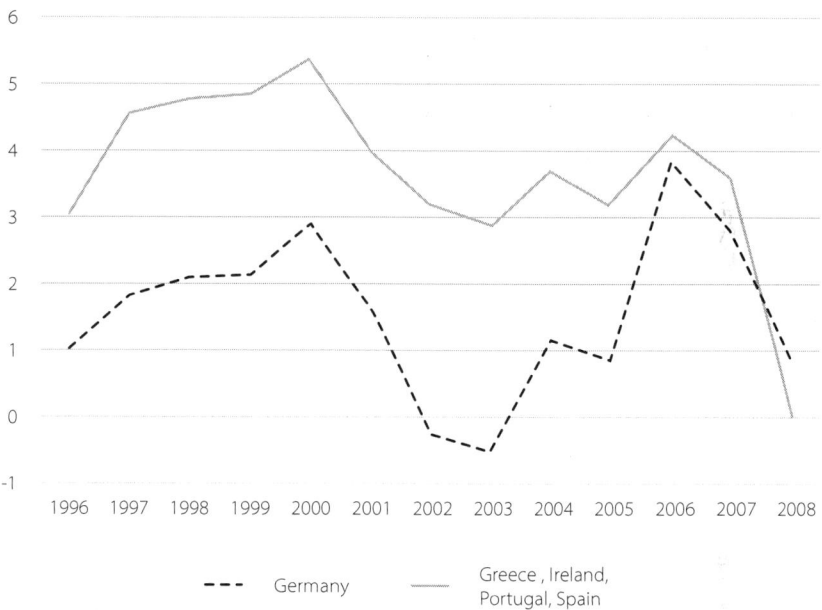

Fig. 43: Real growth in Germany and the 'GIPS' countries (% year-over-year, data: IMF)

These growth figures were associated with an above-average inflation rate in the GIPS countries (▶ Fig. 44). Between 1996 and 2008, average inflation was around two percentage points higher than in Germany, which impacted real interest rates. In simplified terms, the real interest rate is the difference between the nominal interest rate (i.e., the contractually agreed interest rate) and the inflation rate. From the lender's point of view, the interest payment initially represents an increase in wealth, but this is offset by the loss of purchasing power in the amount of the inflation rate. From the borrower's perspective, his payment obligation increases with the nominal interest rate, whereas inflation reduces the real value of his debt. Since nominal interest rates in the eurozone converged from 1999 onwards, different inflation rates led to real interest rates in the GIPS countries that were lower than those in Germany, to the point that they even became negative in some cases. This meant that it was comparatively easy for private households, companies and governments in Greece, Ireland, Portugal and Spain to take out loans. This fact further fueled the boom in consumer, investment and government spending. Because the high domestic demand could not be satisfied with domestic goods and financed with domestic funds alone, imports of goods and services increased. This development led to rising foreign debt in the GIPS economies. Accordingly, the current account deficit of the GIPS countries rose, while Germany increased its surplus.

Fig. 44: Inflation in Germany and the 'GIPS' countries (%, data: IMF)

A current account balance – regardless of whether it is a surplus or deficit – is not inherently 'good' or 'bad,' just as little as a country with a persistent current account surplus or deficit is inherently an economically strong or weak country. For current account deficits to lead to a current account crisis, both the causes and financing of these current account deficits must be problematic.

When countries are in the process of catching up economically, there tends to be pent-up demand regarding consumption, investment and state infrastructure. The catch-up process can go along with current account deficits because domestic demand for those goods is so high that it cannot be fully satisfied by domestic production capacities. If, in the course of this catch-up process, pent-up demand for consumption decreases and corporate investment and the development of state infrastructure have increased the country's production potential and economic competitiveness, imports may fall and exports rise, thereby reducing the current account deficit and possibly even evening out the balance. Such a development would have been particularly desirable in the European monetary union because the currency union and the single market were expected to initiate such catch-up processes and thus to create the convergence which the monetary union requires. Unfortunately, the desired effect did not take place. Apparently, domestic demand was only partially directed towards goods that contributed to an increase in production capacity and competitiveness. In addition, a lot of money was invested into real estate, creating a bubble (Spain, Ireland), and into an inefficient state sector (Portugal, Greece). At the same time, the trade unions managed to push through high wage agreements, which were not matched by adequate increases in productivity. Companies' wage costs therefore grew faster than production, and unit labor costs rose considerably. This is because the positive economic development ensured strong demand, particularly in the area of non-tradable goods (private and public services, construction sector). At the same time, however, productivity increases are unlikely in this area due to the lack of international competitive pressure and the specific production characteristics of these sectors (the efficiency of hairdressers, nurses or teachers can only be increased to a limited extent). Instead of becoming more competitive, the GIPS countries became less so in the first decade of the monetary union. Ultimately, current account deficits did not decline as anticipated; instead, they widened, and rather than converging, national economic structures became increasingly divergent (▶ Fig. 45).

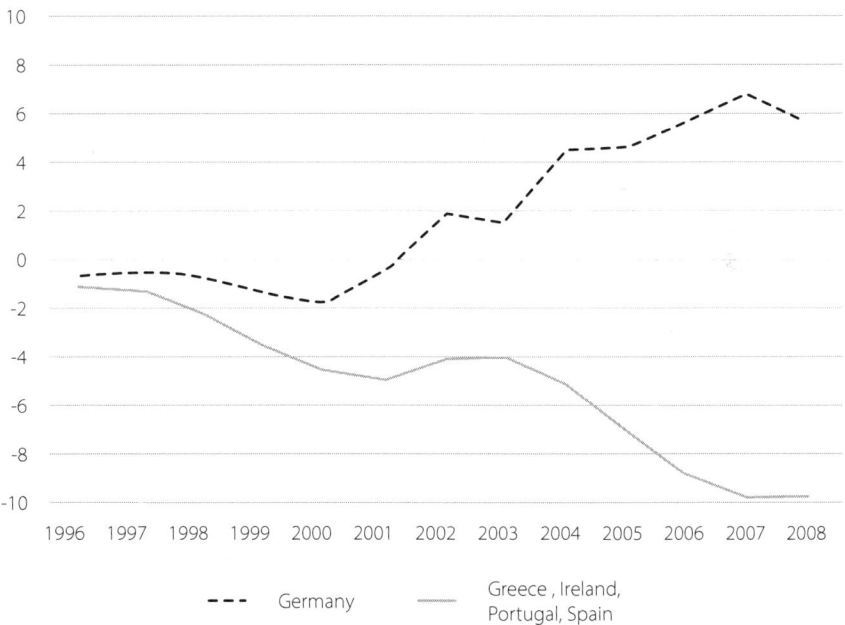

Fig. 45: Current account balances of Germany and the 'GIPS' countries (% of GDP, data: IMF)

In other words, Greece, Ireland, Portugal and Spain did not use the very favorable framework from the mid-1990s onwards to their long-term advantage, i.e., they did not make their economies fit for the type of intensified competition that had been underway for some time, namely since the establishment of the single market in 1993 and of the monetary union in 1999. This was made worse by the fact that the latter deprived those countries of the possibility to devalue their currency. Though the refinancing of government debt had become much cheaper, the GIPS countries did not seize the opportunity to modernize their infrastructure and improve the institutional framework for domestic companies. Also, their labor and product markets were not made sufficiently flexible, and everything remained the same in terms of wage policy mechanisms. Painful structural reforms did not take place in the GIPS countries because politicians, citizens and companies did not feel under any acute pressure to act due to the favorable interest rate situation. The monetarists' expectation that the monetary union would catalyze economic and political transformations conducive to the euro's long-term success ultimately proved unfounded. Neither the economic cycles or economic structures nor the institutional framework converged. In retrospect, it is easy to see how influential the specific economic set-up of these crisis countries was in the long-term. Thus, the sectoral focus of the national economies, the institutional framework such as competition, tax and insolvency law, the labor market structures, the regulation of product markets or even the type and extent of state intervention in the economy, all these had developed over decades, if not centuries. Competition problems had been repeatedly defused with the help of exchange rate devaluations in these formative years. In 1999, however, this instrument was discontinued. Overall, the assumption that countries such as Greece, Portugal and Spain (Ireland is an exception here) would adapt to the requirements of the single market and the monetary union within a few years proved to be overly optimistic (▶ Fig. 46).

The current account deficits of the GIPS countries were therefore not an expression of a successful catching-up process, but rather of a lack of adaptation to the requirements of the single market and the monetary union. It has thus been shown that one of the prerequisites for a negative assessment of current account deficits in fact applies, namely their problematic cause.

The second prerequisite – i.e., the problematic financing of the current account deficit – is based on what has been shown in chapter 1.2, namely that current account deficits lead to an increase in liabilities to foreign countries. Ideally, the financing of the current account deficit should be diversified so that countries do not depend too much on one single financing channel. In addition, long-term financing is advantageous so that an abrupt change in conditions on the international banking and financial markets has no impact on current account financing in the short and medium term. As it soon turned out, these conditions were not met. The capital flows were very heavily channeled through the banking sector. German and French banks, in particular, transformed their countries' export surpluses into interbank loans to financial institutions in the peripheral eurozone. They also invested heavily in sovereign bonds issued by the GIPS nations. This meant that the financing of current account deficits was dependent on the willingness and ability of German and French banks to continue to function as lenders on the money market and to take government bonds, particularly from Portugal and Greece, onto their balance sheets.

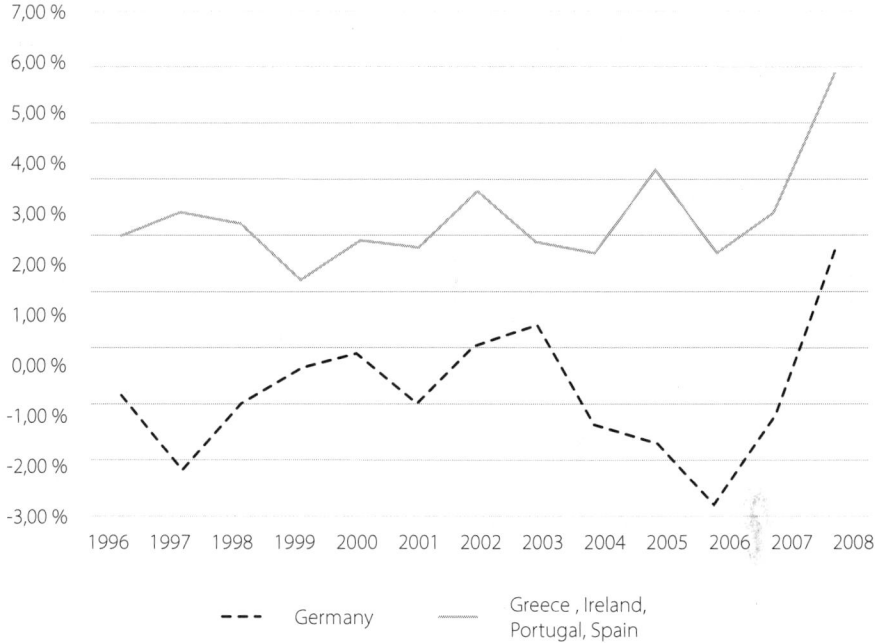

Fig. 46: Growth in unit labor costs in Germany and the 'GIPS' countries (% year over year, data: ECB)

In summary, this means that the classification of the euro crisis as a current account crisis stems from the fact that the single market, together with the single interest rate policy and the elimination of exchange rate risks within Europe, has fostered two undesirable developments:

- The uniform interest rate policy with diverging inflation rates led to low and in some cases negative real interest rates in the later crisis countries. This triggered a special economic situation. Despite or because of falling unemployment figures and abundant tax revenues, structural reforms were not made to prepare the national economies for the fact that competition in Europe had intensified significantly in 1993 and 1999, respectively.
- The current account imbalances (surpluses in the core countries, deficits in the periphery) led to massive capital flows from Germany, France and the Netherlands to Greece, Ireland, Portugal and Spain, among others. The inflowing capital financed private consumption in all four crisis countries as well as a real estate boom in Spain and Ireland and inefficient state structures in Portugal and Greece.

5.2.2 The euro crisis as a banking crisis

The euro crisis can also be interpreted as a banking crisis in three different ways:

- Most directly, it was a banking crisis in Spain and Ireland, where local credit institutions had fueled a real estate bubble through excessive lending. When the bubble burst, more and more real estate loans defaulted and the banks got into serious difficulties.
- The problem of the commercial banks in the peripheral countries (especially Spain and Ireland) quickly developed into a problem for the banks in the core countries of the eurozone. As shown in section 5.2.1, the current account deficits of the peripheral countries were financed to a large extent by capital inflows from the core countries. These capital flows were channeled very heavily through the banking sector. The banks in the core countries granted loans to the banks in the peripheral countries on the interbank market. When rumors of problems in the Spanish and Irish real estate and banking markets emerged, they stopped these loans, causing liquidity problems for the Spanish and Irish banks in particular. The vulnerability of these banks stemmed, in part, from an increasing dependence on short-term interbank lending for refinancing in the years preceding the crisis, which progressively supplanted the traditionally more stable deposit-based funding. Furthermore, banks – particularly those in Germany and France – amplified their exposure to sovereign debt by acquiring substantial volumes of government bonds from peripheral eurozone countries, notably Greece. When these core country banks had to write down their (Greek) government bonds in the course of the sovereign debt crisis, they came under pressure.
- The purchase of government bonds draws attention to another dimension of the euro crisis as a banking crisis, namely the sovereign-bank nexus. This refers to the interdependence between states and banks. Banks very often invest a relatively large proportion of their assets in (domestic) government bonds because they are a liquid and usually safe investment. Also, contrary to all other assets that banks usually hold, such government bonds do not have to be backed by equity according to minimum capital requirements (at least in the EU). In addition, government bonds serve as collateral for interbank loans or open market transactions with the central bank. If a state threatens to run into payment difficulties, the banks have to write down their government bond holdings. This can place them in a position of financial distress, which only state intervention may be able to ease. Of course, this does not only apply to difficulties resulting from write-downs on government bond portfolios. Whenever banks get into difficulties, the taxpayer has to step in if the banks in question are classified as 'too big to fail' or 'too interconnected to fail.' Problems on the part of the state can therefore cause the banks to get into difficulties, and banking problems can potentially place an existential burden on the state budget. In extreme cases, these two effects exacerbate each other (so-called 'feedback loop').

The sovereign-bank nexus was particularly important for the further progression of the crisis in Europe.

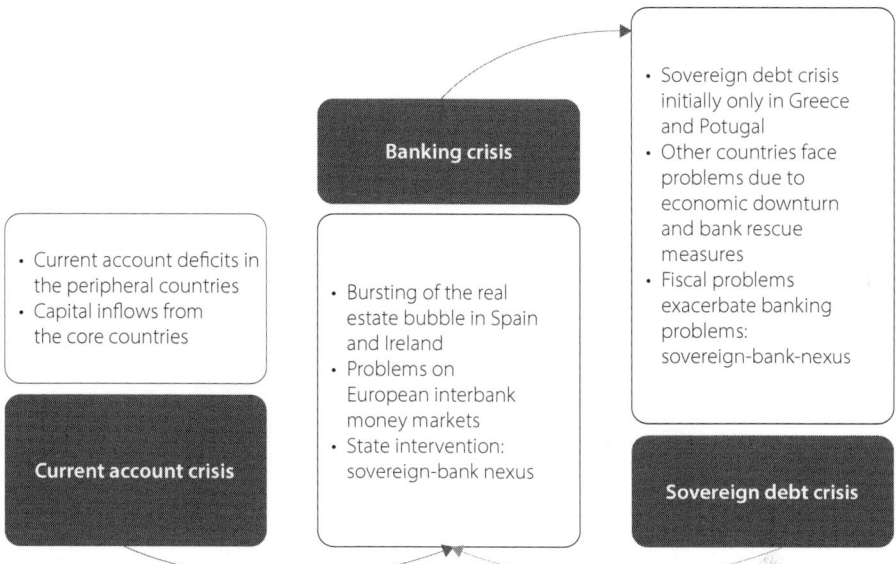

Fig. 47: Dimensions of the euro crisis

5.2.3 The euro crisis as a sovereign-debt crisis

From 2010 onwards, the euro crisis developed into a sovereign debt crisis. At the center was Greece, where sovereign debt was the cause of the crisis. To a lower extent, the same applies to Portugal. In the other crisis countries and in the core countries of the eurozone, however, the sovereign debt problem had its roots in the current account and banking crisis. A more detailed consideration of the sovereign-bank nexus is necessary to shed more light on the relevant mechanism here. At its center is the market for government bonds.

Governments take out loans by issuing government bonds. In simple terms, the buyer of a government bond acquires the right to receive interest payments during the maturity and to receive the nominal price back at the end of that period. The loan granted by the initial purchase of the government bond is thus repaid. Government bonds are traded on the capital market during their term, which results in prices (rates) that may deviate from the nominal value. These prices or rates then determine the yields and spreads of the bond in circulation.

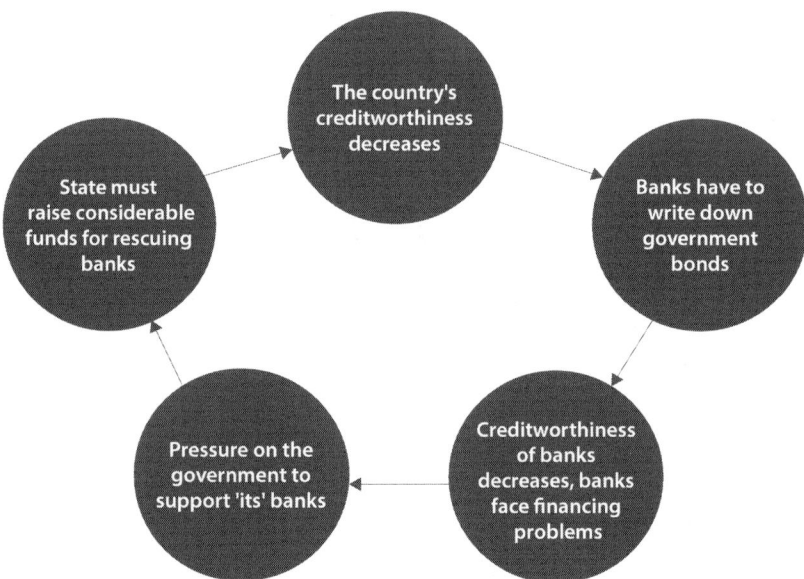

Fig. 48: The sovereign-bank nexus

In detail, the basic relationships are as follows: The nominal value (face value) generally corresponds to the purchase price, i. e., the loan amount granted to the state when the bond is first purchased on the primary market. Bonds sold by the initial purchasers before maturity are traded on the secondary market. The price of a bond on the secondary market depends on various factors, not least the credit rating (i. e., the ability and willingness of the issuer to repay the loan). If the creditworthiness of an issuer decreases, capital market investors will only buy the government bonds in question at a lower price, i. e., with a safety discount that reflects the increased risk. The distinction between the nominal value on the one hand and the price on the other is reflected in the two variables nominal interest and yield. Here is a (highly simplified) example: A state issues a government bond with a nominal value of EUR 100 and a nominal interest rate of 6 %. The holder of the bond therefore receives six euros once a year. Shortly afterwards, there are rumors of payment difficulties on the part of the issuing state. The first purchaser of the government bond therefore wants to sell it, but only finds a buyer at a price of 60 euros. The price discount of 40 % reflects the increased credit risk. The new holder of the government bond continues to receive an annual interest payment of six euros for his investment of 60 euros. This results in a yield of ten percent: six euros interest payment for a purchase price of 60 euros.

Bonds from different countries have different yields depending on the credit rating of the country in question. The difference between the government bond yield of a given country and that of a country with a particularly good credit rating ('benchmark bond,' which usually has a triple A or AAA rating) is known as the 'spread.' The higher the spread of a bond, the less favorable the credit rating of the issuer. In the European Monetary Union, German government bonds ('Bundesanleihen' or 'Bunds') are the benchmark.

It is important to know that a finance minister has to be active on the bond market practically all the time. This is due to maturing bonds issued in previous years. Even if government revenue and expenditure are currently balanced, i. e., no actual new borrowing is necessary, new bonds must be issued in order to be able to use the issue proceeds to repay old bonds, i. e., to keep the overall debt level stable. If the government from the example above wants to issue new bonds (either to redeem old bonds with the issue proceeds or to take out completely new loans), it must provide these new bonds with a nominal interest rate of ten percent from the outset. If the interest rate of the new bonds was lower, no one would buy them, as investors could buy the old bonds in circulation at a yield of 10 %. The conditions on the primary market (for newly issued bonds) follow those on the secondary market, where previously issued bonds are traded.

In practice, this has the following consequences for the banking sector (▶ Fig. 48): If capital market players lose confidence in the fiscal soundness of a state, its rating is lowered and the prices of outstanding government bonds fall. As a result, the banks have to revalue the (usually) extensive portfolio of government bonds on their balance sheets, which can lead to write-downs. The banks' balance sheet situation deteriorates. If this leads to rating downgrades for individual banks or the banking sector as a whole, banks find it more difficult to obtain funding on the capital market: on the one hand, because investors either do not want to invest in bank shares and bonds that have become riskier or only do so at lower prices to compensate for the increased risk; on the other hand, because the write-downs on government bonds mean that they have fewer collateral available for interbank loans and open market transactions with the central bank. If these refinancing difficulties lead to a crisis at one or more banks, the home state of the affected banks may have to step in to help (which further exacerbates its fiscal problems), and the vicious circle is complete.

If banking problems form the starting point of the development, capital market players change their risk assessment regarding the sustainability of the national budget. The possibility of a bank bailout is included in the forecasts for future expenditure. This may result in a rating downgrade; in any case, the yield on government bonds is likely to rise. Refinancing government debt will become more expensive. This in turn can lead to write-downs on bank balance sheets, which again constitutes a vicious circle.

These mechanisms work even if neither the state nor the banks have encountered problems. The mere (possibly unfounded) expectation of capital market players [1] that a country's banks could get into difficulties and have to be bailed out by the state or [2] that the state could face refinancing difficulties, which in turn would negatively impact bank balance sheets, can lead to a drying up of liquidity for the state and/or banks. This is because any player who thinks that other players might think that the state and/or banks could run into problems and drag each other into a downward spiral will withdraw their financial investments from the government bond and banking sector. Once this happens, the government and/or banks will have real financing difficulties, which can trigger the downward spiral explained above. The beginning of a sovereign debt/banking crisis can therefore also be a self-fulfilling prophecy.

The first bank bailouts by the state in Germany took place in the summer of 2008. It involved banks that had invested in American mortgage securities. Because the German fiscal situation at the time was comparatively favorable (the severe crisis at the beginning of the decade had been followed by several years of upswing) politicians were able to stabilize the German banking market with guarantees and capital. Soon afterwards, considerable problems arose on the Spanish and Irish banking markets. The necessary support measures and the economic crisis strained national budgets in Spain and Ireland. The direction of the sovereign-bank nexus is clear here: the problems emanated from the banks, which caused fiscal problems, not the other way around, as both countries had been considered "fiscal policy role models" in the years before the financial crisis because they had easily met the Maastricht fiscal criteria (▶ Fig. 49).

The situation was different in Greece. Here, the special economic situation resulting from low interest rates from the turn of the millennium onwards not only boosted private consumption, but also led to an enormous expansion of public services and the welfare state. At the same time, the regulation of the labor and product markets was expanded so that the competitiveness of the Greek economy declined significantly. Rising government spending unmatched by revenues resulted in government deficits despite favorable economic conditions. The considerable financing problems of the Greek state that came to light at the end of 2009 put pressure on the European banking sector, as many banks – not least in Germany and France – had substantial holdings of Greek government bonds on their balance sheets. At the beginning of 2010, capital market players (investors and rating agencies) then began a comprehensive reassessment of the risks in European bank balance sheets and national budgets – in a sense a self-fulfilling prophecy. Whereas the sovereign-bank nexus had previously been more of a national problem (states supported 'their' banks and therefore ran into budget problems), it was now Europeanized. It became apparent that the banks had invested in government bonds across borders. A vicious circle loomed that would affect a very large part of the eurozone.

5.2 Dimensions of the euro crisis

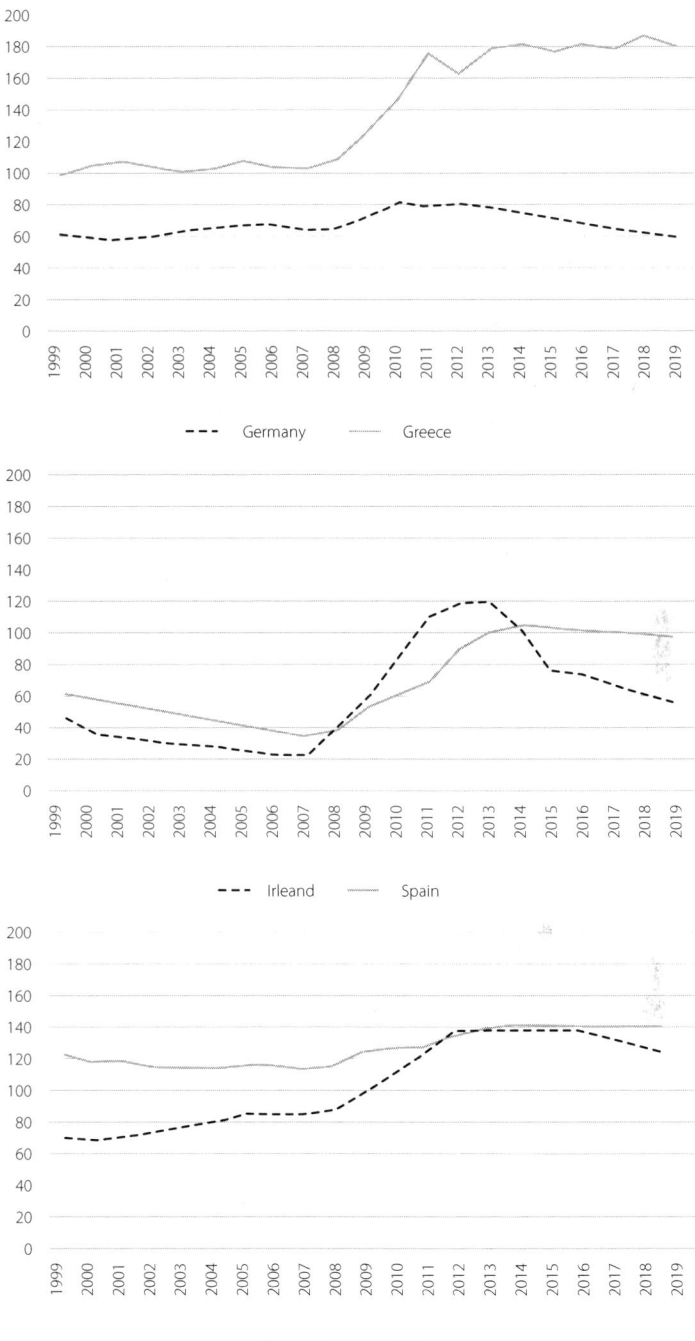

Fig. 49: Public debt 1999–2019 (General government debt, % of GDP, data: ECB)

5 Crisis years: The monetary union on the brink of collapse (2008–2015)

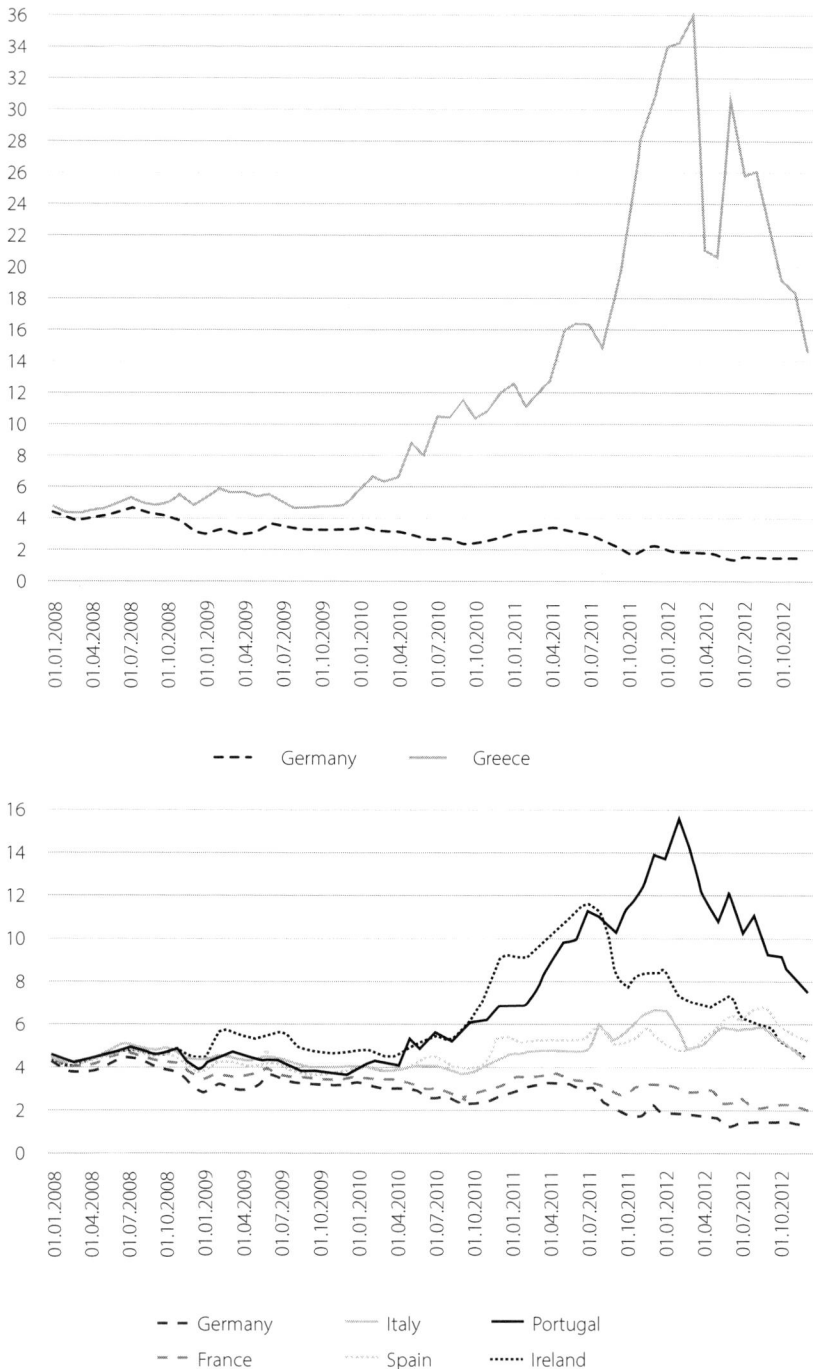

Fig. 50: Ten-year government bond yields in the eurozone (%, data: ECB)

A look at the evolution of government bond yields illustrates the trend in the years 2008 to 2010 (▶ Fig. 50). After there had been almost no difference between the yields of eurozone countries' bonds at the beginning of 2008, there was a minimal divergence in the course of 2008. While yields of many government bonds still tended to fall, those on Greek government bonds rose from the middle of the year. Irish bonds followed suit at the beginning of 2009, when the problems of the banks there and the need for massive government support measures became apparent. The government bond yields of the other euro countries (including Spain) continued to fall (slightly) in 2009. In early 2010, there was a three-way split in the trend: Greek, Irish and Portuguese yields rose permanently and sharply, Spanish and Italian yields moved sideways well into the second half of the year and German and French yields continued to fall. From the second half of 2010, yields of Spanish and Italian government bonds also rose sharply. With Portugal and Italy, two other euro countries that had not previously played an important role came into focus. Against the backdrop of pronounced nervousness among investors, their failure to use the good years before the crisis to restructure their national budgets proved fatal.

This led to a disintegration of the European government bond markets. The crisis countries Greece, Ireland, Italy, Portugal and Spain were not expected to be able to solve their financing problems; therefore, demand for their government bonds collapsed. This led to rising yields, which further exacerbated their financing problems. Now, investment capital flowed into the "safe havens" of Germany and France rather than into the periphery of the eurozone, which led to rising bond prices and falling yields in the two core countries. The eurozone was split in two.

5.3 The discussion about the institutional causes of the crisis

In 2010, an intensive discussion started, initially about the institutional causes of the crisis and quite quickly also about what conclusions could be drawn from the crisis and whether or how the architecture of the eurozone needed to be reformed. This discussion continues to this day. There are two opposing points of view. The first one (the Maastricht defenders) considers the Maastricht construction of the monetary union to be an overall success. It argues that the main failings occurred in individual member states that did not align their policies with the requirements of the single market and the monetary union. According to this position, the later crisis countries failed to flexibilize labor and goods markets and to improve the legal framework, which resulted in relatively few companies that were able to withstand European competition. The opposing view (held by the Maastricht critics) considers the monetary union to be incomplete from the outset; its 'original sin,' it is argued, was that there was no central economic policy institution that could react to and influence the macroeconomic situation with and alongside the European Central Bank. Furthermore, the Maastricht critics argued that the crisis countries were not the only ones to blame for the crisis. Thus, Germany in particular had pursued an exaggerated policy of wage restraint and social cuts in the 2000s, which had worsened the relative competitive position of the later crisis countries and thus triggered the current account crisis. According to the argument, the core issue was not the current account deficits of the peripheral countries, but rather in Germany's persistent surpluses.

There was general consensus that the sovereign debt crisis was linked to one economic characteristic of the eurozone: from 1999 onwards, the monetary union made it possible for public and private debtors in eurozone countries to borrow in other European countries (as long as they were part of the eurozone) without exchange rate risk. In other words, creditors were able to lend their money to debtors in other eurozone countries without incurring any exchange rate risk. However, despite the lack of exchange rate risk, debtors were to a certain extent borrowing in foreign currency. The euro was not provided by the respective national central bank, but by the ECB. This meant that there was no local institution that could step in as a lender of last resort for private debtors (especially for the banking system) or the state in the event of a crisis. Also, it was no longer possible to ease the burden on debtors by inflating the currency or to increase the competitiveness of domestic companies by devaluing the currency. It was already clear to everyone involved in the 1990s that this could become a problem.

The Maastricht architects had assumed a decentralized, market-based response to potential difficulties ('double decentralization' ▶ Ch. 3.1). Competitive pressure would put governments and companies throughout the eurozone under pressure to adapt, so that structural reforms on the political side and programs to increase efficiency on the economic side would become unavoidable. At the same time, the Stability and Growth Pact would make it impossible for member states to whitewash structural problems by means of constant state intervention in the economy. The Europeanization of parts of fiscal policy was rejected because it could have created negative incentives for the governments of the member states. It was argued that money flows from Brussels could deprive national politicians of the incentive to pursue an economic policy that was in line with stability and growth. The defenders of the Maastricht regulations did not consider possible current account imbalances within the monetary union as a problem, but rather as an expression of deeper trade and financial market integration. The combination of the 'no-bailout clause,' the ban on monetary state financing and fiscal rules was intended to transfer the monitoring of national policies in the eurozone to the financial markets. Capital market investors would sanction unsustainable financial and economic policies of individual member states through yield premiums on the basis of information from rating agencies. This would increase the interest burden and thereby make the work of finance ministers more difficult, which governments should respond to by pursuing a more solid fiscal policy and growth-promoting structural reforms. The economies of the member countries could be brought back into balance by adjusting prices and wages to restore competitiveness and, potentially, by the temporary migration of workers to areas of the monetary union.

In the 1990s already, critics of the Maastricht eurozone architecture and the Stability and Growth Pact considered such a scenario unrealistic. In an actual crisis, they argued, the mere focus on competition and the market was not expedient. Instead, fiscal policy was to react decisively; on the one hand, it should do so in a discretionary way, employing targeted anti-cyclical measures; on the other hand, it should allow the automatic stabilizers to take effect. They argued that the existing strict fiscal rules and the lack of financial support from other member states or the Union had, particularly in times of crisis, the exact opposite effect in that it led to pro-cyclical policy by national governments. If structural difficulties or asymmetric shocks worsened the economic situation and thus the budget situation, these governments could not react adequately because they lacked fiscal leeway. Instead of investing, i. e., boosting the economy in the short term and thus putting it on a higher growth path in the long term, the governments would have to save money, which would further exacerbate the situation. The crisis had exposed what the surveillance and co-ordination rules of the Stability and Growth Pact, which were reformed in 2005, had been ever since their introduction in 1997: a poor compromise between the need for at least partial Europeanization of fiscal policy and the refusal of member states to relinquish sovereignty rights.

Skeptics had also from the outset been critical of the sanctioning of fiscal policy misconduct by the capital markets. For them, such sanctions basically meant that countries already facing financial difficulties would have to service even higher debt caused by higher yields. This would be counterproductive. In addition, at an early point already, questions were raised on whether the capital markets functioned well enough to act as fiscal watchdogs. Thus, behavioral finance research showed that capital market transactions are characterized by irrationality. Similarly, it was unclear whether or not government bondholders trusted the 'no bailout clause.' All in all, it was quite possible that "the capital markets" would initially not react to undesirable developments in financial policy or do so late – and then react too strongly.

Proponents of both positions felt vindicated by the crisis, a fact that shaped the discussions on how to proceed. In the short term, it was imperative to avert the immediate threat to the eurozone, while in the long term, it was essential to reinforce the structural foundations of the monetary union in order to mitigate the likelihood of future crises. The different positions of Maastricht critics and supporters had to be taken into account in the decision-making process.

Fig. 51: Main arguments in the discussion about the causes of the euro crisis

	Maastricht critics	Maastricht defenders
Main cause of the crisis	Maastricht rules are not suitable for preventing crises, but actually exacerbate them.	Individual member states have not complied with the rules; yet the set of rules is important.

Fig. 51: Main arguments in the discussion about the causes of the euro crisis – Continuation

	Maastricht critics	Maastricht defenders
Central line of argument	Tough fiscal rules make sensible economic policy at national level almost impossible. Countries like Germany are increasing their competitiveness at the expense of other eurozone countries.	Relaxation of the rules or Europeanization of fiscal policy creates negative incentives for national governments: Incentives for stability-oriented fiscal policy and growth-promoting structural reforms become weaker.
Reform proposals	Relaxation of the rules Partial Europeanization of fiscal policy	More consistent implementation of the rules

5.4 The 'rescue packages', the European Stability Mechanism (ESM) and the crisis year 2015

When it became increasingly clear in early 2010 that Greece was heading towards insolvency, intensive negotiations began on how to stabilize the country. Various factors had to be taken into account and balanced under great time pressure. First of all, it was important to ensure the functioning of the Greek state and to prevent the crisis from spreading to other eurozone countries. At the same time, the potential aid was not to send any signals that national governments or the capital markets could interpret as a free ticket for escalating national debt in the future. The heads of state and government of the eurozone always kept in mind that any support for Greece would not only be met with legal concerns due to the 'no bailout clause,' but also face considerable political resistance. After all, the no bail-out requirement had been a central pillar of the Maastricht eurozone architecture. In Germany in particular, politicians – not least the leading party, the Christian Democratic Union (CDU) – had campaigned for the euro with the claim that there would be no liability for the debts of other states. This meant that Chancellor Merkel now urgently needed to justify the new policy. She had to convince both a skeptical public and her party's MPs. There was also fierce criticism in other countries sparked, among other things, by the fact that the stabilization of Greek public finances 'saved' not so much the Greek people as rather Greece's creditors, i. e., the owners of the government bonds. To a considerable extent, the move therefore also involved German and French banks.

In May 2010, a compromise was finally reached. It provided for a combination of loans, non-European control and conditionality of aid payments:

- Loans totaling 110 billion euros were to ensure Greece's solvency until 2013. The total sum was made up of loans from the euro countries (80 billion) and the International Monetary Fund (IMF) (30 billion). As there were no supranational mech-

anisms for such purposes, the aid was organized bilaterally, i.e., each eurozone country granted Greece a loan individually.
- The involvement of the IMF, a non-European institution that was very familiar with support payments to countries in financial difficulties thanks to decades of experience, was to ensure a professional view from outside and thus keep intra-European relations on a rational footing.
- In order to put Greece's economy and national budget on a sustainable footing, comprehensive restructuring and reform programs were devised. The measures on the agenda included massive staff cuts in the public sector, reductions in subsidies, far-reaching privatization, cuts to public services and the liberalization of goods markets. A new committee, whose members were delegated by the EU Commission, the ECB and the IMF, was to assess on a quarterly basis whether progress was made on reforms. Only when this 'troika' approved of how these measures were implemented, the next loan instalment was to be disbursed. This procedure was referred to as the 'conditionality' of the support.

The conditions were not only intended to reduce the Greek state's expenditure and strengthen the competitiveness of the Greek economy, but also to appease critics of the rescue measures. Last but not least, the aim was to send an unmistakable signal to potential future aid recipients that a sound fiscal policy is worthwhile, because a failure to manage public finances in line with stability would bring considerable difficulties even if the European solidarity community supported that country. However, this did not change the fundamental fact that risks from the private sector, namely the default risks of government bondholders, had been transferred to the public sector. An expected or implicit guarantee had materialized into rescue programs. The 'no bailout clause' (▶ Ch. 3.3.1) of the Maastricht Treaty was effectively no longer valid.

At the same time, a "temporary rescue fund" was created, which was to be accessible to all euro countries and prevent panic on the European government bond markets. In May 2010, 'the markets' even started to scrutinize France; in several southern European countries yields also threatened to rise so sharply that it became increasingly difficult to refinance government debt. In addition, Ireland was the focus of investor attention due to its extensive bank rescue program. The temporary rescue fund was designed to be active for three years (until 2013). What it had in common with the Greek program was that the loan was to be paid out in instalments if previously agreed conditions were fulfilled and that (at Germany's insistence) the IMF was still involved. However, the loans were not granted bilaterally, but by the EFSF (European Financial Stability Facility), a private-law corporation set up specifically for this purpose. The EFSF refinanced its lending to weak euro countries by issuing bonds on the capital market. Its total lending capacity amounted to 440 billion euros. The member states of the monetary union guaranteed the activities of the EFSF with a total of 780 billion euros. This guarantee total, which surpassed the lending capacity by far, ensured that the EFSF bonds received an AAA rating. The best credit rating was to result in low interest rates. Alongside the EFSF was another EU Community instrument, the EFSM (European Financial Stability Mechanism). This enabled the

EU Commission to take out loans of up to 60 billion euros in order to support ailing member states. The IMF agreed to contribute up to 250 billion euros. The recipients of funds from the temporary protective shield were Ireland (2010–2013), Portugal (2011–2014) and Greece (second Greek program, 'Greece II'), because the first aid program ("Greece I") had not been sufficient to put the country back on its own financial footing. The European funds were to flow from 2012 to 2014, whereas the IMF loan was disbursed until 2016. The loans of the second Greek package also included undisbursed instalments of the first.

It was a special feature of "Greece II" that it required the participation of the private sector. This had been first agreed on by German Chancellor Angela Merkel and French President Nicolas Sarkozy and was then approved by the other heads of state and government. The private creditors exchanged their bonds for new bonds with a lower nominal value and longer terms of up to thirty years. With this 'haircut,' they waived around half of the original nominal value of their bonds. The absolute volume of the waiver amounted to around 100 billion euros. The 'haircut' was highly controversial: Although it satisfied the public's desire for capital market players to share in the costs of overcoming the crisis, it also sent a clear signal to investors that government bonds issued by eurozone countries entailed a real risk of default. This signal was to cause turbulence on the government bond markets shortly afterwards, prompting ECB President Mario Draghi to hold his famous "whatever-it-takes" press conference (▶ Ch. 6.1.3).

In Germany, constitutional complaints were filed against both the first bailout for Greece and the establishment of the EFSF and EFSM. The complainants claimed that the Maastricht 'no bailout clause' and the principle of democracy had been violated. In its 'Maastricht ruling' of 1993, the Federal Constitutional Court had made it clear that the comprehensive transfer of sovereignty rights to European institutions was only permissible if the future monetary union was constructed as a stability union. According to the judges in Germany's highest court, this required strict compliance with the relevant treaty provisions.

According to the complainants, the extensive aid programs clearly violated this requirement. In addition, the guarantees and loans violated the German parliament's budgetary rights and the principle of democracy under Article 20 of German Basic Law. The EFSF and Greek loans could, for example if the eurozone were to break up, result in almost incalculable burdens for German taxpayers who had not had their say in this. The constitutional complaints failed. They were to be followed by numerous others in the long course of the fiscal and monetary policy measures taken to overcome the crisis, which kept both the Federal Constitutional Court and the European Court of Justice busy for years.

5.4 The 'rescue packages', the European Stability Mechanism (ESM) and the crisis year 2015

Fig. 52: Aid measures for euro countries in financial difficulties

Program	Recipients of support loans	Credit period	Agreed scope
"Greece I"	Greece	2010–2012	110 billion €
Temporary rescue mechanism	Ireland	2010–2013	85 billion €
	Portugal	2011–2014	78 billion €
	Greece ("Greece II")	EFSF/EFSM: 2012–2014	130 billion €
		IMF: 2012–2016	28 billion €
European Stability Mechanism (ESM)	Cyprus	2013–2016	9 billion €
	Spain (bank rescue fund)	2012–2013	41 billion €
	Greece ("Greece III")	2015–2018	86 billion €

While Ireland, Portugal and Greece were program countries of the temporary rescue mechanism, negotiations were underway on a permanent crisis mechanism, which was then established in 2012 as the European Stability Mechanism (ESM). This is not an EU body, but an international financial institution based in Luxembourg. Decisions on financial aid are made by the Board of Governors, which consists of the finance ministers of the eurozone countries. Like the EFSF, the ESM finances itself on the capital market by issuing bonds. The ESM's capital (cash contributions and callable guarantees) totals 700 billion euros. The national contributions are based on the national shares in the ECB's capital, so that e. g., the German share is 190 billion euros. While maintaining a triple-A rating, this capitalization enables a lending volume of up to 500 billion euros. Again, a constitutional complaint was filed in Germany against the ESM. It was claimed that there was the danger of unlimited budgetary risks and that the Bundestag's budgetary rights were undermined. Yet the Federal Constitutional Court did not uphold the complaint and only stipulated that when the ESM Treaty was ratified, it had to be ensured that the liability limit was not to exceed the German share of the capital stock without a separate resolution by the Bundestag.

The prerequisites for receiving an aid payment ("stability support loan" in ESM terminology) are that the applying eurozone country faces imminent or urgent serious financing problems, that its sovereign debt is sustainable and that stability support is essential for maintaining financial stability in the eurozone as a whole and in its member states. If the applicant's sovereign debt is classified as unsustainable, it must be restructured. This means that the government bond creditors have to make concessions in terms of interest and repayment. Legally, this is made possible by a clause that has been mandatory for all government bond issues in the eurozone since 2013 and that stipulates that creditors can initiate a restructuring by majority vote. The legal possibility notwithstanding, such restructuring can be a considerable burden for the national and European banking system. It should therefore only be considered a last resort.

ESM programs also follow the principle of conditionality. A memorandum of understanding on structural reforms and restoring the sustainability of public finance is negotiated with the applicant member state. The aid is then paid out gradually in instalments if milestones set in the memorandum of understanding have been reached. ESM stability assistance can take various forms, including loans to refinance government debt or to recapitalize distressed financial service providers or the purchase of government bonds. The ESM program countries Cyprus and Spain had to apply for stability aid because the crisis had severely affected their banking sector. In this case, the euro crisis was a banking crisis. The Spanish banks had to deal with the legacy of the real estate boom of the years before 2008. The Cypriot banking sector was traditionally closely linked to Greece and therefore suffered considerably from the problems in that country and, in particular, the debt 'haircut' associated with the second Greek program.

Greece became an ESM program country for different reasons. The crisis here was still a sovereign debt crisis. When the second bailout package expired at the end of 2014, it was clear that Greece would continue to need help. While the troika and the Greek government were negotiating the 2015 budget and the heads of state and government deliberated 'Greece III,' domestic political problems in December 2014 led to an early election of the parliament in January 2015. The left-wing populist Syriza party emerged victorious, and its leader Alexis Tsipras became prime minister. Syriza had won the election with an anti-troika campaign. After years of structural reforms with significant cuts to state benefits, pension payments and wages, the body of representatives from the EU Commission, ECB and IMF had become the symbol many Greeks had come to loathe for what was perceived to be foreign domination and dependence on aid. Even after the election, Tsipras and Finance Minister Yanis Varoufakis promised the Greeks that the days of enforced austerity were finally over. This rhetoric met with little approval in Brussels and the other capitals. While the Greek government was constantly trying to meet its financial obligations with bankruptcy looming, negotiations on the necessary third bailout program dragged on until the summer. Despite the extremely tense budgetary situation, Tsipras and Varoufakis were not prepared to make the austerity and reform commitments demanded by the donor countries. German Finance Minister Wolfgang Schäuble emerged as Varoufakis' opponent in this dispute.

In July 2015, Schäuble announced that he could imagine a temporary exclusion of Greece from the eurozone, a 'temporary Grexit.' This reignited a discussion that had already begun in 2010. The question was whether individual members should leave the eurozone or whether it should be fundamentally restructured. Such a restructuring could, for example, have meant splitting the monetary union along the 'core vs. periphery' dividing line into a 'northern euro' and a 'southern euro.' In 2015, proponents of a Grexit argued that 'business as usual' was not politically feasible neither in Greece nor in the donor countries. The austerity and reform requirements imposed since 2010 had repeatedly put enormous strain on Greek democracy. The constitutional order was at risk and the country in danger of falling under the influence of foreign powers (namely, Russia and China). It was therefore extremely risky, they argued, to continue on the path of enforced austerity. With its own currency, Greece could devalue nominally and thus restore its competitiveness. Politicians and the population would have room to breathe again and could restructure the state, economy and banking system. This would make it possible to reintroduce the euro at a later date.

The Grexit opponents could not follow this argument. A nominal devaluation in the course of leaving the eurozone would inevitably lead to higher, possibly barely sustainable import prices. Whether price competitiveness would really improve was an open question, they argued. There was a risk of a self-reinforcing spiral of devaluation, inflation and wage increases, which could ultimately plunge Greece into poverty. The country would also not be able to service its liabilities in euros with a devalued currency. There was a risk of national bankruptcy vis-à-vis foreign creditors and of a complete loss of confidence on the international capital markets. This in turn could spread to other countries and trigger bank runs there because once there was suspicion in a crisis country that this country would follow Greece's path and be the next country to leave the eurozone, its citizens would try to avoid converting their euro deposits into a new national currency by withdrawing cash. In the eyes of depositors and investors, the currency union would then be nothing more than a fixed exchange rate system that could be reversed at any time.

But it did not come to that. After some back and forth, which included the resignation of Finance Minister Varoufakis, a referendum and new elections, Greece received ESM stability aid from 2015 to 2018.

5.5 The reform of the eurozone architecture

5.5.1 Overview of the main features of the discussion

The various aid programs in the years from 2010 onwards served to manage the crisis. At the same time, an intensive discussion began on the question of how to avoid future crises. This discussion led to a far-reaching reform of the eurozone architecture with a threefold objective:

- Because the fiscal rules that were in force until the outbreak of the crisis – including the essential Stability and Growth Pact that had been revised in 2005 – had not prevented the crisis, the relevant regulations were comprehensively revised and expanded.
- New instruments of macroeconomic coordination were also to help limit current account imbalances within Europe.
- The EU heads of state and government considered the sovereign-bank nexus the Achilles' heel of the monetary union. They therefore sought a banking union and wanted to reorganize macroprudential financial market supervision.

Some of the measures were highly controversial. While there was broad agreement on how to reduce the sovereign-bank nexus, there were two opposing camps in the debate on fiscal policy and macroeconomic imbalances. These two camps had already emerged during the 1990s, when the Maastricht regulations and the Stability and Growth Pact were at issue (▶ Ch. 3.3.1 and 3.4), and at the outbreak of the 2009/2010 crisis (▶ Ch. 5.3), when the institutional causes of the crisis were discussed. One side considered the Maastricht construction, which essentially goes back to the Delors Report, to be fundamentally good, but nevertheless argued for individual clarifications and extensions. The other side argued for a systematic revision of the institutional foundations of the eurozone. At the heart of the debate was the allocation of fiscal policy competences.

Supporters of a fundamental overhaul of the eurozone architecture argued for the greatest possible Europeanization of fiscal policy. A central fiscal capacity of the monetary union, which would have to be financed by issuing bonds (Eurobonds), could serve as insurance against shocks and as an equalization mechanism in the event of structural differences between the member states. European solidarity should not be limited to granting aid loans under strict conditions in the event of a crisis, because then it would be too late. Rather, the eurozone had to be constructed in such a way that countries would not get into a crisis in the first place because they could already count on the support of the solidarity community. The central fiscal capacity could already help member states when financial problems were just beginning to emerge. Only under these circumstances was it possible for governments to make targeted investments in improving state and economic structures. According to this line of argument, this was precisely what the purely decentralized approach to fiscal policy prevents from happening, if the overly strict rules of the Stability and Growth Pact also had to be followed. In a downturn, this would lead to an unnecessary austerity policy that did not solve the problems of the affected countries, but instead unnecessarily exacerbate them. As a result, the national debt ratio increased rather than decreased – and the social upheavals brought the democratic system into disrepute. Therefore, not only was it necessary to Europeanize fiscal policy, but also to loosen fiscal rules. After all, it was precisely in a monetary union, where there is a lack of monetary and interest rate policy instruments, that members needed the ability to act in terms of fiscal policy. Furthermore, it was generally the wrong approach to only try to prevent future crises with a view to potential 'deficit sinners.' It was true that the budgets of the euro countries must be sustainable in the long term. However, this was prevented by the fact that Germany, as the economically strongest country, operated too frugally and imposed its austerity policy on the rest of the monetary union. The debt brake and the cautious wage policy of the collective bargaining parties were dampening government demand as well as private consumption in Germany and, as a result, corporate investment. Too little domestic demand led to export surpluses and capital exports. Germany was not the engine but the brake on overall economic demand in the eurozone. Its current account surpluses must be limited. What was needed was not only regulation with regard to government deficits and debt levels, but also international current account surpluses. Instead of a debt brake, the surplus countries of the center and the north needed a 'current account brake,' the Maastricht critics argued.

The defenders of the Delors/Maastricht concept could not follow this fundamental criticism. For them, the problems of the eurozone did not represent a fundamental failure of the set of rules itself; rather, European institutions and national governments had only insufficiently complied with these rules. The (rule-based) establishment of fiscal policy competencies at member state level was still correct. Both a (partial) Europeanization of fiscal policy and the relaxation of the Stability and Growth Pact could enable national governments to at least partially externalize the negative effects of unsound budget management, i. e., to impose them on third parties – be it (in the case of ESM stability aid) the taxpayers in other member states or all citizens of the eurozone, if the unsustainable fiscal policy is reflected in higher inflation rates. Moral hazard, i. e., irresponsible behavior as a result of false incentives, was thus inevitable: painful structural reforms and a sustainable fiscal policy to avoid future problems would not be implemented if external aid could be counted on in the event of a crisis. The moral hazard argument lies at the heart of this school of thought. Insurance could only make sense if the members of the solidarity-based community were equally likely to become a problem case. This was, however, not the case in the eurozone. Due to structural problems, some countries were exposed to more frequent and stronger asymmetric shocks than others. There were also member states with stronger and weaker growth. A fiscal policy insurance policy therefore threatened to become a transfer union in reality. The idea of a 'current account brake' also met with reservations. Interstate capital flows and positive or negative current account balances in the monetary union were the result of regional specialization and therefore desirable market processes. The single market and the monetary union had been established not least for this purpose.

Against this backdrop, the proponents of the Maastricht framework expected national governments to create the conditions for financial leeway in the future and make future crises less likely through budget consolidation and policies aimed at increasing competitiveness. Moreover, reducing government deficits only has a limited impact on economic growth as long as the focus is on cutting spending rather than raising taxes. Before the introduction of the euro, the crisis countries had still been able to work with external devaluations, i. e., the nominal devaluation of their currency. These external devaluations tended to have an inflationary effect. National governments would have to accept that this option no longer existed and that they could only devalue internally, i. e., in real terms: Companies in their countries would have to be competitive on the domestic market against competitors who also calculated in euros. This would require a moderate wage policy, a reduction in state activity and social spending as a prerequisite for lower taxes and social security contributions as well as structural policy reforms in the service of more flexible labor and product markets. This would increase the export power of the respective economies and reduce external imbalances. Competition between governments for the best financial and economic policy would make the eurozone as a whole more stable and competitive and thus benefit all parties involved. If the regulatory framework was constructed appropriately, national governments would then cause positive externalities rather than negative ones. A downward spiral would become an upward spiral. Summing up, this argumentation leads to a clear conclusion: There is no reason to fundamentally change the Maastricht setting.

5.5.2 The reorganization of the fiscal and economic policy rules

The principle of "solidarity only with conditionality" followed in the 'rescue programs' was also reflected in the reorganization of the fiscal rules. Although the ESM was set up as a permanent aid mechanism for member states in need, there was no adjustment to fiscal policy competencies at the same time: Responsibility for fiscal policy remained with the governments of the euro countries, and they still had to comply with European rules. The ESM only paid out its stability aid gradually in instalments, depending on the implementation of the reform steps previously agreed in a memorandum of understanding" (▶ Ch. 5.4). Thus, the opponents of the basic fiscal policy framework of the monetary union laid down in the Maastricht Treaty and the Stability and Growth Pact did not prevail. In principle, everything remained the same.

However, guided by the desire to make future crises less likely, a whole series of changes and additions were made to the rules between 2011 and 2015. These reforms were guided by the realization that the Stability and Growth Pact, which had come into force in 1998 and had been amended in 2005, had clearly not been able to prevent the euro crisis. The basic idea of dividing the rules of the pact into a preventive and a corrective arm remained unchanged, but both parts were modified. The new Fiscal Compact, the European Semester (see below) and a special matrix to take account of the structural policy efforts of the member states were also added. Last but not least, it was agreed to pay more attention to macroeconomic imbalances. Overall, the aim was to strengthen fiscal policy discipline and economic policy coordination, while at the same time granting the member states economic policy leeway to a certain extent. The two Maastricht fiscal criteria continued to play an important role, but they were integrated into a broader assessment scheme.

Since 2005, the preventive arm of the Stability and Growth Pact had essentially been geared towards a medium-term structural budget balance. The member states aimed to achieve a certain structural budget balance (as a percentage of gross domestic product) within a certain period of time. This indicator shows how large the difference would be between government revenue and expenditure if the economy was neither in recession nor in an upswing. This is referred to as a fictitious situation with 'normal capacity utilization.' Governments had to submit a stability program to be agreed with the Commission, showing how they intended to achieve the medium-term budget target (defined as a structural budget balance at a certain level). The 2011 reform of the Stability and Growth pact combined this rationale with the goal of reducing the overall debt level. For countries with a public debt below 60 % of GDP, the structural budget balance had to improve by 0.5 percentage points annually, and by one percentage point for countries with public debt above 60 %. When assessing the consolidation performance of the member states, the Commission took into account the respective economic situation. In a favorable environment with rising tax revenues and falling (social) expenditure, greater efforts were expected than under difficult macroeconomic conditions. One-off efforts (e. g., privatization of state property or one-off taxes) were assessed with a view to their lack of sustainability. Deviations from the stability program were possible if the government in question implemented structural reforms that improved growth in the medium and long term and thus also the state revenue base. If a national government's budgetary policy deviated significantly from the adjustment path to the medium-term target, the Commission could issue a warning and submit recommendations for adjustment measures; if these measures were not implemented, a sanction could be imposed in the form of an interest-free deposit by the respective country. This meant that sanctions were for the first time also possible in the preventive arm of the Stability and Growth Pact.

The corrective arm of the Stability and Growth Pact continued to focus on the question of whether the two Maastricht fiscal criteria had been met. In principle, the parameters of 3 % of GDP (budget balance) and 60 % of GDP (debt level) remained unchanged. There were two major exceptions: On the one hand, an event beyond the member state's control and, on the other hand, an exceptionally severe economic slump. From then on, the exceptional case could also be determined for the eurozone as a whole.[29] In addition, the fiscal criteria were considered to have been met even if they were exceeded, if the deficit or debt level was sufficiently close to the target value or only missed it in exceptional cases. What is meant by a sufficient approximation to the target value was specified with regard to the debt criterion: over a period of three consecutive years, the debt level had to fall annually on average by one twentieth of the difference between the actual debt level as a percentage of gross domestic product and the target value (60 %). Here is an example: if the debt level in the initial situation was 100 % of gross domestic product, the deviation from the target value was 40 percentage points. This meant that the member state in question had to reduce its debt level by 1/20 of 40 percentage points, i. e., by two percentage points per year, in order for the correction mechanism of the Stability and Growth Pact not to take effect. If the Commission identified an unjustified deviation from the deficit and/or debt criterion, it presented recommendations on the basis of which the member state was to return to a compliant fiscal policy. If the proposed measures were not implemented within a certain period of time, sanctions in the form of interest-free deposits or penalty payments were again possible. There was one decisive innovation here: previously, sanctions had to be proposed by the EU Commission and then decided on by the Council of Ministers. This had resulted in the 'sinners judging sinners' problem (▶ Ch. 3.4 and 4.2). The sanction mechanism was now sharpened.

---

29 This so-called 'general escape clause' has been activated once so far, namely in the course of the Covid19 pandemic and the Russian invasion of Ukraine for the years 2020 to 2023.

The sanction was automatically effective if it was not rejected by the Council with a qualified majority.

The reforms of the years 2011 to 2015 not only amended the Stability and Growth Pact, but also introduced completely new instruments and procedures into the basic economic policy structure of the monetary union. These new elements had two objectives: firstly, to emphasize national responsibility for stability-oriented fiscal policy; secondly, to extend the focus beyond fiscal policy to other areas of economic policy. The first objective was served by the 'Fiscal Compact' and the 'European Semester,' the second by the 'Macroeconomic Imbalance Procedure.'

Since its adoption in 1997, the regulations of the Stability and Growth Pact have been perceived in many countries as being imposed from outside. Many governments, when faced with economic problems in their country, used the European requirements in domestic political discussions to point to 'the pact' with its allegedly excessive and unrealistic requirements. This reduced acceptance and thus indirectly the effectiveness of the regulations. The reforms following the sovereign debt crisis were therefore intended to point to the actual intention of the Stability and Growth Pact – namely to ensure the long-term sustainability of public finances – at national level. The Fiscal Compact of 2013 served this purpose, providing for all member states to introduce a national debt brake, according to which structural government borrowing could not exceed 0.5 % of GDP. The medium-term budget target of the reformed Stability and Growth Pact was therefore to become an integral part of national legislation and thus national policy. The 'European Semester' serves a similar purpose. This measure involves the preparation of national budgets with European support in the first half of each year. The aim is to anchor realistic and stable budget planning in the national budget preparation procedures from the very beginning. Undesirable developments are to be avoided from the outset instead of being the subject of dispute afterwards in the preventive or even corrective arm of the Stability and Growth Pact. To this end, the Commission presents growth forecasts for the coming years in January, on the basis of which the finance ministries of the member states then calculate the expected revenue and expenditure. In the past, national growth forecasts had repeatedly proved to be too optimistic. As a result, deficits were often higher than expected and medium-term budget targets were missed. In the interest of realistic budget planning, the Commission's growth forecasts were not the only part of the European Semester: national governments must now also submit their (medium-term) budget plans to the Commission, on the basis of which the medium-term budget target is to be achieved. The Commission examines these documents and, if it is dissatisfied with the figures submitted, asks the government(s) concerned to revise their plans. All national budget plans are finally forwarded to the Council, which discusses them.

With the Fiscal Compact and the European Semester, European policymakers accommodated those critics of the Stability and Growth Pact who considered the unsound fiscal policy of some national governments to be the main cause of the sovereign debt crisis. Others considered countries such as Germany to be responsible. With their cautious wage and fiscal policies, they had ensured that the gap between the surplus and deficit countries in the eurozone had become too wide. According to this line of argument, Germany in particular had improved its competitiveness at the expense of the peripheral countries and, due to its weak domestic demand, had not functioned as an importer of goods from other eurozone countries. The resulting current account balances had contributed to the cross-border debt that had turned the global financial crisis into a European sovereign debt crisis. It was therefore urgently necessary to subject not only fiscal policy but also economic policy in general to greater European control. Following this reasoning, a new 'macroeconomic imbalance procedure' was integrated into the European Semester. Every year, the Commission uses ten indicators (including, for example, the current account balance, real estate price trends and the unemployment rate) to examine whether a macroeconomic imbalance exists. If so, the member state concerned must submit a plan to correct the imbalance. If it fails to do so or if the measures contained therein are not effective in the opinion of the Commission, a sanction (in the form of a fine of up to 0.1 % of GDP) may be imposed. However, the 'macroeconomic imbalance procedure' has not played a significant role either in public debate or in economic policy practice ever since its establishment in 2011.

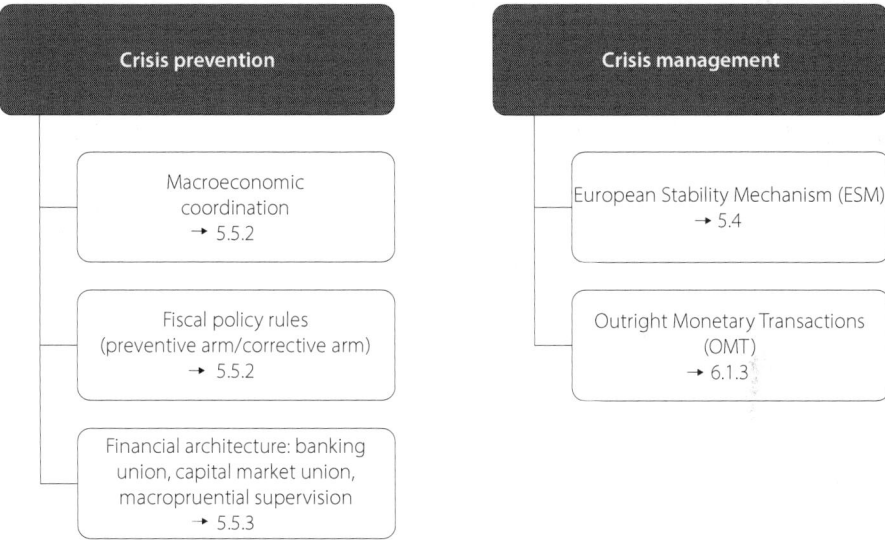

Fig. 53: Economic policy coordination in the euro zone

5.5.3 The reform of the financial architecture

The unforeseen effects of the Lehman insolvency, the collapse of the eurozone interbank market and the almost incalculable risk potential of the sovereign-bank nexus revealed that the monetary union would only have a good future if it had a consistent financial market architecture. The new focus on the financial markets represented a paradigm shift. Banks and financial markets had gradually disappeared from macroeconomic models – and thus from macroeconomic thinking – over the previous decades. This initially only applied to academia, but soon also affected central banks and capital investors, and finally politics. In the theory of optimal currency areas, the financial sector played only a subordinate role – if any at all – as well as in the political discussion of the 1990s. Moreover, there was no historical experience to fall back on: The Maastricht combination of monetary union and single market with the free movement of capital was new. The European Monetary System was also not a suitable object of study due to the capital controls that were possible until the end of the 1980s. The US, as a single currency area with open borders for goods, services, people and capital, was so different from the eurozone that hardly any learning effects could emanate from there. Financial market-based interdependencies such as the financing of the current account deficits of Greece, Ireland, Portugal and Spain by means of cross-border interbank loans and government bond purchases by commercial banks from the core countries of the monetary union were either not seen at all or underestimated in terms of their risk potential.

In the run-up to the Maastricht conference, there was widespread agreement that an integrated financial market would be associated with more intensive competition on the financial services and capital markets. This could lead to more cost-effective payment transactions, broader investment opportunities for savers and more comprehensive financing options for investors and governments, and therefore to a better distribution of risks and a more efficient allocation of capital overall. The integrated European financial market was expected to be the prerequisite for households and companies to be able to operate optimally in the single market. However, apart from the abolition of capital controls, no adequate institutional framework has been created for this common financial market. The crisis then showed that this was a mistake. The eurozone lacked suitable regulations regarding the capital markets union, macroprudential supervision and the banking union:

- Capital markets union:
  For an integrated financial market to develop its positive allocative effects, it is not enough to simply abolish explicit capital controls. Rather, an almost unmanageable number of implicit barriers to market entry needs to be removed. These can be found in tax law as well as insolvency law, in the area of pension subsidies as well as in the structuring of real estate financing and, last but not least, in the field of capital market regulation in the narrower sense, which includes, for example, stock corporation law and the regulation of stock exchanges. The Capital Markets Union project is an ongoing task on which the Commission and the member states are working continuously, but on which they are only making slow progress because it involves a large number of detailed regulations that often affect the interests of the member states. However, these practical implementation problems do not change the fact that the need for a capital markets union is not disputed in principle.

- Macroprudential supervision:
  The term 'macroprudential' can be translated as 'taking a reasonable overall view.' It therefore refers to a well-founded view of the financial system as a whole. Macroprudential supervision complements monetary policy and microprudential supervision, i.e., traditional banking supervision. The aim is to recognize the emergence of systemic risks at an early stage. Systemic risks result from a wide range of interdependencies between financial market players. These can cause problems in one part of the system that lead to unexpected problems in other parts, which in turn can have negative effects elsewhere and ultimately cause the entire system or at least large parts of it to become unstable. The history of financial crises shows that the probability of crises increases with the extent of private debt, among other things. There was no systematic monitoring of the relevant developments in the eurozone before the financial crisis. This changed in 2010, when the European Systemic Risk Board (ESRB) began its work. The ESRB is intended to serve as an early warning system for systemic risks in the eurozone. Its highest decision-making body consists of the President and Vice-President of the ECB, the presidents of the national central banks, a representative of the European Commission, the chairmen of the European supervisory authorities EBA, EIOPA and ESMA (see below) and three members who contribute academic expertise and expertise on technical issues.
- Banking union:
  In contrast to the capital markets union as well as the macroprudential supervision, the banking union (defined as the institutional framework for a common banking market in Europe) had not been on the European political agenda before the crisis. Although there was a common framework for the state supervision of credit institutions in the form of the regulations agreed at the Bank for International Settlements in Basel ('Basel II'), the practical implementation of this set of rules was undisputedly a national domain. This reflected the fact that the national banking systems in Europe had their own peculiarities (such as the three-pillar model in Germany with savings banks, cooperative banks and private commercial banks) and – at least until the beginning of the millennium – were hardly interlinked.

It soon became clear that the banking union would be the most difficult part of the new financial architecture, not only because of the many problems with implementing it in detail, but also because of national conflicts of interest and differing attitudes to key issues.

The imposition of stringent state regulation on credit institutions, even within market economies, is economically justified due to the high risk of market failure associated with their unregulated operation. Such failures can lead to inefficient resource allocation and socially suboptimal outcomes, necessitating governmental oversight. The banking business is associated with information asymmetries, i.e., knowledge of the facts that are relevant to business relationships is unevenly distributed between the parties involved. It is thus difficult or impossible for depositors to assess whether their bank is taking disproportionate risks when granting loans or in the investment business. The same applies to banks that lend money to other banks on the interbank market. The resulting uncertainty can encourage panic. Once there is mistrust about the creditworthiness of individual banks, a self-fulfilling prophecy looms: anyone who thinks that others think that their respective bank could be insolvent assumes that the others will withdraw their money from their bank. This would inevitably result in the illiquidity of these banks, because they would have to forego a considerable proportion of their refinancing funds within a very short space of time – regardless of their actual solvency. To prevent this from happening, it is rational for all depositors and banks on the interbank market to withdraw their money as a precaution. The banking system then actually collapses. Economies of scale in the banking business exacerbate the problem. The banking market tends to have oligopolistic market structures with a few dominant providers that are considered systemically relevant due to their size and interconnectedness with both other financial service providers and the real economy: The collapse of any one of these dominant providers would have catastrophic macroeconomic consequences – which is usually followed by calls for a 'bailout' or 'support' with taxpayers' money.

Before the financial and sovereign debt crisis, the regulation of credit institutions was largely a national domain. Although there were already institutions such as the Committee of European Banking Supervisors (CEBS) in London or the Basle Committee on Banking Supervisors (BCBS), these had more of an advisory and coordinating function (CEBS) or their role was limited to defining certain minimum standards of banking supervision (BCBS). These supranational institutions had no operational powers at all. National banking supervisors, in turn, lacked the incentives to deal with the cross-border business of banks. If the supervisory authority in one eurozone country was of the opinion that a bank under its supervision in another member state was granting excessive loans and thus taking on too much risk, it was not necessarily in the national interest to restrict this lending. After all, the resulting profits initially strengthen the national banking market, while the problems arise in the form of a credit bubble and an overheating economy (at least initially) in another country. Apart from this, the national banking supervisors in the European banking market were subject to the inaction bias. Early and strict intervention in the business activities of domestic banks would have reduced future risks but weakened the relative competitive position of the domestic industry – at least as long as the other national supervisors remained inactive. As a result, no one wanted to be the first to tighten regulatory standards.

For example, before the start of the crisis in 2008, the purely nationally oriented bank supervisors in Germany and France did not draw any conclusions from the fact that 'their' banks were heavily involved in the lending business in southern Europe and also invested heavily in Greek government bonds. Furthermore, the risks of the cross-border business activities of systemically important institutions were generally not recognized. When these transnationally active commercial banks got into difficulties in the course of the crisis from 2008 onwards, the national authorities did not have the mechanisms in place to wind them down in an orderly manner. Ultimately, this meant that the taxpayer had to step in and finance the rescue of troubled financial institutions. This caused considerable resentment in the affected member states of the monetary union.

Calls for a fundamental reform of microprudential supervision (i.e., focused on each individual institution) became louder. It was recognized that a cross-border functioning banking market with multinational institutions that was regulated in line with stability considerations was a prerequisite for the functioning of the monetary union as a whole. Without banking stability, there could be no macroeconomic stability in Europe. Healthy banks were also a necessary means of breaking the sovereign-bank nexus. It was therefore largely undisputed that European banking regulation was an important addition to the single market. After all, the European competitive order required a level playing field for all market participants in the banking market.

Against this backdrop, better control of the sector was to prevent future difficulties at individual institutions from the outset and also uncover transnational dependencies in order to make crises such as those since 2008 less likely in the future. If banks were nevertheless to get into difficulties, the general view was that taxpayer involvement should be avoided as far as possible. Furthermore, the insolvency of individual banks must not destroy confidence in the entire sector and drive other banks, which were actually solvent, into illiquidity in a bank run. Against this backdrop, the desired European banking union was to consist of three components:

1. A European banking supervision (Single Supervisory Mechanism, SSM)
2. A Single Resolution Mechanism (SRM)
3. A common deposit insurance scheme (European Deposit Insurance Scheme, EDIS)

The Europeanization of banking supervision required a European set of rules for the sector that would have to be implemented in all member states according to uniform standards. In principle, this could be achieved in two ways: Either by establishing binding common regulations, which were, however, to be implemented by national supervisory authorities; or by shifting the competence to the European level with a European supervisory authority, which would have virtually automatically resulted in a uniformly formulated and implemented set of rules. The argument against such a European supervisory authority was that it might be too far removed from the specific features of the national banking markets and might have hindered rather than promoted the development of a European banking market with its sometimes impractical provisions. The principle of subsidiarity argued in favor of decentralizing the implementation of common supervisory rules. However, the fact that a central supervisory authority would be 'further away' from the supervised institutions can also be interpreted positively: in this case, it may be more difficult for lobbyists in the banks to influence supervisory practice. A further rationale for establishing a European supervisory authority lies in the inefficiencies that would arise if multiple national regulators were to simultaneously assess the operations of a multinational banking group. Such overlapping oversight could lead to frictional losses and regulatory duplication, undermining supervisory effectiveness. And finally, a decentralized implementation of common regulations would again have entailed the risk that the national supervisory authorities would have acted too cautiously out of consideration for 'their' banks.

The discussion about the pros and cons of Europeanizing banking supervision led to a compromise. In 2011, the 'European System of Financial Supervision' (EFSF) was created. It consists of the national supervisory authorities and:

- the European Systemic Risk Board (ESRB)
- the European Banking Authority (EBA)
- the European Securities and Markets Authority (ESMA)
- the European Insurance and Occupational Pensions Authority (European Insurance and Occupational Pensions Authority, EIOPA)
- the Joint Committee of the European Supervisory Authorities (JSA). The EBA, ESMA and EIOPA coordinate their activities in this committee.

Even though the three supervisory authorities EBA, ESMA and EIOPA are referred to as such, this does not mean that they directly supervise the market participants in their area of responsibility. Rather, the task of the EBA, which is central to the banking union, is to coordinate and harmonize national supervisory activities. At the heart of this is a 'single rule book,' which contains the central provisions relating to the European banking market. These include, for example, minimum and maximum requirements for capital adequacy, leverage and liquidity. A coordinating institution such as the EBA is necessary because a large part of operational banking supervision remains a national responsibility. Against this backdrop, the EBA guarantees the uniform application of European rules with its 'single rule book.' However, the 114 most important ('significant') institutions[30] in the eurozone are directly supervised by the ECB as part of the Single Supervisory Mechanism. To fulfill this function, the ECB establishes 'Joint Supervisory Teams' composed of both ECB staff and representatives from the national supervisory authorities of the countries where the respective institution operates. These teams collaborate closely to ensure consistent and effective oversight across jurisdictions. Whether a bank is classified as 'significant' depends on its balance sheet total, its economic significance for individual member states or for the eurozone as a whole, the extent of its cross-border business activities and the question of whether or not it has received direct state support payments from the ESM.

The establishment of the Single Supervisory Mechanism (SSM) at the ECB was initially highly controversial. Its critics feared a conflict of interest if a central bank is also responsible for macroprudential regulation and banking supervision in addition to its monetary policy responsibilities. For example, in times of rising inflation rates,

---

30 The figure may of course change if institutions are no longer or newly classified as 'significant.'

a restrictive monetary policy is generally appropriate to maintain price stability. However, the resulting increase in costs and shortage of liquidity for the banking system and the real economy could have serious negative effects on the stability of the financial sector if higher interest rates led to loan defaults and a fall in asset prices (e. g., property prices). If the central bank also has banking stability in mind in this case, it could be inclined to take a somewhat less aggressive stance against price increases than would actually be macroeconomically appropriate. This would have a negative impact on its monetary policy credibility. However, if it were to focus on consistently combating inflation, this could cause considerable problems for the banks. The central bank would then have to answer the question of why it, as the banking supervisory authority, did not prepare the financial sector better for the risk of rising interest rates. Once again, its reputation could be damaged.

The fact that the implementation of the SSM was nevertheless delegated to the ECB had not least very practical reasons. The central bankers in Frankfurt were the only institution in Europe with the necessary knowledge and spatial and technical capacities. The aim was to counter the conflicts of interest described above with a 'Chinese wall,' i. e., a strict organizational separation of the employees responsible for monetary policy and those in charge of banking supervision, between whom there must not be any exchange of information. The ECB emphasizes its Chinese Wall also spatially: thus, its banking supervisors are not housed in the ECB tower in Frankfurt's Eastend, but in a separate rented building in the city center.

Thus far for the single supervisory mechanism (SSM). The institutions involved have been working within its framework since the end of 2014. The second pillar of the banking union, the single resolution mechanism, has a more complicated history. Banking supervision is intended to make it less likely that credit institutions will get into difficulties, but it will not be able to completely prevent this from happening. Precautions must therefore be taken for this eventuality. In principle, there are various ways of dealing with this – contingent upon the severity of the bank's financial distress. If it is fundamentally solvent, but its room for maneuver is restricted by an excessive number of non-performing loans and/or insufficient capital resources, one option is to play for time, so to speak, i. e., to gradually reduce the non-performing loans and gradually build up the necessary capital. State subsidies or the direct participation of the state in this bank may be able to accelerate the recovery process. Time and again, banks in difficulties are also rescued, again with state support, by being taken over by other banks or by merging with them. These possible solutions fall under the umbrella term 'restructuring.'

The most radical reaction – apart from the option of allowing the bank to go into uncontrolled insolvency – is orderly liquidation. In a market economy, this is the way to deal with companies that are not viable. Keeping so-called 'zombie banks' that no longer have a viable business model alive artificially would mean a misallocation of resources. On the one hand, the capital tied up in the bank could be put to better use elsewhere in the economy; on the other hand, there would be a risk that the state-funded bank would not only be a zombie bank, but that it would also be in a position to keep non-viable companies ('zombie companies') alive with its loans thanks to the financial support of the state. The state-financed rescue of banks that are not actually viable therefore not only stands in the way of restructuring the financial sector, but also the real economy.

In the case of both restructuring and resolution, the question must be answered as to the extent to which equity and debt capital providers share in the burdens and whether certain claims against the bank, such as the salary claims of its employees, are privileged. The two extreme cases are the total loss for shareholders and creditors in the event of insolvency on the one hand and their complete protection against losses by the state or the central bank on the other. If the bank undergoes restructuring rather than liquidation, a secondary consideration is whether existing management should retain their positions.

Answering these questions infringes on the (property) rights of those involved and is usually associated with massive burdens for taxpayers, which is why it must be carried out within the framework of a democratically legitimized, constitutional procedure. This supports assigning authority at the national level, as taxpayers are likely to fund any necessary restructuring. Aligning financial responsibility with decision-making justifies this approach. However, banks may have an easier game against the governments of the member states when it comes to lobbying at the expense of taxpayers. This is not least because they will often fall on sympathetic ears with national governments, which are usually keen on preventing takeovers of domestic credit institutions by foreign providers or even their disappearance from the market in order to preserve 'national champions.' This threatens to bring about an implicit subsidization of the respective domestic financial sector by the national governments and, in extreme cases, the described survival of de facto insolvent institutions ('zombie banks'). National interests would thus undermine the functioning of the European banking market. These externalities justify a European responsibility for regulating the restructuring and, if necessary, resolution of ailing financial institutions.

The Single Resolution Mechanism (SRM) finally came into force in 2014. The aim is to replace the frequent and hectic rescue of banks with taxpayers' money ('bail-out') during the financial crisis with either an orderly resolution or a restructuring with the transparent participation of all stakeholders ('bail-in'). The liability cascade is as follows: equity providers, debt providers, depositors (taking into account the deposit guarantee of € 100,000) and only at the very end taxpayers, whose participation should be an exception. The decision on the respective share of the individual groups is made on a uniform European basis. The single resolution board (SRB) is only responsible for banks that are supervised by the ECB or operate on a cross-border basis. However, the national supervisors from the member states in which the bank in question operates are involved in the decision-making process. The resolution or restructuring of those institutions that do not fall under the direct responsibility of the SRB is the responsibility of the national authorities. If the financial resources of a bank's shareholders and creditors are not sufficient for its orderly resolution or restructuring, the single resolution fund (SRF) can be used first. This comprises 1 % of the covered deposits of all institutions licensed in the member states. In addition, in-

direct financing of bank restructuring via affected member states is possible through the European Stability Mechanism (ESM).
The Single Supervisory Mechanism (SSM) and the Single Resolution Mechanism (SRM) are fully operational. In contrast, the third pillar of the banking union, the deposit insurance scheme, is still incomplete.

Many citizens have invested a large proportion of their assets in banks. The loss of these assets in the event of a bank collapse would have a considerable social impact. Therefore, from a socio-political point of view, there is a case for some form of deposit protection. However, its economic justification is crucial. Deposit guarantee systems are an effective means of countering the self-fulfilling prophecy of a bank collapse. Against this background, the EU countries have agreed to harmonize their national deposit guarantee schemes. The core of this harmonization is that 100,000 euros per depositor and institution must be covered in all member states.

However, there is still no uniform European deposit guarantee scheme. The need for such a system is not disputed in principle. Yet there are considerable differences of opinion regarding its specific design. As long as deposit protection remains a national responsibility, there is a risk that bank customers in Europe will judge the quality of national protection systems differently. Confidence in the protection of 100,000 euros per customer and bank could vary from country to country. Banks in countries where deposit protection is perceived as weak would then have to offer higher interest rates in order to attract depositors. In the event of a European banking crisis, depositors in countries with perceived weak deposit protection would also be likely to transfer their account balances to countries with perceived strong deposit protection. This would not only cause the banking systems of individual member states to collapse and subsequently – via the sovereign-bank nexus – affect the respective national budgets, but would also be accompanied by a fragmentation of the European banking market. Advocates of a European deposit guarantee scheme argue that this must be prevented at all costs in order to create a genuine European banking market.

This is countered by the practical problem that the current national deposit insurance systems are structured very differently. Genuine harmonization in the sense of the same rules and European financing would require far-reaching changes. A compromise solution could consist of a hybrid system in which the national institutions are retained, but in the event of a crisis could, under certain conditions, fall back on reinsurance organized and financed at European level. This would allow Germany, for example, to avoid having to intervene in the autonomy of the three-pillar system (private commercial banks, savings banks, cooperative banks) and their respective guarantee systems.

Irrespective of these technical implementation problems, the idea of a European deposit guarantee scheme is also facing fundamental criticism. Germany and other member states are calling for countries with weak banking systems to be restructured first before a Europeanization of insurance against default risks for depositors might be considered. Risk sharing must be preceded by risk reduction. Otherwise, the introduction of European deposit protection would create the wrong incentives, the argument goes.

6 'The only game in town:' The ECB in charge of everything? (2015–2022)

6.1 Overview: The evolution of the ECB's monetary policy since the start of the financial crisis

6.1.1 The ECB's response to the problems on the banking market

Initially, many observers considered the US real estate crisis to be a problem that was limited to the American banking market. Yet over the course of 2007, European credit institutions were also gradually drawn into the downward spiral. In Germany, this trend initially affected IKB (Industriekreditbank) and Sachsen LB in the summer of the year and later also Hypo Real Estate (▶ Ch. 5.1). Both institutions had invested in securitized US mortgage loans because they lacked a viable business model. These investments had to be written off to a large extent. In addition, the Spanish and Irish mortgage markets were soon to become the focus of events. The European banking crisis that was slowly but surely emerging was therefore imported from the US, but also home-made – at least in some eurozone member states. The collapse of the long-established American investment bank Lehman Brothers on September 15, 2008 then triggered a worldwide chain reaction that was to fundamentally shake confidence in banks and between banks in Europe as well. The solvency problems of individual banks caused a general liquidity crisis on the banking market: as a result, all banks, even the solvent ones, faced problems financing their business activities.

After decades of progress towards integration, the crisis also led to a re-fragmentation of the European financial markets as distressed banks turned to the governments of their home countries for support. The way governments dealt with the problems of 'their' banks varied greatly. Some countries recapitalized troubled banks right at the beginning of the crisis. While the impact on the state of public finances in Germany, for example, was manageable, the sovereign-bank nexus fully came to bear in Ireland. The rescue of Anglo Irish Bank drove the national deficit to around a third of Irish GDP in 2009, making it necessary to provide the country with financial support from the ESFM and the IMF the following year (▶ Ch. 5.4). Other members of the monetary union, such as Italy and Spain, also found it difficult to comprehensively restructure their banking systems. Spain later had to resort to ESM support loans for this purpose. Some countries, not least Italy, were either unwilling or unable to mobilize their own financial resources to the extent necessary or to apply for European support. Accordingly, the bad loans in these countries had to be reduced gradually

6.1 Overview: The evolution of the ECB's monetary policy since the start of the financial crisis

– by liquidating the individual exposures when this seemed economically viable for the bank in question. The banks in these countries were also reluctant to grant new loans in order to comply with regulatory requirements. The reduction of portfolios already on the balance sheet and caution in new business had a negative impact on the supply of credit and liquidity in parts of the eurozone; elsewhere, the banking business was already flourishing again, especially where the institutions had received early and comprehensive help. The goal of a single European banking and financial market had receded into the distance.

For the ECB, the development came as a surprise. After a fairly successful start of the monetary union, the banking crisis had caught the euro central bankers in Frankfurt on the wrong foot. This also applied to the events in Spain and Ireland. The price level on the Spanish and Irish real estate markets and the development of mortgage lending had been monitored increasingly closely in the years leading up to the crisis. That the central bank had not taken any concrete measures reflects two aspects: firstly, the ECB had gradually moved away from monetary analysis and instead emphasized the 'economic pillar' when gathering information (▶ Ch. 4.1). Real economic data such as GDP growth or the unemployment rate now played a greater role in the preparation of monetary policy decisions than financial data such as the growth in bank lending or the development of the money supply. Secondly, when politicians and academics discussed the institutional set-up of the monetary union in the 1990s, hardly anyone had the risk of financial bubbles in mind. In the early years of the monetary union, the bursting of the internet bubble was indeed a problem that needed to be tackled from 2000 to 2002; yet this crisis was rather considered a global problem, whose causes did not primarily lie in the structure of the eurozone. Macroprudential issues were not the focus of European central bankers until the change in the European financial market architecture from 2012 onwards (▶ Ch. 5.5.2).

Against the backdrop of the profound crisis, the ECB gradually changed its concept of and approach to monetary policy in 2007/2008. As early as the beginning of the 1990s, the future European Central Bank's strictly rule-oriented focus on the primary goal of price stability, its strong independence and the ban on monetary state financing had been criticized, not only in France and Southern Europe (▶ Ch. 3.3.1), but also in the Anglo-Saxon world. Quite tellingly, the title of a scholarly article published in 1992 sums up this skeptical mood: "The ECB: a bank or a monetary policy rule?"[31] Citizens in these countries would have preferred a central bank with an active role in economic policy. This wish now became reality: Within just over a decade (i.e., between 2010 and 2022) the ECB abandoned the strategic direction it had been committed to since its foundation in the summer of 1998. The institution that emerged was a European Central Bank that had little in common with the originally envisioned

---

31 Sweeney, R/Garber, P./Pattison, J. Folkerts-Landau, D. (1992), 'The ECB: a bank or a monetary policy rule?', in Grilli, V, P Masson and M Canzoneri (eds), Establishing a Central Bank: Issues in Europe and Lessons from the US, CEPR Press, Paris & London. https://cepr.org/publications/books-and-reports/establishing-central-bank-issues-europe-and-lessons-us

'European Bundesbank' (▶ Ch. 3.3.1). In other words, the Maastricht specifications had been abandoned without a formal treaty amendment.

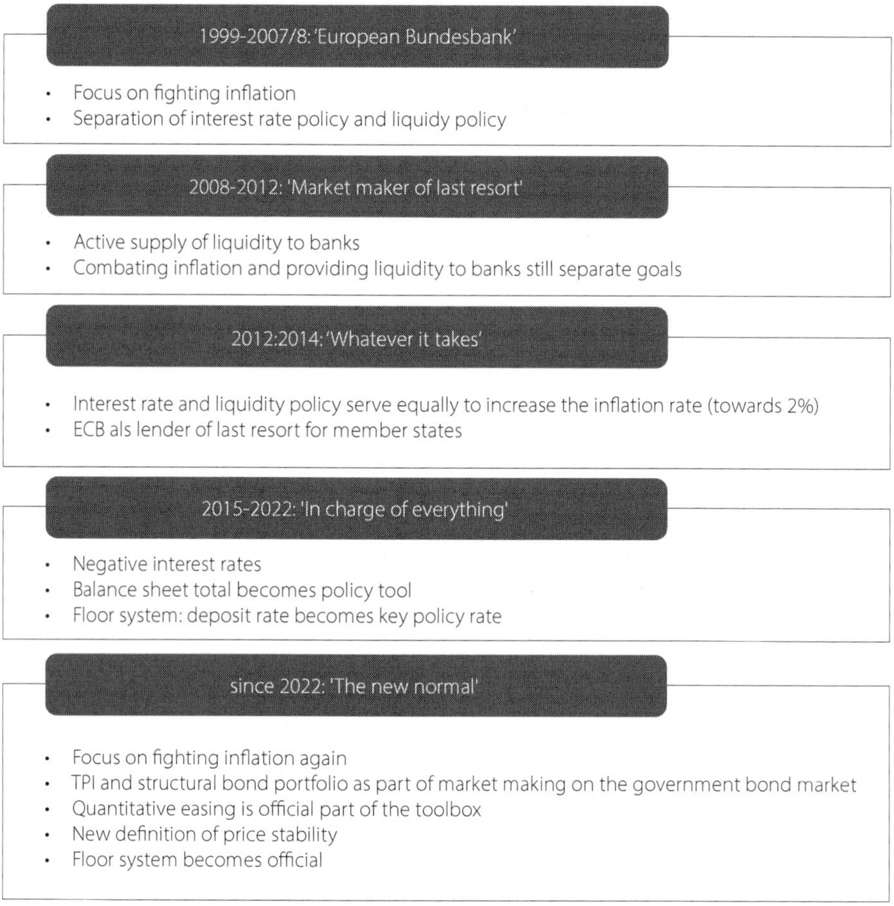

1999-2007/8: 'European Bundesbank'
- Focus on fighting inflation
- Separation of interest rate policy and liquidy policy

2008-2012: 'Market maker of last resort'
- Active supply of liquidity to banks
- Combating inflation and providing liquidity to banks still separate goals

2012:2014: 'Whatever it takes'
- Interest rate and liquidity policy serve equally to increase the inflation rate (towards 2%)
- ECB als lender of last resort for member states

2015-2022: 'In charge of everything'
- Negative interest rates
- Balance sheet total becomes policy tool
- Floor system: deposit rate becomes key policy rate

since 2022: 'The new normal'
- Focus on fighting inflation again
- TPI and structural bond portfolio as part of market making on the government bond market
- Quantitative easing is official part of the toolbox
- New definition of price stability
- Floor system becomes official

Fig. 54: The five phases of the ECB's monetary policy (Based on: Baglioni, A. (2024): Monetary Policy Implementation, 2024, p. 123)

At the beginning of the development there was the ever more pressing need to counter the liquidity crisis on the European banking market over the course of 2007/2008. The conventional approach to monetary policy was based on the separation of interest rate policy on the one hand (which signals the direction monetary policy takes), and the provision of liquidity for the banking system on the money market on the other hand. Interest rate policy was geared towards fighting inflation, whereas the provision of liquidity was intended to ensure the functioning of the banking system. Liquidity was provided as an elastic response to the demand for liquidity from commercial banks. The amount of central bank money – and thus the balance sheet total of the central bank – fluctuated with the liquidity needs of the credit institutions. In its open market operations, the central bank was careful not to acquire government bonds on a permanent basis. Instead, they were acquired as part of repo transactions and automatically sold again a little later, or they merely served as collateral for lending to commercial banks. In September 2007, ECB President Trichet summed up the two coexisting central bank policy objectives as follows: "Again, let us not confuse the appropriate functioning of the money market and the monetary policy stance."[32] In this context, "functioning of the money market" stands for liquidity policy and 'monetary policy stance' for interest rate policy.

Jean-Claude Trichet was born in Lyon, France in 1942. He studied economics and administrative sciences and later became head of the French Treasury and governor of the Banque de France, among other things. The French government wanted him to become the first president of the ECB, but was unable to get its way. Instead, a highly controversial compromise was reached which stipulated that the Dutchman Wim Duisenberg was given the post on the condition that the first eight-year term of office would be split and that he would step down after fours year to hand the office over to Trichet. Trichet's presidency began in 2003 and lasted until 2011. After leaving the ECB, he became involved in the European think tank Bruegel in Brussels. [Photo: ECB]

The separation of interest rate policy and liquidity policy was basically maintained until 2011, as inflationary pressure continued until then. In the course of the financial crisis, the ECB lowered the key interest rate from 4.25 % in mid-2008 to 1 % in May 2009, then kept it constant for almost two years and finally started a short cycle of interest rate hikes in 2011 in response to rising inflation rates and inflation expectations.

While its interest rate policy still followed the classic pattern, the ECB began to break new ground in terms of liquidity in 2008 at the latest. With the collapse of Lehman Brothers in the fall of 2008, banks lost mutual trust to such an extent that overnight liquidity balancing between banks with liquidity surpluses and those with liquidity deficits no longer worked. The ECB became a liquidity broker between the commercial banks. Banks with surpluses parked their liquidity in the deposit facility, while banks with deficits made use of the marginal lending facility. However, the latter played an increasingly minor role because the ECB supplied the commercial

---

32 Trichet, J.C. (2007): Introductory statement, press conference, September 6th, 2007, https://www.ecb.europa.eu/press/press_conference/monetary-policy-statement/2007/html/is070906.en.html

banks with enormous amounts of liquidity. In the first phase of the transition from conventional to unconventional monetary policy (2007–2009), these measures were still designed to be temporary. They were intended to help banks bridge a possible maturity mismatch between assets and liabilities until the financial crisis was over. In normal times, such a maturity mismatch is a natural characteristic of modern banking business; yet in a crisis, it becomes its Achilles' heel. Banks finance themselves to a large extent with funds that they have to at least theoretically be able to repay at any time or at least at very short notice. An example for such funds are current account deposits (which customers can withdraw at any time) or loans from other commercial banks (so-called interbank loans with a term of one day to several months). Yet these funds are usually invested in long-term assets. Overall, this mechanism is referred to as maturity transformation. The bank converts short-term funds into long-term loans, for example. This is not a problem as long as the bank can secure its refinancing. If the banks lose their customers' or other banks' trust, i.e., if these either withdraw their deposits or do not extend interbank loans, the banking sector runs into liquidity problems. Banks must then react to such a situation by attempting to liquidate asset positions, i.e., by selling securities or terminating or not renewing loans. The immediate economic effect of the crisis would therefore be the risk of commercial banks massively reducing their lending, which in turn would have considerable negative consequences for private household consumption and corporate investment. From 2007 onwards, the ECB responded to this risk by devising a package of so-called 'enhanced credit support policies:'

- In 2007 and 2008, the ECB made dollar loans available to European banks on the basis of an agreement with the US Federal Reserve. Against the backdrop of the crisis on the US banking market, the aim was to ensure that banks would not run the risk of no longer being able to refinance their activities in the US. The ECB therefore acted as lender of last resort in US dollars.
- From October 2008 onwards, the main refinancing operations were carried out at a fixed interest rate with full allotment; provided they could provide collateral, commercial banks were able to obtain as much liquidity as they wanted. The liquidity of the banking system thus finally became endogenous, i.e., it was no longer determined by the ECB.
- The ECB extended the term of the longer-term refinancing operations from 3 to 12 months with the aim of giving banks more planning security with regard to their liquidity position.
- The monetary policy collateral framework was expanded. Banks were now able to deposit securities and credit claims as collateral for monetary policy transactions that the ECB had previously not accepted ('qualitative easing'). This made it easier for credit institutions to access central bank liquidity.
- From the summer 2009 onwards, the ECB made targeted purchases of covered bonds (CBPP 1 and 2, the first and second Covered Bond Purchase Programmes): These are bonds that are backed in particular by real estate loans. For credit institutions, they play an important role in refinancing the mortgage business.

These measures still reflect the separation between interest rate and liquidity policy. The ECB continued to influence the development of the price level via the level of key interest rates, but at the same time it provided the banking system with a considerable amount of liquidity, either in general (full allotment for main refinancing operations, extension of the term for longer-term refinancing operations, 'qualitative easing') or specifically for certain market segments (CBPP 1 and 2, dollar supply for European banks).

The increasingly generous supply of liquidity to the banking system since the financial crisis gradually brought about a technical change in the operational implementation of monetary policy. The supply of liquidity to commercial banks was so abundant that the weekly refinancing transactions at the main refinancing rate were no longer decisive. As a result, the main refinancing rate was no longer the key interest rate on which interbank interest rates were based. As the commercial banks no longer lent each other money due to the enormous surplus liquidity, the ECB's deposit rate de facto became the relevant interest rate for reserves. Thus, the former corridor system (▶ Ch. 4.1), which stipulated that interbank interest rates were to move between the deposit rate and the marginal lending rate with the main refinancing rate as the central anchor was abandoned. It was replaced by a 'floor system,' in which the lower limit of interbank interest rates is controlled.

6.1.2 The ECB's response to the sovereign debt crisis

Between 2010 and 2012, the ECB gradually changed both its approach and its communication strategy. In May 2010, it took a major step towards what would later be referred to as 'unconventional monetary policy' with the Securities Markets Programme (SMP). For the first time, bonds were not purchased in order to supply banks with liquidity and to influence short-term money market interest rates, but to have a targeted impact on national government bond markets. The purchased bonds could be held until final maturity, and there was no previously announced maximum limit on the intervention volume. The previous practice of not taking government bonds onto the balance sheet until final maturity was abandoned. However, this was not to impact the monetary policy line as a whole. The liquidity created by the SMP purchases was therefore siphoned off again through targeted operations (the collection of term deposits). This means that the ECB bought government bonds from commercial banks and credited the proceeds of the sale to their account at the ECB. This automatically led to an increase in central bank liquidity (reserves). To prevent this increase from happening, the ECB simultaneously offered the banking system attractive term deposits of the same amount. The liquidity created was therefore immediately withdrawn from the banking sector. However, in an environment with an abundant supply of reserves, this had more of a signaling effect than an actual impact on the liquidity position of the banking system. It was to be made clear that the government bond purchases would not lead to an increase in the money supply or any risk of inflation.

This meant that the separation between monetary policy (in the sense of combating inflation) and liquidity policy (in the sense of influencing liquidity conditions on the interbank market) continued to exist. However, the latter was given a new twist and, simultaneously, a new rationale: The ECB diagnosed a disruption to the transmission mechanism in the eurozone, which according to ECB officials was caused by extremely high yields on the government bonds of countries such as Italy, Portugal, Spain, Ireland and Greece. It argued that these yields reflected an irrational assessment of the default risks of these members of the monetary union. Monetary policy decisions by the ECB Governing Council would therefore not have the same effect in all member states. Specifically, what was at risk was the central bank's ability to stimulate the economy throughout the eurozone by means of an expansive monetary policy.

This argument is based on the fact that government bond yields are very important for the credit market, because they function as an important benchmark for both corporate bond yields and bank lending rates. Higher interest rates for government bonds mean that, in relative terms, all other types of investment become less attractive. Conversely, this means that those seeking financing – either as home builders looking for a mortgage loan or as companies looking to finance an investment project – can only obtain the necessary funds if they are also prepared to pay a higher interest rate. In addition to this indirect link, government bond interest rates can also serve as a direct benchmark for loan interest rates if a loan agreement explicitly states that the interest rate is based on the applicable yields on certain government bonds plus a fixed premium. Overall, a rise in government bond interest rates will therefore sooner or later also negatively impact the financing conditions for private households and companies. This could – at least according to the ECB – mean that, due to high government bond yields, bank interest rates did not fall in times of crisis despite key interest rate cuts. This made it more difficult for the central bank to implement an expansive monetary policy in the affected countries.

Between May 2010 and February 2012, the ECB purchased Italian government bonds in particular, but also Spanish, Greek, Portuguese and Irish government bonds with a total volume of just over 200 billion euros as part of the SMP. ECB President Trichet was careful to emphasize that the SMP was "temporary in nature."[33] In other words, the aim was to reassure the government bond markets concerned and to lower government bond yields without creating the impression that monetary state financing was taking place.

Two longer-term refinancing operations (LTROs), which would go down in history as the so-called 'big Berthas,' had a similar effect to the SMP on the government bond markets in the crisis countries. At the end of 2011 and beginning of 2012, the ECB provided commercial banks with potentially unlimited amounts of liquidity at favorable conditions. A total of around 1,000 billion euros was called. Spanish and Italian banks

---

33   Trichet, J.C. (2010): Introductory statement, press conference, December 2nd, 2010, https://www.ecb.europa.eu/press/press_conference/monetary-policy-statement/2010/html/is101202.en.html

in particular took advantage of this instrument, investing the acquired liquidity in government bonds (especially those of their home countries) – which in turn limited their yields. With the two LTROs, the ECB thus also stabilized national bond markets at the turn of 2011/2012, even though in contrast to the SMP, it achieved this effect only indirectly this time. A special feature of these longer-term refinancing operations was the repayment option after one year. Twelve months after the implementation of the two LTROs, the amount of liquidity provided was therefore in the hands of the commercial banks. If they decided to repay the amounts borrowed, central bank liquidity decreased, even if this was not necessarily in the ECB's interest.

6.1.3   "Whatever it takes"

In 2012, two developments emerged that contributed to the ECB's strategic realignment: New turbulence on the government bond markets and persistent disinflation, i. e., a decline in inflation rates.

The eurozone had already suffered a fundamental loss of confidence in the course of the crisis. Yet in 2012, doubts resurfaced as to whether the eurozone would continue to exist. From spring 2012, Italy and Spain in particular faced a noticeable increase in spreads because markets reacted to the increased redenomination risk of Italian and Spanish government bonds (▶ Fig. 55). The underlying reason was that many investors who believed that these two countries in particular might leave the eurozone were afraid their governments would then repay their national debt not in euros, but rather in reintroduced national currencies with an uncertain value ('redenominated').

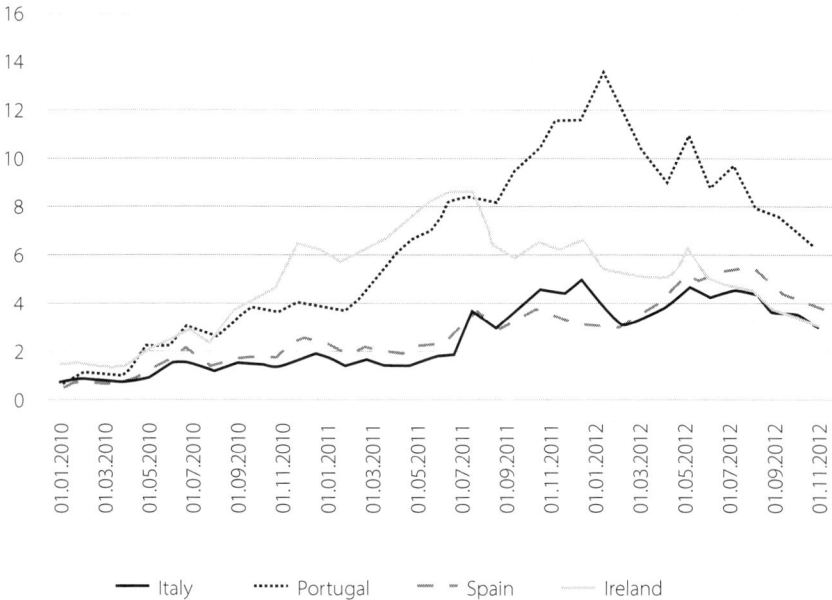

Fig. 55: Spreads on ten-year government bonds 2010–2012 (percentage points, data: LSEG Datastream)

This fear of redenomination led to a flight of capital from the crisis countries to the eurozone core countries. In the latter, the rising demand for government bonds led to falling yields and therefore better financing conditions for private households and companies. While the crisis on the government bond markets in the crisis countries therefore increased interest rates, the opposite was true in the core countries. The unrest on the government bond market therefore not only impacted financing conditions in the real economy in a way that was undesired by the ECB; moreover, it had different consequences in different parts of the eurozone and thereby led to a fragmentation of the monetary union. In the eyes of the ECB, the monetary policy transmission was massively disrupted. 'One size fits all' threatened to become 'one size fits none' (▶ Ch. 4.1). In addition, it was argued that the future path of inflation could no longer be predicted or even controlled in a monetary union that was on the verge of collapse. After all, a monetary entity that market participants expected to break apart at any time could neither be analyzed nor could its economic policy be managed with the usual instruments.

6.1 Overview: The evolution of the ECB's monetary policy since the start of the financial crisis

Mario Draghi was born in Rome in 1947. After studying economics in Italy, he received his doctorate from MIT in Cambridge (USA) in 1977. Draghi became a professor of economics and worked for the World Bank in Washington D.C. In the 1990s, he became a director general in the Italian Finance Ministry, paving the way for the introduction of the euro in his home country. After a short stint at the investment bank Goldman Sachs, Draghi served as Governor of the Banca d'Italia from 2005 onwards before becoming ECB President in 2011. In 2019, after his eight-year term of office, he left the ECB. In 2021 and 2022, he served as Italian Prime Minister. Afterwards, Draghi worked as an advisor to the European Commission, publishing a report on the future of European competitiveness in September 2024. [Photo: ECB]

In reaction to this precarious situation, ECB President Mario Draghi went public and made the following famous statement during a speech at an investment conference in London on July 26, 2012: "But there is another message I want to tell you. Within our mandate, the ECB is ready to do whatever it takes to preserve the euro. And believe me, it will be enough."[34] This statement signaled the ECB's commitment to do anything necessary to preserve the euro. This holds true even if Draghi's formulation "within our mandate" qualified his statement to some extent. This reference to the Maastricht Treaty was a reminder of the European Central Bank's primary task: to ensure price stability and to only pursue secondary objectives if this did not contradict the primary objective. In any case, the ECB was not allowed to finance government debt and pay down government liabilities with central bank money created for this purpose.

On this basis, the ECB initiated the OMT program in September 2012. The SMP program ended with the OMT. 'OMT' stands for 'outright monetary transactions.' The OMT government bond purchases thus differed fundamentally from those under traditional monetary policy, which were generally designed as repurchase agreements, i.e., they consisted of a purchase agreement that was simultaneously linked to a sale at a slightly later date. The government bonds were therefore only held on the central bank's balance sheet for a short time. In addition, traditional monetary policy transactions with government bonds did not specify any particular issuer. The only decisive factor was whether the rating of the bonds in question met the requirements of the collateral framework (▶ Ch. 4.1). Regarding the OMT government bond pur-

---

34 Draghi, M. (2012): Speech at the Global Investment Conference, London, July 26th, 2012, https://www.ecb.europa.eu/press/key/date/2012/html/sp120726.en.html

chases, the ECB stressed the fact that they were potentially "unlimited in size."[35] In order to bring the program at least formally in line with the requirements of the Maastricht Treaty, monetary policy objectives and government financing needed to be separated. To this end, the ECB chose to specifically design the program as follows:

- Only government bonds from ESM program countries were to be purchased. The conditionality of the ESM (structural reforms, budget consolidation) was thus transferred to the OMT.
- Only government bonds with a term of between one and three years could be purchased.
- The ECB aimed at full disclosure about the extent of OMT purchases.
- The amount of central bank liquidity was not to increase. The amount of reserves generated by OMT purchases would be withdrawn from the banking system elsewhere.

The OMT was never activated. Its mere announcement managed to calm the government bond markets and remedy the disruption to the transmission mechanism in the eurozone previously diagnosed by the ECB.

Nevertheless, the 'Whatever it takes' approach was subject to fierce criticism from two sides. Supporters of an even more active ECB policy criticized the conditionality of government bond purchases associated with the ESM. This would legitimize and reinforce the rationale of the EU support measures (aid loans only against the fulfilment of fiscal and structural policy conditions), which merely exacerbated the crisis. It was contended that crisis-affected countries would be disproportionately burdened by restrictive policy measures and, conversely, required unconditional fiscal and monetary support to facilitate economic recovery. Yet this view was a minority position. The loudest criticism came from among the ranks of OMT critics who fundamentally rejected the program. They argued that rising government bond yields were likely to reflect a decline in the solvency of the issuer, which the respective government would have to respond to by consolidating its budget and by initiating structural reforms. In such a situation, the OMT program would only function as an insurance policy against solvency problems and therefore reduce that government's incentive to pursue a stability-oriented, growth-friendly policy. Overall, according to this line of argumentation, the program would thus exacerbate the problems in the long term or at least delay their solution. Another argument was that the ECB became a de facto 'lender of last resort' for states, which violated the prohibition of monetary state financing. The bank would make it much easier for finance ministers to finance their budgets by increasing (potential) demand for government bonds and thus lowering their yields – and therefore alleviate the interest burden on public budgets. Finally,

---

35 Draghi, M. (2012): Introductory statement to the press conference (with Q&A), September 6th, 2012, https://www.ecb.europa.eu/press/press_conference/monetary-policy-statement/2012/html/is120906.en.html

the OMT critics made the point that the permanent purchase of government bonds also entailed considerable risks. If a country whose bonds the ECB had on its balance sheet left the eurozone, considerable write-downs would have to be made. The insolvency risk of individual member states would thus be shifted to the other states.

The ECB countered that the European government bond markets had been in an exceptional situation in 2012. The spreads on the government bonds of individual member states could not be explained based on fundamental analysis. According to the ECB, the crisis countries (particularly Italy and Spain) had been threatened by a vicious circle of rising yields, which would have led to decreasing solvency (due to the rising interest burden) and, as a result, another round of rising yields. Against this backdrop, the mere suspicion that a country might have to leave the monetary union could have become a self-fulfilling prophecy. If, in the wake of ever-increasing yields, member states might no longer have been able to refinance themselves, leaving the eurozone would have been their only option. ECB officials argued that, together with the ESM, the OMT had prevented such an economically unjustified downward spiral. The argument was that to this day, the OMT served as an insurance policy because its very existence assured market participants that a complete or partial break-up of the eurozone was not a realistic scenario. A risk premium for redenomination risks was therefore unnecessary.

The ECB responded to the counterargument that the OMT would have negative incentive effects (moral hazard) by pointing to the conditionality of the ESM as well as to the fact that possible purchases were limited to bonds with a term of up to three years. Governments would therefore still be forced to implement fiscal and structural policy reforms and market discipline would continue to apply across the long end of the bond market. That the ECB's bond purchases were only to impact the fundamentally unjustified part of the spread was put forward as yet another argument against the moral hazard argument, showing that monetary state financing was not to be expected from OMT.

What the OMT supporters conceded was that risks were in fact redistributed as criticized by the OMT critics. Yet they argued that monetary policy was always associated with such a redistribution of risks because it had very different effects on market participants and on the members of the currency area. According to them, this was an inevitable side effect of a monetary policy that is primarily geared towards price stability. Yet regarding the OMT, the redistribution of risks was a zero-sum game because it was unrealistic to assume that the non-crisis countries would shoulder the insolvency risk of the crisis countries for good without tangible changes. Against that backdrop, the OMT proponents argued that, rather, the OMT reduced the risks in the entire monetary union since it would prevent the described scenario of a downward spiral towards a (partial) break-up of the eurozone from becoming a reality. As a result, even stable Euro area members would profit from the OMT scheme.

A legal challenge was brought before the German Federal Constitutional Court against the OMT program, alleging infringements of the principle of proportionality and the prohibition of monetary financing of sovereign debt. The Federal Constitutional Court referred the case to the European Court of Justice for a preliminary ruling, which classified the OMT as a legitimate part of the ECB's monetary policy and saw no violation of EU primary law. The Federal Constitutional Court subsequently ruled in 2016 that the Bundesbank was allowed to participate in the OMT.

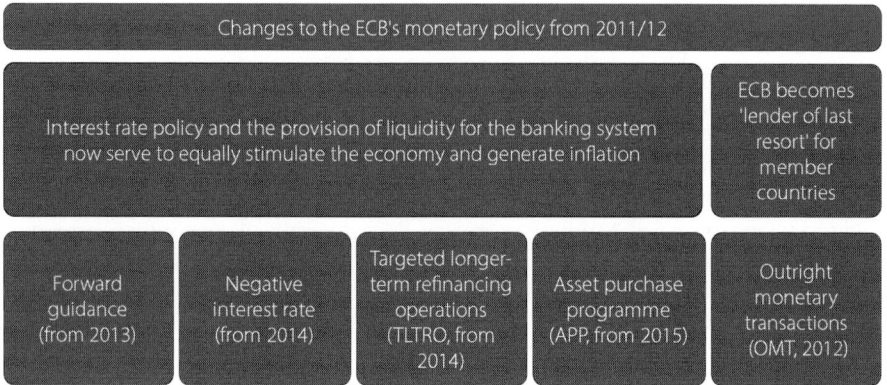

Fig. 56: Unconventional monetary policy measures of the ECB

In 2012, it thus seemed as if one of the eurozone's two major problems had been solved, at least for the time being. The second problem that the ECB saw, namely the ongoing disinflation process could not be solved by the OMT. This disinflation process began after the monthly inflation rate had reached its last peak of 3 % at the end of 2011. The rate then fell relatively steadily, reaching a low of minus 0.6 % in January 2015. The only time that the monthly inflation rate in the monetary union had reached that level had been in July 2009, i. e., at the height of the economic crisis. Negative values were also recorded in April 2016 and in the fall 2020 (both minus 0.3 % ▶ Fig. 63). The ECB attributed the falling inflation rates to the fact that bank lending was too slow, particularly in the crisis-hit countries of southern Europe. The passive approach to liquidity provision pursued since the introduction of the euro was based on the assumption that the banking system's demand for liquidity reflected the economy's need for liquidity. However, the banks in Southern Europe, not least the Italian banks, were unwilling or unable to provide credit at sufficient levels from a macroeconomic point of view. The uncertain future prospects and the high level of bad loans in some cases made it rational for too many commercial banks to act very cautiously when granting loans. The ECB argued further that the creation of liquidity in the banking system therefore did not meet the overall economic requirement to sufficiently stimulate the economy in southern Europe and thus break disinflation. This credit crunch could not be dealt with using the traditional means of monetary policy because the commercial banks in Southern Europe would exercise restraint in lending for the described reasons, even if the ECB supplied liquidity more generously. The underlying reason, it was argued, was the fact that the transmission mechanism was considerably disrupted. In addition, key interest rates had already approached the lower interest rate limit and could not be lowered any further.

The ECB used this line of argument to justify its final departure from the traditional monetary policy approach. According to the central bank, the separation between monetary and liquidity policy had become obsolete because both monetary and liquidity policy now had to serve the same goal: to stimulate the economy and raise the inflation rate to a level of just under 2%. It was now necessary to pursue an active liquidity policy to support the interest rate policy.

To achieve this goal, the ECB subsequently introduced new instruments, including forward guidance, negative interest rates and the so-called TLTRO:

- Forward guidance means that a central bank provides a credible outlook on its future monetary policy. The aim is to stabilize the expectations of market participants in a volatile environment that is characterized by great uncertainty. With this in mind, ECB President Draghi announced in the summer 2013 that interest rates would remain at the current level or stay below it for an extended period of time. This is known as the 'lower for longer' approach.[36] Forward guidance helps to make interest rate policy more expansionary once the effective interest rate floor (see below) has been reached. The underlying mechanism here is the creation of expectations. Provided it is credible, forward guidance gives market participants certainty about the future level of short-term interest rates. This allows the central bank to add a medium-term component to its interest rate policy, despite the fact that the latter actually only relates to the short-term money market. The prospect that short-term interest rates remain 'lower for longer' also influences inflation expectations as desired by the ECB, because market participants expect a consistently expansionary monetary policy over the period of the forward guidance.
- The so-called 'effective lower bound' (=lowest possible level of nominal interest rates) is not zero percent, but slightly lower. Over the course of 2014, the deposit rate was lowered into negative figures, first to -0.1% in June and then to -0.2% in September. The deposit rate ultimately reached its lowest point of -0.5% in September 2019. Significantly lower interest rates are not expedient, as that would make it worthwhile for market participants to hold their liquidity in the form of cash if negative interest rates were perceived as too high. In addition, extremely low key interest rates can be diametrically opposed to the central bank's central objective of stimulating lending. In an extremely low interest rate environment, lending rates fall to historic lows (which is desirable in terms of monetary policy). At the same time, however, banks can only lower deposit interest rates minimally

---

[36] Draghi: "The Governing Council expects the key ECB interest rates to remain at present or lower levels for an extended period of time." Cf. Draghi, M., Introductory statement to the press conference, July 4th, 2013, https://www.ecb.europa.eu/press/press_conference/monetary-policy-statement/2013/html/is130704.en.html

into negative figures – if at all – because their customers would otherwise choose other forms of short-term money storage. This is where the effective lower bound floor comes into play. In this environment, the banking sector finds it increasingly difficult to generate an adequate interest margin (defined as the difference between lending and deposit interest rates). Income from interest on loans falls faster than expenditure on interest on deposits. The lending business no longer generates sufficient net interest income. As a result, in order to preserve their equity, banks could restrict lending as a result of the low interest rate policy instead of expanding it. The interest rate which causes this effect is known as the 'reversal rate.'

- Also in June 2014, the ECB launched the first of three targeted longer-term refinancing operations (TLTRO). These required participating banks to meet certain conditions in return for being provided with liquidity at particularly favorable conditions. Thus, their net lending had to comply with certain quantitative requirements. If they did not manage to do so, the liquidity received had to be repaid. The three TLTRO programs each had a term of four years. The volume utilized by the banks peaked at around 2 trillion euros. The second program started in March 2016, and the third was launched a year later. The commercial banks were able to repay the TLTRO early, i. e., they could reduce their liquidity in the form of central bank money on their own. Conversely, this meant that the ECB could not directly control its liquidity supply, but that it was dependent on the commercial banks' behavior with regard to holding reserves: as with the 2011/2012 LTROs, it was not only up to the commercial banks to decide whether and to what extent they would make use of the targeted longer-term refinancing operations, but also when and to what extent they would repay them.

6.2 Quantitative Easing

6.2.1 The Asset Purchase Programme

The ECB's fundamental change of course described in section 6.1.3 culminated in mid-2014 with the announcement that the bank intended to launch a comprehensive Asset Purchase Programme (APP). The program covered securitizations (asset-backed securities), bonds and covered bonds, corporate sector bonds and, last but not least, government bonds (public sector bonds). This method of conducting monetary policy is known as 'quantitative easing.' With a share of 80 % of the APP, the purchase of government bonds was quantitatively the most significant part. It was also highly controversial. The following comments therefore focus on the Public Sector Purchase Programme (PSPP).

As in the case of previous monetary policy changes, the central bankers justified their move with the fact that they needed to ensure the transmission of monetary policy throughout the eurozone. According to the ECB, two developments in the summer 2014 impaired the transmission of its monetary policy impulses:

- Many commercial banks used the opportunity to repay loans from the longer-term refinancing operations (LTRO) initiated at the turn of the year 2011/2012 ahead of schedule (▶ Ch. 6.1.2). Much to the displeasure of the ECB, the liquidity of the banking sector fell noticeably as a result. Figure 57 shows how LTROs rose to a volume of more than EUR 1,000 billion at the beginning of 2012, before early repayments became possible a year later and the level then fell to below EUR 400 billion by summer 2014. As a result, this development reduced the expansionary impulse of the oversupply of liquidity to the banking sector.
- The ECB observed a fragmentation of the European market for bank loans to the real economy. The demand for credit from private households and companies varied depending on the economic situation in each member state. Where the economy was sluggish, consumers and investors submitted few loan applications. The ability of commercial banks to grant loans also varied depending on the member state. Where banks still had to clear their loan portfolios of bad loans and also had difficulties meeting regulatory capital requirements, they were reluctant to lend.

From the second half of 2014, the ECB also saw a far-reaching weakening of overall economic demand in the entire eurozone as well as the risk that inflation expectations would become anchored to the downside. It was feared that citizens no longer trusted the central bank to keep the inflation rate below, but close to, 2%. According to the ECB, this could have led to a deflationary downward spiral, which had to be prevented at all costs. As the key interest rates were close to the effective lower bound, a way was sought to achieve the greatest possible monetary policy effect on the fragmented European financial market – which is why the APP was launched. The size of the central bank's balance sheet became the ECB's central policy variable. European monetary policy now had a fundamentally different direction than at the beginning of the monetary union in 1999, when the ECB had kept bank liquidity tight and controlled financing conditions on the interbank market – and thus indirectly in the real economy – by setting the interest rate for the main refinancing operations (MROs) in such a way that it achieved its primary goal of price stability. At the time, the volume of MROs and longer-term refinancing transactions amounted to around 200 billion euros (▶ Fig. 57). With the onset of the financial crisis in 2007/2008, the main refinancing operations lost importance at the expense of (targeted) longer-term refinancing operations (LTRO, TLTRO) and securities purchases. The APP thus represents the end point of a development that started with the temporary calming of the interbank market from 2007 to 2009, then focused on maintaining functioning individual government bond markets (since 2010) and finally aimed at economic stimulation and inflation generation (phases 2 to 4 in Figure 57).

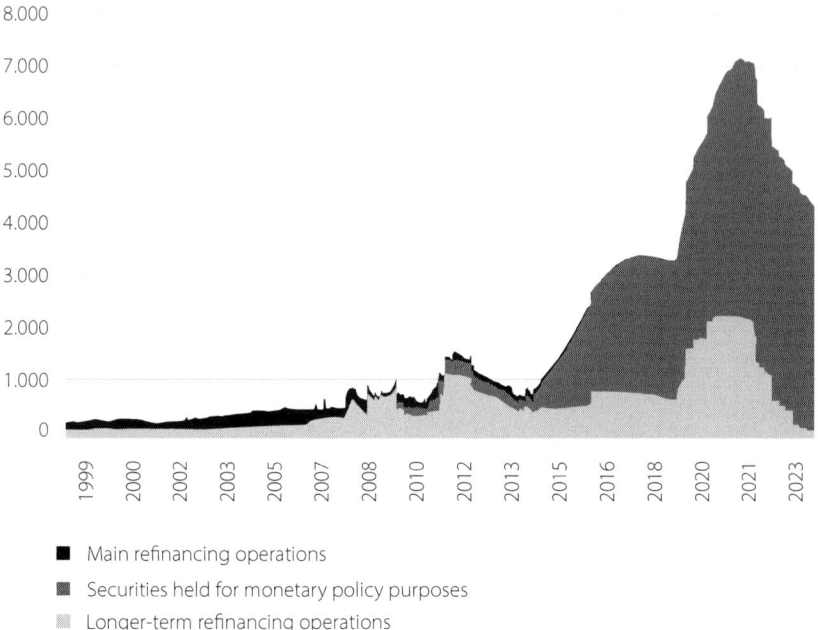

Fig. 57: Monetary policy-relevant assets in the ECB's balance sheet (billion euros, data: ECB)

Considering that the Federal Reserve, the Bank of England and the Swiss National Bank had already started quantitative easing (QE) in 2009, the ECB did not break new monetary policy grounds with the targeted expansion of its balance sheet. Yet because of the reservations some national central banks (including the German, Dutch and Finnish central banks) initially held against this tool, the toolbox in the European Monetary Union was only expanded in this direction a few years later. Critics of the new approach feared, among other things, losses for taxpayers if individual member states went bankrupt and/or had to leave the eurozone. This is where a key difference between the eurozone on the one hand and the US, the UK and Switzerland on the other comes into play: the European Central Bank cannot buy European government bonds (because they do not exist), but must instead essentially operate on the markets for national government bonds.

The ECB used a special design of the government bond purchase program (PSPP) to counter both the default risk described above and the suspicion that the government bond purchases could exceed the limit for monetary financing of the budgets of individual member states:

- In order to avoid any impression that individual member states might be favored by the purchases, purchases are made according to a percentage key that corresponds to the euro countries' shares of ECB capital and that is based on population size and gross domestic product.

- In order to not cross the line into monetary government financing, the Eurosystem buys a maximum of one third of the bond volume per issue and issuer.
- The national central banks take 80 % of the bond volume purchased onto their balance sheets. At the same time, each national central bank only buys the bonds of its own country so that the default risk is predominantly carried by the respective member state. The ECB only takes the remaining 20 % of the volume onto its own balance sheet. Half of the ECB purchases are national government bonds and half are bonds issued by supranational institutions (including, for example, the European Investment Bank).
- Greek government bonds could not be purchased because their rating did not meet the ECB's requirements for eligible securities.

The purchases started in March 2015 (▶ Fig. 58). While the monthly volume initially amounted to 60 billion euros per month, it was then increased to 80 billion euros and finally gradually reduced to zero euros by the beginning of 2019. This reduction in purchases is referred to as 'tapering.' From January to October 2019, there were no net purchases and the number of securities in the APP portfolio was kept constant. This process is called 'roll-on.' Here, as many new securities are purchased as old ones expire, i.e., are redeemed. At the end of 2019 – even before the pandemic began – the ECB resumed monthly net purchases amounting to 20 billion euros. From spring 2020 onwards, the APP ran parallel to the PEPP (Pandemic Emergency Purchase Programme; ▶ Ch. 6.3); in addition to the regular monthly purchases, another EUR 120 billion were spent on securities over the course of 2020. In April and May 2022, there were also net purchases slightly in excess of the specified EUR 20 billion per month. This was followed by another roll-on phase until February 2023. From March to June 2023, purchases and sales were designed to reduce the APP bond portfolio by EUR 15 billion per month. There have been no more APP purchases since July 2023. The portfolio is now automatically reduced as the securities purchased since 2015 expire and are redeemed ('roll-off').

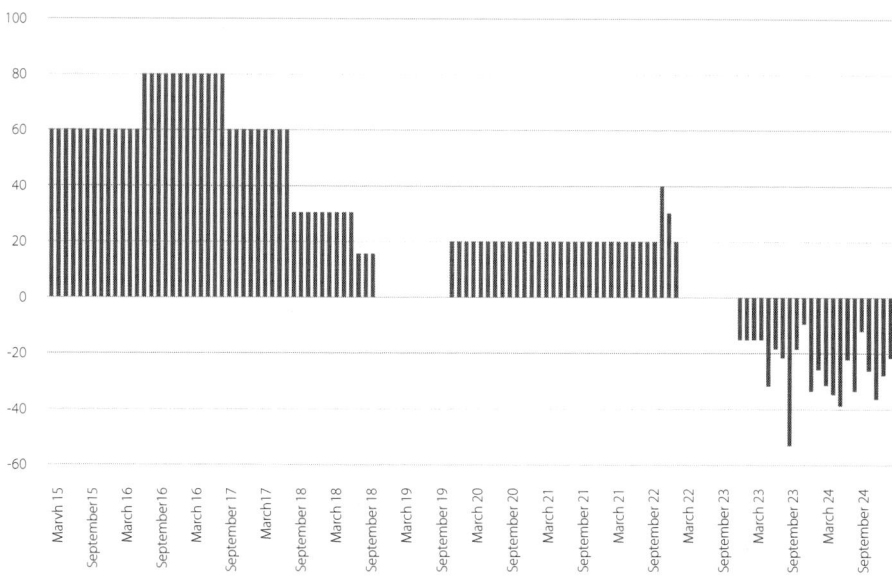

Fig. 58: Asset Purchase Programme, monthly purchases (billion euros, data: ECB)

The bond purchases are to work in two ways:

- The ECB purchases the bonds from commercial banks and credits them with the equivalent value as central bank money (reserves, liquidity). This increases the commercial banks' excess liquidity, which makes it easier for them to grant loans. Conversely, this means that companies and private households have easier access to credit, which stimulates investment and consumption and therefore also the inflation rate and economic activity. This macroeconomic effect applies to all types of assets acquired. The purchase of securitized assets and covered bonds also makes it easier for banks to lend directly. The more easily commercial banks can securitize and sell loans or use them to issue covered bonds, the easier it is for them to grant new loans.
- The ECB's bond purchases increase the prices of bonds and thus reduce their yields. Banks and investors then shift their activities to other assets, which in turn increases those assets' prices and reduces yields. As a result, interest rates fall across the yield curve, which in turn has a stimulating effect on investment and consumption. The lower interest rate level also causes capital to flow abroad. This results in a nominal devaluation of the euro, which can be expected to lead to an increase in exports. This as well stimulates the price level and economic activity.

In both cases, the effect is reinforced by the fact that this unconventional policy measure signals the central bank's determination to pursue an expansive monetary policy, which then automatically stabilizes inflation expectations and tends to stabilize or even increase inflation itself.

The ECB claims the APP as a success as long-term interest rates had fallen as desired and there had been positive effects on lending by commercial banks. Also, economic growth figures had improved and unemployment had been lower than in the hypothetical alternative scenario without the APP.

6.2.2 Criticism of the government bond purchases

The asset purchase program was criticized from the outset. The longer the program ran and the more the stock of government bonds grew on the ECB's balance sheet, the louder the criticism became. It was generally doubted that the risk of a deflationary downward spiral feared by the ECB existed at all. Critics argued that such a development would have required a self-reinforcing spiral of low consumer and investment spending, generally weak sales and falling prices, but that the low and selectively negative inflation rates at the turn of the year 2014/15 and in spring 2016 had been statistical outliers which were mainly due to falling energy prices at the time. According to this position, the problem at that time had therefore not been a general weakness in demand in the eurozone, but rather the 'imported' fall in prices for the primary energy sources oil and gas, most of which were imported from abroad. These imports had lowered the inflation rate directly (i.e., via private household expenditure on petrol, diesel and natural gas for heating) and indirectly (i.e., via energy costs as an important component of companies' price calculations). There had therefore been no need for monetary policy action – at least not to the extent the ECB had taken.

As usual, the ECB had used the development of the headline inflation rate to measure price level changes. Yet its critics pointed to two available common alternatives to the headline inflation rate, namely the core inflation rate and the GDP deflator, which supported their analysis:

- The core inflation rate is calculated using the same methodology as the general inflation rate, but represents the price trend excluding energy and food prices. The described effect that a fall in energy prices alone lowers the European inflation rate or even pushes it into negative territory does therefore not affect the core inflation rate and can be ignored in the analysis.
- Both the official and the core inflation rate measure the prices paid by private households with a representative consumption structure, the so-called 'basket of goods.' This basket of goods includes, besides other necessities, energy sources and food (which the core inflation rate ignores), plus a considerable number of imported goods and services. Therefore, if inflation is measured using this method, cost and price trends abroad are factored in. The GDP deflator – also known as 'domestic inflation' – allows a completely different perspective. It determines

how the prices of domestically produced goods develop and is therefore a suitable measure of domestic cost and price trends.

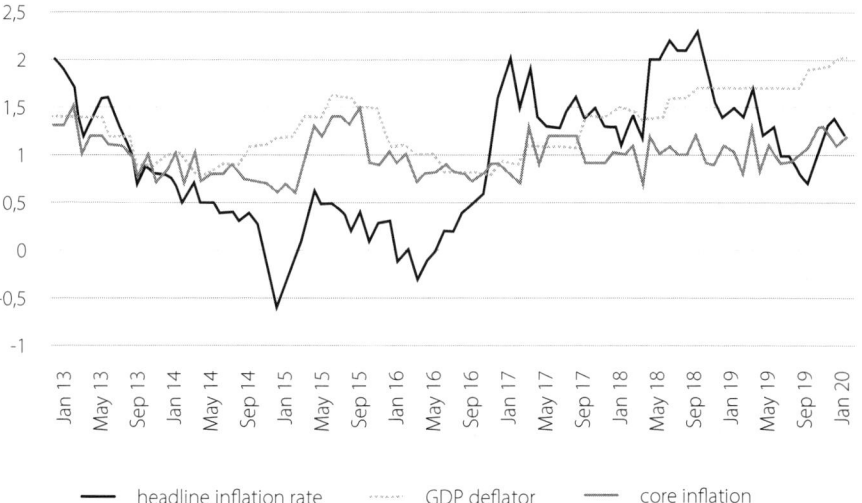

Fig. 59: Inflation dynamics across different measurement concepts (%, data: ECB)

Both the core inflation and the rate of change in the GDP deflator were consistently above 0.5 % during the period under review (i.e., from the start of the discussion about extensive purchase programs in early 2013 until the start of the COVID-19 crisis) and they were even above 1.5 % in 2015, when the purchases began (▶ Fig. 59). The APP critics cite these figures as evidence for their thesis that the ECB presented and ultimately implemented a solution to a problem that did not exist.

In addition, there was an intensive debate in the following years about the possible side effects of this type of unconventional monetary policy. It was argued that even if the APP had in fact the desired effect on the economy and the price level, the side effects of the bond purchases needed to be taken into account as well. The following arguments were put forward:

- The lower interest rates had triggered a 'hunt for yields.' As there were no, or even negative, interest rates on safe investments – even those with a relatively long investment horizon – many market participants shifted to alternative assets, such as real estate or equities, which caused price bubbles in these markets. This development had benefited those parts of the population who had already owned such assets before the start of the APP. Poorer households, however, had completely missed out on this effect. Quantitative easing therefore continued to involve 'upward' redistribution of wealth.

- If interest rates remained low for too long, there was a risk that the asset markets, parts of the banking system and the real economy would eventually run into difficulties when interest rates rose again. As a result, the central bank could come under 'financial dominance:' This means that for fear of triggering a crisis in the financial sector, the central bank might delay tightening its monetary policy despite the fact that such a step was indispensable to combat inflation. The primary goal of maintaining price stability may then take a back seat to concerns about the fate of some financial market players.
- The different demand for credit and the different situations of commercial banks in the member states had led to commercial banks in the core countries in particular expanding their lending. Yet in the peripheral countries, the APP essentially had had the effect that banks with relatively weak capital resources had been able to delay the reduction of non-performing loan portfolios and extend their loans to companies with dubious business models. The 'dezombification' of the banking system and the real economy in the peripheral countries could thus have been avoided (▶ Ch. 5.5.3). In addition, the relative devaluation of the euro associated with the APP had strengthened the export-oriented economies in the core eurozone. All in all, the APP had increased the heterogeneity of the monetary union.
- Low government bond yields created negative incentives for national governments. There was less pressure to consolidate public budgets and implement growth-promoting structural reforms if the state, banks and the real economy were able to finance themselves easily.
- Last but not least, it was argued that the resulting risk of 'fiscal dominance' was very dangerous for the central bank. The low interest rate level achieved through the extremely loose monetary policy eased terms for finance ministers because it lowered the interest burden on the budget. If the interest rate level now actually had to rise again in order to ward off the risk of inflation, the central bank could possibly shy away from a more restrictive monetary policy because of fears that higher interest rates could trigger a new sovereign debt crisis.

In addition to this economic criticism, serious legal concerns were also raised about the government bond purchase program. In Germany – as with the OMT – a complaint was filed with the Federal Constitutional Court. The complainants argued that the ECB was violating its mandate, which stipulated that the primary goal was to be price stability. They also argued that the central bank was in violation of the ban on monetizing government debt. The judges in Germany's highest court referred the case to the European Court of Justice (ECJ) for a preliminary ruling.

In December 2018, the ECJ ruled that the ECB, by virtue of its independence, was relatively free in determining how it wanted to achieve its mandate. In view of the risk of deflation the central bank had diagnosed, the government bond purchase program was permissible and did not constitute a breach of the Maastricht agreements. In addition, the ECJ argued that the specific design of the APP had ensured that potentially harmful side effects, for example the unjustified redistribution of default risks, were limited and that the principle of proportionality was maintained by the program. According to the ECJ, there was also no breach of the prohibition on monetizing public debt. The court did in fact agree that monetary policy must not create false incentives and that thus neither the buyers of government bonds on the primary market nor the member states as their issuers must always and everywhere be able to rely on the central bank as the 'buyer of last resort,' so to speak. The ECJ however ruled out that the APP constituted monetary state financing given the specific regulations of the program (including the distribution of purchases according to capital ratio, the quantitative limitation to one third of the bonds per issuer and per issue as well as the unclear duration of the program).

The German Federal Constitutional Court did not fully agree with the reasoning of the European Court of Justice. In May 2020, it ruled that the ECB's purchase of government bonds was unconstitutional. Although the PSPP did not constitute monetary state financing, it violated the principle of the proportionality that state measures had to comply with. The court argued further that by possibly causing fiscal and financial dominance, the PSPP had affected the future ability of the ECB to fulfill its mandate. In addition, when implemented the program caused considerable side effects, for example for all market participants whose economic freedom was limited by the extremely low interest rates. The judges announced that Germany's Bundesbank would therefore no longer be allowed to participate in the government bond purchase program if the ECB did not prove within three months that its actions were in fact proportionate because it could not reach its goals through less invasive measures. The ECB complied by justifying its course of action to the German government and parliament, the Bundestag. Its explanation of why it considered the concerns of the Federal Constitutional Court to be unfounded put an end to the legal dispute over the PSPP.

6.3 The monetary policy response to the Covid pandemic

The Covid-19 pandemic posed an unprecedented challenge to the governments of the eurozone countries and the European Central Bank. First and foremost, the member states had to limit the acute risk to the health of their citizens. To this end, they implemented contact restrictions, school closures and border controls. These measures and the general uncertainty caused by the pandemic threatened to have a massive impact on the economic situation and caused considerable unrest on the financial markets. Also, government bond yields rose, developing quite differently within the eurozone and causing spreads to widen.

In response to the evolving situation, the ECB reactivated its Targeted Longer-Term Refinancing Operations (TLTRO), last implemented in 2017, with volumes exceeding € 2,000 billion in 2020/2021 (▶ Fig. 60). Concurrently, it introduced a new asset purchase initiative – the Pandemic Emergency Purchase Programme (PEPP). In principle, the same types of securities could be purchased as with the APP; however, the PEPP purchases almost exclusively covered government bonds. In contrast to the APP, Greek government bonds could also be purchased and deviations from the capital ratio were possible. In other words, the ECB was free to choose the percentage country weightings in its government bond portfolio. Also, there were no longer any limits regarding issuers or individual issues as had been the case with the APP. Given the enormous scope of the program, which was launched alongside the ongoing APP, there would otherwise have been a shortage of eligible securities because the PEPP had a total – if even not fully utilized – volume of 1,850 billion euros.

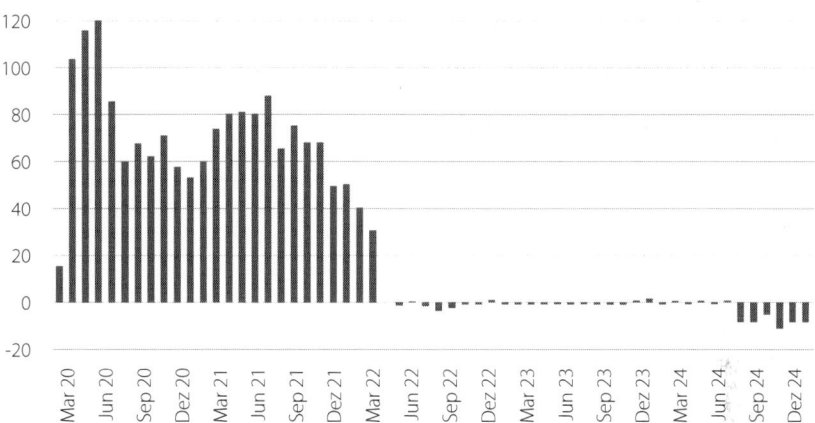

Fig. 60: Pandemic Emergency Purchase Programme, monthly purchases (billion euros, data: ECB)

Initially, in March 2020, the new program was to comprise 750 billion. Yet in June it was increased by 600 billion and in December again by a further 500 billion euros. In contrast to the APP, the ECB did not purchase predetermined monthly volumes. Rather, it acted relatively freely (▶ Fig. 60). The last net purchases took place in March 2022. After that, the portfolio was kept constant until June 2024. The funds raised through the redemption of expired securities were reinvested (roll-on). A scheduled roll-off then took place in the second half of 2024, reducing the PEPP portfolio by € 7.5 billion every month.

The ECB balance sheet for 2024 still featured a total of more than four trillion euros. At this point, ten years had passed since the decision to launch the APP. During this period, the central bank had, intentionally or unintentionally, become the 'market maker of last resort' for the European financial markets – and the government bond markets in particular. The OMT program and the ESM had de facto become obsolete. Also, the ECB had ensured sufficiently favorable financial policy conditions, and governments could rely on being able to sell their government bonds at affordable conditions at any time and thus maintain or even increase their debt with little or no consequences.

7 Present and future

7.1 Inflation is back

The massive bond purchases under the Asset Purchase Programme (APP) and the Pandemic Emergency Purchase Programme (PEPP), as well as the targeted longer-term refinancing operations (TLTROs) caused the monetarily relevant part of the ECB's balance sheet to rise to over € 7 trillion in the course of 2022 (▶ Fig. 57). The excess reserves (▶ Ch. 4.1) of commercial banks developed accordingly. In other words, monetary policy was strongly expansionary. In March 2020, the governments of the eurozone countries also activated the general escape clause of the Stability and Growth Pact for the current year, so that they were no longer restrained by any (European) expenditure and/or deficit provisions. The escape clause was once again invoked from 2021 to 2023, with Russia's attack on Ukraine and the accompanying energy crisis serving as justification from 2022 onwards. The member states used the resulting financial leeway to support private households and companies with subsidies, loans and guarantees that were worth trillions. As result, fiscal policy as well as functioned as an expansionary stimulus.

Christine Lagarde, born in Paris in 1956, began her professional career as a lawyer with Baker McKenzie, an international law firm, which she also headed from 1999 to 2005. She was then a member of the French government, initially in the Departments of Trade and Agriculture and Fisheries and finally as Minister of Economy and Finance. In 2011, Lagarde became Managing Director of the International Monetary Fund (IMF) in Washington, D.C. before taking office as President of the European Central Bank in 2019. Her term of office ends in October 2027. [Photo: ECB]

As a result, while the demand for and supply of services were constrained by contact restrictions in most countries, the demand for goods remained strong during the COVID-19 crisis. The global disruptions to passenger and, in some cases, freight transport caused by the pandemic led to global supply constraints, which in turn resulted in price increases of important intermediate products (including computer chips) and energy already during the pandemic. At the end of 2021 and in the first half of 2022, the previously pent-up demand for goods and services became effective on global goods markets within a short period of time as Covid restrictions were eased and eventually lifted. At the same time, Russia's invasion of Ukraine caused an energy crisis and price increases on the agricultural market, because Ukraine is a very large producer of agricultural goods.

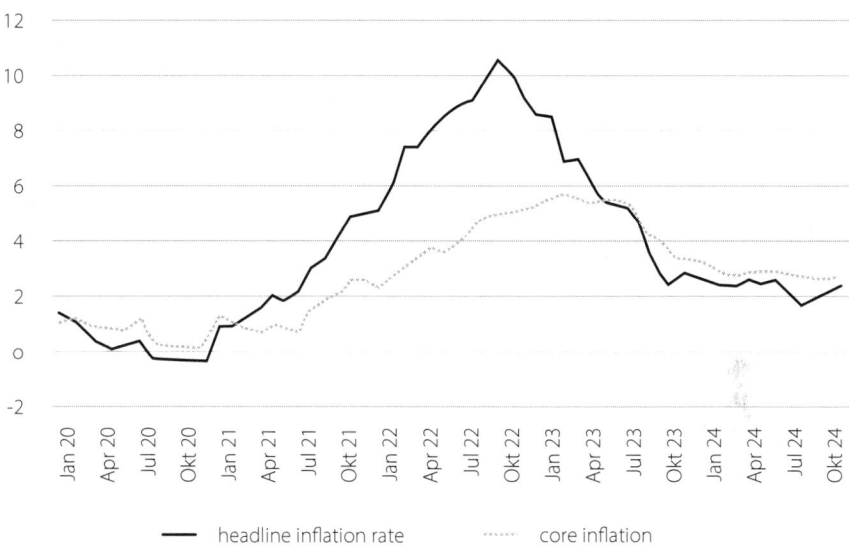

Fig. 61: Inflation in the eurozone during and after the COVID-19 pandemic (%, data: ECB)

As a result, the inflation rate rose sharply in the course of 2021, as monetary and fiscal policy remained highly expansionary (▶ Fig. 61). After the pandemic, the European countries once again deployed massive financial resources to protect private households and businesses, this time against the war-induced energy price shock. The ECB had previously justified its expansionary monetary policy until summer 2022 by pointing to the supply-side nature of the inflationary surge, which it expected to be temporary. It argued that a central bank could not influence energy prices anyway, and that monetary policy would only take effect with a delay of at least nine months. By then, energy prices might already be back to normal, and the COVID-19-related backlog in demand as well as supply bottleneck might have been reduced. Weak economic development with potentially deflationary tendencies remained the ECB's main concern in the medium term, it stressed. A restrictive monetary policy could not solve the temporary inflation problem, but rather would increase the latent risk of deflation. This was the position held by the ECB until early summer 2022. It is possible that the central bankers initially exercised restraint because they considered the potential impact of a rapid interest rate hike on government bond markets and the financial system to be more problematic than high inflation rates.

Yet this kind of wait-and-see attitude was met with opposition early on already. Its critics argued that if the ECB allowed inflation to rise for too long, it risked a rise in inflation expectations, which in turn might induce a wage-price spiral. Due to the labor shortage, employees were in the position to push through higher wage demands in order to limit their inflation-induced loss of purchasing power. Higher wages would then drive up costs for companies and lead to further general price increases. The worst-case scenario would be an entrenchment of the inflation rate well above the target value of two percent. They also argued that the ECB could very well tackle higher energy prices, if only indirectly, because oil as well as other fossil fuels (e. g., American liquefied natural gas), were invoiced in dollars on the world market. A more restrictive monetary policy by the ECB would have strengthened the euro against the dollar and thus mitigated the effect of higher energy prices (calculated in US dollars) on private households and companies in the eurozone. In addition, a more restrictive monetary policy would also have dampened energy demand from private households and companies in the eurozone, which would have slowed down energy price inflation further.

The ECB Governing Council ultimately agreed with this line of argument, announcing a monetary policy U-turn in the summer of 2022. In doing so, it had to overcome two challenges: Firstly, it had to resolve the conflict that central banks have always faced, namely that of the objectives price stability on the one hand, and economic growth on the other. It is the aim of a restrictive monetary policy to dampen aggregate demand for goods and services to such an extent that it corresponds with aggregate supply because companies are able to raise prices as long as demand exceeds supply. However, the reduction in demand necessary to combat inflation regularly results in slower growth and higher unemployment. Secondly, the ECB Governing Council had to manage the transition to a restrictive monetary policy against the backdrop of a decade of extremely expansionary liquidity provision to the banking system. In the summer of 2022, the ECB still had securities – in particular government bonds from eurozone countries – with a volume of around € 5 trillion on its balance sheet (▶ Fig. 57). Rapidly reducing these securities would have resulted in falling prices and rising yields and thus have caused considerable unrest on the financial markets. For banks, such a development would have implied write-downs on their government bond holdings, and for finance ministers, higher interest costs. Against this backdrop, an abrupt change in monetary policy could have led to rising spreads for some member states and – at least according to the ECB's current line of argument – to the disruption of the transmission mechanism.

The ECB tackled the first challenge, namely the conflict between price stability and economic growth, by clearly prioritizing the former as its primary objective under the EU Treaty. Between July 2022 and September 2023, there were ten interest rate hikes, which raised the deposit rate relevant under the "floor system" (▶ Ch. 6.1.1) from -0.5 % to 4 %. The ECB Governing Council thereby not only influenced lending rates and thus consumption and investment, but also sent an unmistakable monetary policy signal that it was determined to keep inflation expectations at 2 %. At the end of 2022, forward guidance (▶ Ch. 6.1.3) was also discontinued as a communication tool. From that point onwards, the central bank communicated its monetary policy ideas on a short-term basis and on the basis of currently available data.

The ECB overcame the second challenge, namely the transition to a restrictive monetary policy with as little collateral damage to the financial markets as possible, by strictly separating interest rate and balance sheet policy. Specifically, this meant that excess liquidity was reduced, on the one hand, by repaying targeted longer-term refinancing operations. The ECB's related credit claims fell in several steps from over € 2 trillion at the end of 2022 to close to zero at the end of 2024. On the other hand, the ECB began to cautiously reduce its securities holdings. These holdings had reached their highest level in late summer 2022 at just under € 5 trillion, were then kept more or less constant until spring 2023, as described in section 6.2, and subsequently slowly reduced. There were no more reinvestments under the APP from March 2023 onwards; since then, the portfolio has been declining in line with the repayments. The PEPP volume was kept constant from April 2022 to July 2024 and reduced by € 7.5 billion per month in the second half of 2024. The balance sheet total is to be reduced by the gradual repayment of bonds until the balance sheet reaches the optimal size and structure according to the ECB Governing Council.

The European Central Bank thus ruled out that it might return to the monetary policy approach it followed in the early years of monetary union. At that time, it was keen to act in a 'market-neutral' manner. This meant, among other things, that it would not purchase securities on a long-term basis, but only temporarily as part of its open market policy (repo transactions) or that it would accept them as collateral when granting loans to commercial banks (▶ Ch. 4.1). In the future, however, the ECB intends to maintain a 'structural bond portfolio.' Its contents will be specifically selected so that the bond portfolio is conducive to the objectives of European monetary policy. Market-neutral short-term transactions can therefore be complemented by longer-term securities investments. The possibility of returning to balance sheet policy through asset purchases, as already practiced under the large-scale asset purchase programs (APP and PEPP), has also become an explicit part of the ECB's strategy.

7.2 The 2021 revision of the ECB's strategy

The ECB adopted its first strategy in 1998. The core elements of this strategy are the operationalization of the contractually stipulated objective of price level stability, the description of the central monetary policy instruments and the disclosure of the methods used to obtain and process the information relevant to the central bank's work (▶ Fig. 62). After having been adjusted in 2003, the officially communicated strategy remained unchanged for a very long time, although the ECB had abandoned its original approach with the OMT program, the negative interest rate policy and the massive securities purchases. In 2020, the ECB Governing Council then deemed it appropriate to initiate a strategy review process.

Fig. 62: The development of the ECB strategy

	Definition of price level stability	Most important monetary policy instrument	Relevant information for decision-making
1998	Inflation rate below 2% (to be achieved in the medium term)	Key interest rate (interest rate for main refinancing operations)	2-pillar policy approach (with reference value for the growth rate of a monetary aggregate)
2003	Inflation rate below, but close to 2% (to be achieved in the medium term)	Key interest rate (interest rate for main refinancing operations)	2-pillar policy approach (Growth of monetary aggregate only for information purposes)
2021	Symmetrical target is an inflation rate of 2% (to be achieved in the medium term)	Key interest rate (from 2024 officially: deposit rate) Optional: balance sheet total (quantitative easing); Forward guidance and long-term lending to credit institutions remain part of the toolbox	Integrated analysis framework (Financial information underpins analysis of the real economy and inflation expectations)

From 2021 onwards, the ECB pursued a new strategy. It abandoned quantitative easing and announced that the primary monetary policy instrument would no longer be the balance sheet total, but rather once more the key interest rate. The purchase of assets, long-term lending to banks and forward guidance nevertheless remain part of the toolbox. The 'two-pillar policy' approach has now become an 'integrated analytical framework.' Monetary and financial information is to underpin the analysis of real economic developments and inflation expectations. That the ECB took this step shows that it considers money in circulation and credit developments to be important factors when it comes to understanding the transmission process. It also indicates that the price level and financial stability are inextricably interconnected. These interactions include, among other things, the influence that house prices have on the overall price level. In the future, these price changes should be taken into account when calculating the inflation rate. With the so-called 'green monetary policy,' risks resulting from climate change are now also to be included in the monetary and financial stability policy analysis.

Defining the central bank's target of price stability has always been an elementary part of the ECB's strategy. Starting with an "inflation rate below 2%" in 1999, the target was then defined as "below, but close to 2%" in 2003. In 2021, the ECB finally formulated a 'symmetrical 2% target.' With it, the primary objective set for central bankers by the Maastricht Treaty of maintaining price stability in Europe is considered to have been achieved if the inflation rate is 2%. At the same time, any deviation from that goal is considered equally problematic, regardless of whether the actual inflation rate exceeds or falls below the 2 % target. This policy reflects the conditions prevailing at the time the 2020/21 strategy was formulated. After a decade of low interest and inflation rates, many economists and market participants regarded addressing deflationary pressures at the effective interest rate floor as the central challenge for monetary policy (▶ Fig. 63). In such a situation, a symmetrical inflation target enables central bankers to stabilize inflation expectations through a very specific type of forward guidance: Thus, the central bank can announce that it will tolerate an overshooting of the inflation target in the future (possibly over several years) until an average inflation rate of 2 % is reached over a defined time period. In other words, an inflation rate of over 2 % will then be permitted if that helps the central bank to offset previously lower figures and reach the intended average inflation rate of 2 %. If this policy goal is communicated credibly, inflation expectations can be maintained at 2 % even in a deflationary environment.

Such considerations soon became obsolete because of the considerable price increases from 2022 onwards. Rather than dealing with deflationary developments as expected, real inflation soon became the key challenge for the ECB. Yet the symmetrical inflation target had, notwithstanding the new market realities, met with criticism from the outset already. Such criticism was based on two considerations: On the one hand, price stability – which is the contractually stipulated objective of the ECB – strictly speaking means an inflation rate of 0 %. It therefore requires some goodwill to consider a target inflation rate of 2 % to be in line with the contractual conditions. Also, it is more than questionable that the measurement errors that are often used to justify an inflation target above 0 % can be expected to amount to two percentage points. On the other hand, critics question the validity of the alleged risks of deflation, which have been put forward since 2014 at the latest (▶ Ch. 4.1 and 6.2.2). They agree with the ECB's claim that deflation also represents a breach of the contractual objective of price stability. However, by constantly warning against this problem, the central bank in their views justified a policy that de facto was not symmetrical, but rather biased in favor of higher inflation rates. On average, according to the critics' line of argumentation the central bank did therefore not aim at price level stability (defined as an inflation rate so far above zero that measurement errors are taken into account), but at inflation rates significantly above zero.

Another topic that met with a mixed response were the ECB's internal debate on whether climate protection goals should play a role in the bank's future activities. The Governing Council of the ECB ultimately opted for a cautious approach and decided that the effects of climate change are to be incorporated into the analysis of economic development. The analysis addresses the economic implications of physical climate-related events – such as extreme weather phenomena – and the associated risks for the banking sector and financial markets. It also examines the effects of transition risks on monetary policy, as well as on banking and financial stability. Transition risks refer to the possible consequences of the climate-friendly restructuring of national economies. This concerns questions such as, for example, which impact continually increasing CO_2 pricing has on how the inflation rate develops or how the electrification of the transportation and energy sectors will affect the creditworthiness of companies in these sectors. It is self-evident that these questions must be raised and that the monetary and financial stability policy analysis must be adapted accordingly. The consequences of physical and transition risks associated with global warming have an impact on monetary policy as well as banking and financial stability and must therefore – like all other relevant developments – be taken into account by the ECB.

Fig. 63: Euro area inflation rate 1999–2024 (%, data: ECB)

However, there have repeatedly been calls – both from within and outside the ECB – for the use of monetary policy or banking supervisory instruments to fight climate change itself (and not just the economic risks it poses). Such calls are problematic despite the fact that they are usually justified with the following passage from the Treaty on the Functioning of the European Union (Art. 127 (1)): "The primary objective of the European System of Central Banks (hereinafter referred to as 'the ESCB') shall be to maintain price stability. Without prejudice to the objective of price stability, the ESCB shall support the general economic policies in the Union with a view to contributing to the achievement of the objectives of the Union as laid down in Article 3 of the Treaty on European Union." Even though Article 3 of the Treaty on European Union explicitly includes "a high level of protection and improvement of the quality of the environment" among the Community's objectives, this does not mean that the ECB may, or even should, pursue climate policy as long as price stability is ensured. First of all, it would be necessary to determine whether the ECB's toolbox even contains suitable instruments to achieve such goals. Theoretically, one could use the traditional instruments of monetary and financial stability policy to not only curb price inflation and increase the stability of the financial system, but to also reduce greenhouse gas emissions. To this end, the central bank could, for example, define 'green' or (in contrast) 'brown' bonds whose issuers do or do not meet certain requirements regarding their ecological footprint. For example, bonds issued by manufacturers of wind power plants could be considered 'green' bonds, whereas the operator of a coal-fired power plant would be more likely classified as 'brown.' Green bonds could then be preferred in securities purchase programs, open market transactions or as collateral when lending to commercial banks. If this was the case, commercial banks would have an incentive to take more 'green' instead of 'brown' securities on their balance sheets, as they could profit from favorable terms and conditions when using such securities in their transactions with the ECB. This would make it easier for 'green' companies to finance their business activities, but more difficult for 'brown' companies, and would overall accelerate the transition to a climate-neutral economy.

The ECB has decided against this far-reaching variant of taking climate policy aspects into account for good reasons. As the simple example of 'green' and 'brown' companies and bonds shows already, the decisions that would be made if such a form of 'green' monetary policy was to be implemented are quite delicate. Consider, for example, the question of whether a nuclear power plant operator would have to be counted as part of the 'green' sector of the economy due to its largely CO_2-free energy production: such a decision is based on value judgments that, in a constitutional democracy, are not to be decided upon by representatives of a central bank, but rather by elected politicians. The same also applies to the redistribution of resources from the 'brown' to the 'green' sector, because it would be based on value judgments too. Last but not least, a central bank should in general carefully consider whether its instruments allow it to achieve any self-imposed goals in addition to price stability. Even if it was in fact possible to use the monetary policy and banking supervision tools as described to support the transition to a climate-friendly economy, one aspect should be clear, namely that there is no measurable, direct link between the emission of greenhouse gases and ECB policy. At this point, the central bank would risk losing credibility, which could negatively impact its chances to successfully carry out its core activities. Such an effect could take place because if the central bank is unable to pursue a 'green' monetary policy with the desired results, it may not be given credit for fighting inflation.

7.3 Is the ECB operating under conditions of fiscal dominance?

The ECB's massive involvement in the market for government bonds raises the question of whether and to what extent monetary policy in the European Monetary Union has to operate under fiscal dominance. It was this risk in particular that had informed the fiscal policy requirements of the Maastricht Treaty and the Stability and Growth Pact (▶ Ch. 3.2.4) as well as the criticism of the monetary policy in the crisis, which had set in with the implementation of the OMT (outright monetary transactions) program at the latest (▶ Ch. 6.1.3). Not only the OMT program (2012), but also the government bond purchases of the PSPP (from 2015, ▶ Ch. 6.2) led to growing unease sparked by fears of fiscal dominance. Many critics pointed to the unclear economic, political and legal interdependencies between the ECB's government bond purchases, the resulting incentives facing national governments and the specific characteristics of the market for government bonds. Lawsuits were filed, but to no avail. Ultimately, the German Federal Constitutional Court and the European Court of Justice (ECJ) granted the European Central Bank considerable leeway on how to achieve the primary objective of price stability (▶ Ch. 6.2.2). The ECB, in turn, emphasized that it only bought government bonds to ensure monetary policy transmission worked. It also argued that OMT and PSPP were specifically designed not to amount to monetary state financing: Thus the breakdown of PSPP purchases according to national share in the ECB capital, the quantitative restriction to one third of the volume per bond issued, the decision not to purchase securities with less than one year to maturity and the exclusion of weakly rated Greek bonds showed that the central bank did not try to bail out individual countries, but to ensure the effectiveness of its monetary policy in the eurozone as a whole.

The COVID-19 purchase program PEPP did, however, no longer contain these restrictions; it also increased the ECB's government bond holdings to a level previously considered impossible (▶ Ch. 6.3). For the critics, now the decisive step towards monetary financing of government debt had been made. The ECB was now able to directly intervene in the government bond market, and it explicitly did so when reinvesting redeemed PEPP bonds: Thus, it invested the money it received from maturing bonds directly in the bonds of individual countries in order to prevent spreads from widening (and thus interest costs in the eurozone countries from diverging ever further). The ECB justified its actions with the alleged need to ensure that the transmission mechanism continued to function in a time of great uncertainty. In doing so, it followed a line of argument that it had developed in 2010 with respect to the Securities Markets Programme (SMP) and also used to justify the OMT and the government bond purchase program (PSPP) (▶ Ch. 6.1.2, 6.1.3 and 6.2.1).

When inflation picked up speed at the end of 2021 and continued to rise in the first half of the year, both the ECB and its critics felt vindicated. The critics thus accused the central bank of having reacted far too late to the steep price increases to protect government bond markets. Notwithstanding, the ECB launched the most intensive cycle of interest rate hikes in its history in the summer of 2022, thus preventing inflation expectations from becoming unanchored. According to the ECB, its actions had demonstrated its willingness and ability to achieve its primary goal of price stability even under adverse conditions.

However, the "Transmission Protection Instrument" (TPI) was created at the same time as the start of the interest rate hike cycle. It was intended to prevent spreads from widening, which was a likely outcome of the interest rate turnaround and the expected end of quantitative easing. To achieve this goal, the ECB was to be able to influence the development of yields on the government bond market with targeted purchases. After all, it was unclear how capital market investors would react to the ECB's gradual withdrawal from the bond market and its departure from its zero interest-rate policy, which began in summer 2022. What was certain was that member states with particularly high levels of debt would find it much more difficult to service their debt in the future.

The discussion about the TPI followed the same lines as the disputes about the OMT. The TPI proponents saw the risk of financing problems for one or more member states which were not justified by macroeconomic fundamentals. This risk would be reflected in yield premiums, which in turn could be the start of a self-fulfilling prophecy: Because higher yields would imply higher interest expenditure for the finance minister or (in the case of several affected countries) the finance ministers, the capital markets might start worrying about debt sustainability and yields might increase further. In extreme cases, an initially excessive spread, possibly caused by market irrationalities, could thereby lead to the insolvency of a eurozone member. In other words, isolated liquidity problems on the government bond market could lead to the insolvency of a eurozone country. From this perspective, a kind of insurance against irrational market behavior was needed to prevent this from happening. In the best-case scenario, it was argued, the mere fact that such an insurance existed would prevent it from being used. If capital market players knew that a country with liquidity problems would receive help, yield premiums would be dispensable and the vicious circle described above would be broken. In the TPI proponents' opinion, the OMT program was the best proof that market participants reacted to such signals: After all, Mario Draghi's "Whatever-it-takes" press conference in 2012 had been so successful in calming capital markets that the program never had to be used.

The TPI critics rejected these arguments. They claimed that it was not the irrationality of financial market players that caused diverging yield trends within the monetary union and the resulting divergence in spreads; rather, the market data reflected these players' differentiated view of the solvency of the individual eurozone countries. The governments of the member states with relatively bad ratings would have to improve their creditworthiness by implementing structural reforms and budget consolidation measures. The TPI, however, could prevent this from happening and thus lead to a moral hazard because the respective countries might be induced to rely on the program's insurance effect. Instead, they might avoid taking the necessary steps to increase their solvency and thus ultimately delay problem resolution or even exacerbate their problems. The TPI critics stressed that this could be the start of a vicious circle. The yield gap between the euro countries would widen if the less solvent countries took no or insufficient measures to increase their solvency because they relied on the TPI. Sooner or later, the ECB would then have to react by buying government bonds as part of the TPI, which would reward the governments that were unwilling to implement reforms and thereby make painful structural and fiscal policy cuts even less likely in the future. According to this line of argument, TPI thus represented a new gateway for fiscal dominance. A situation could arise in which financial market players relied on the ECB as the last bastion to prevent market turbulence.

The TPI would perpetuate the central bank's role as 'market maker of last resort'[37] on the government bond market, which it had played since the SMP program of 2010. As both national politicians and investors firmly believed the ECB would intervene, its failure to do so could lead to a euro crisis. In order to prevent this from happening, the ECB would, in an extreme case, be forced to guarantee government bonds to a large extent, which would ultimately make it the lender of last resort. What began as a selective intervention to correct irrational market behavior could then ultimately lead to the comprehensive monetization of government debt (▶ Ch. 3.3.1).

As in the case of the OMT and the PSPP, the European Central Bank responded to this criticism arguing that the specific design of the TPI prevented fiscal dominance. In order for the ECB to purchase its government bonds to reduce spreads, a country must meet the following criteria checked by the ECB itself:

- The country in question must not currently be in an excessive deficit procedure under the Stability and Growth Pact.
- The country must not be subject to macroeconomic imbalance proceedings.
- The country's public debt must be on a sustainable path, which is assessed by the ECB itself.
- The government must comply with the voluntary commitment under the "Next Generation EU" program.

7.4 The "NextGenEU" program and the future of fiscal policy in the monetary union

The pandemic brought new challenges not only for monetary policy but also for fiscal policy. Just like the ECB, the governments of the member states had to respond to an unprecedented situation. And while the necessary health policy measures had to be taken, the economy also had to be prevented from collapsing in the face of far-reaching lockdowns and strained international supply chains. To this end, the eurozone countries took a wide range of measures, many of which had direct (e.g., support payments to private households and companies) or potential (e.g., loans, guarantees) consequences for public budgets. As tax revenues fell considerably at the same time, significant budget deficits were unavoidable. As a result, the general escape clause of the Stability and Growth Pact was activated (▶ Ch. 7.1). Also, a completely new approach to financing European tasks was taken with the SURE and NextGenEU programs in particular. With SURE ('Support to Mitigate Unemployment Risks in an Emergency'), the EU granted the member states low-interest loans totaling EUR 100

---

37 A 'market maker' is actually a market participant who ensures that other players on the capital markets can buy and sell assets at market conditions. The market maker acts as a counterparty when no other buyer or seller is available, thereby ensuring liquidity in the market.

billion. The national governments were able to use the funds to set labor market policy programs in order to stabilize employment. The EU initiated SURE after the start of the COVID-19 pandemic, financing it through the issue of European bonds. SURE expired at the end of 2022. Due to its combination of quantitative scope (100 billion euros), policy area (labor market policy) and financing (bond issue), SURE represents a paradigm shift in European policy for some observers. The EU had never acted in this way before.

This applies even more to the "Next Generation EU" (NextGenEU) program, which is also financed by European bonds. The heads of state and government reached a general agreement on this program in summer 2020. From 2021 to 2027, NextGenEU and other measures is to increase the volume of the EU budget from 1% to 2% of European GDP. The core of NextGenEU is the Recovery and Resilience Facility, which allows the Commission to distribute up to 750 billion euros to the member states. Almost half of the funds may be given as a grant, while the rest is paid out in the form of loans to be repaid by 2058. NextGenEU is considered a 'recovery program' to help EU member states cope with the COVID-19 pandemic and its consequences. The funds are allocated on the basis of national recovery and resilience plans, which contain measures for which the countries plan to apply for NextGenEU funds. These measures must be clearly geared towards achieving the program objectives of "recovery after the COVID-19 pandemic," "climate protection," "health," "support for structural reforms" and/or "digitalization." Once the grants and loans have been awarded, the EU checks whether the member states are in compliance with the requirements when implementing the measures.

NextGenEU is the first time that the EU has implemented such an extensive bond-financed program. Overall, it leads to a redistribution of financial resources (in the case of grants) and risks (in the case of loans) because while the program is financed through the common budget, countries use it to different degrees. In contrast to the EFSF and ESM crisis mechanisms (▶ Ch. 5.4), the program cannot be categorized as acute emergency aid with conditionality. While the same is true for the structural and cohesion funds that have been used for decades, these financing tools are much smaller and not bond-financed.

The fact that the heads of state and government were able to reach unanimity here and thereby allowed the EU to enter new financial policy territory can certainly only be explained against the backdrop of the special situation in 2020. The COVID-19 crisis is a prime example of a symmetrical shock with asymmetrical effects. No one (at least in Europe) was responsible for the outbreak of the pandemic. Moreover, countries were affected differently for reasons that could not be attributed to national governments. A prime example for such consequences would be the southern member states, whose economic dependence on tourism made them particularly vulnerable to lockdowns. A joint European effort to overcome the crisis – especially in the most affected countries – could therefore not be rejected on the basis of moral hazard arguments.

Although these specifics explain why there was such a high degree of political consensus, NextGenEU also met with reservations. Critics pointed specifically to the

European Stability Mechanism (ESM), which had been created in order to assist member states with financial problems – regardless of whether these financial problems resulted from a pandemic or other causes. Countries supported by the ESM, however, had to accept financial and structural policy conditions as part of the contractual conditionality, which made this way of solving problems relatively unattractive. The skeptics criticized that in contrast to the ESM, NextGenEU made it too easy to access jointly financed or guaranteed grants and loans. Moral hazard was therefore to be expected: Because NextGenEU might serve as a blueprint for how Europeans might manage national problems in future crises, fiscal and structural policy reforms that would help to cushion future crises could then fail to materialize because member states were more likely to rely on similar programs in the future. This is why the German government considered it important to emphasize that NextGenEU was a unique program. Under no circumstances was the EU to claim the permanent right to issue bonds in order to use the issue proceeds to launch new EU-wide programs on a grand scale.

The future will show whether and to what extent the COVID-19 crisis and NextGenEU represent a paradigm shift towards true Europeanization. This would mean that both political leaders and Europe's citizens would, firstly, consider the well-being of the European (monetary) Union as a whole to be more important than the national interests of their respective home countries; secondly, they would have to have, if not the same, then at least similar preferences regarding the main features of economic policy. This is the case because the different variants of monetary integration can only succeed if the participating countries do not differ too much in terms of their interests and preferences as has been shown with regard to the Bretton Woods system, the 'currency snake' and the European Monetary System (▶ Ch. 2.2.5, 2.4.4 and 3.2.1). However, beyond the economic context in the narrower sense, in order for the monetary union to function better, it is necessary that Europeans develop a strong sense of a shared European identity and mutual belonging. As long as European policy amounts to the clash of 27 (in the EU) or 20 (in the eurozone) national domestic policies, one cannot speak of a genuine Europeanization of fiscal policy. If such a state was achieved, the discussion about state revenue and expenditure would focus on the benefit of Europe on the basis of objective criteria and ideological differences, rather than be based on national interests. The persistence of this phenomenon is particularly evident in the quinquennial elections to the European Parliament, which function less as an authentically supranational democratic decision-making procedure and more as national referenda or midterm evaluations of domestic political climates. Very rarely, the election campaigns focus on problems concerning all of Europe; instead, voters seem to evaluate the work of national governments.

Against this background, a whole series of problems have yet to be solved:

- In the discussion focusing on European versus national responsibilities, there is an unresolved juxtaposition of EU and monetary union. Sometimes, all 27 EU states are included, at other times it is only about the euro countries.

7.4 The "NextGenEU" program and the future of fiscal policy in the monetary union

- In addition, one fundamental decision must be made, namely if fiscal policy should become a European responsibility or not, and if so, how far this transfer of competence should go.
- If fiscal policy was to become a European task, this would require that a decision be made regarding the specific form this responsibility should take. On the revenue side, for example, the question arises as to whether or not the EU should be given its own tax and levy sovereignty, and the right to borrow or whether 'Brussels' should simply should receive more money from the member states in addition to already existing revenue sources (i. e., national membership fees, customs duties, plastic waste tax, share of VAT). With regard to the expenditure side, it should be clarified whether Europe should concentrate on providing European public goods (for example in the form of a European missile defense or European energy or transport networks) or whether a larger European budget should also be used to stabilize the eurozone if it was hit by asymmetric shocks or even, more general, for redistribution. In this case, European income and expenditure would primarily be a means to an end. In the event of an asymmetric shock (▶ Ch. 3.2.1), less revenue would flow from the negatively affected countries into the central budget, whereas the expenditure made there 'by Brussels' would remain the same or may even increase. This would stabilize the economic development in the affected country. If all member states were hit by shocks with the same probability, the common budget would merely serve as an insurance. If, however, there were long-term differences in economic performance, the common budget would lead to redistribution from the prosperous to the weaker parts of the EU.
- Even if 'Brussels' was given more fiscal policy powers, the member states would continue to incur most of government expenditure in Europe for the foreseeable future. This means that the design of a set of rules within which national governments operate remains on the agenda.

It remains to be seen whether and to what extent NextGenEU will serve as a blueprint for similar programs, for example in the defense sector. It is unrealistic to expect such programs to be rolled out before the end of the 2020's. Given the unanimity principle, it also seems unlikely that the European budget – be whether in the form of an EU or eurozone budget – should be significantly expanded with the aim to stabilize eurozone countries as described above or to redistribute financial resources.

The European fiscal rules therefore remain at the center of the discussion. The purpose is, first, to prevent excessive national debt in one or more member states from undermining the stability of the entire monetary union. Second, the fiscal rules are intended to ensure that the central bank can focus its monetary policy primarily on the contractually mandated objective of price stability (▶ Ch. 3.2.4). With the exception of Belgium and Italy, which were already very heavily indebted in the 1990s, the initial aim of the Maastricht fiscal criteria was to prevent excessive debt. Now that the debt ratios in many euro countries, including France, have risen significantly over the decades, the fiscal rules are often more instrumental in showing a realistic path back to sustainable public finances (▶ Fig. 64). At the same time, national governments should be able to continue to structure their income and expenditure countercyclically if necessary and have sufficient incentives to pursue growth-friendly policies.

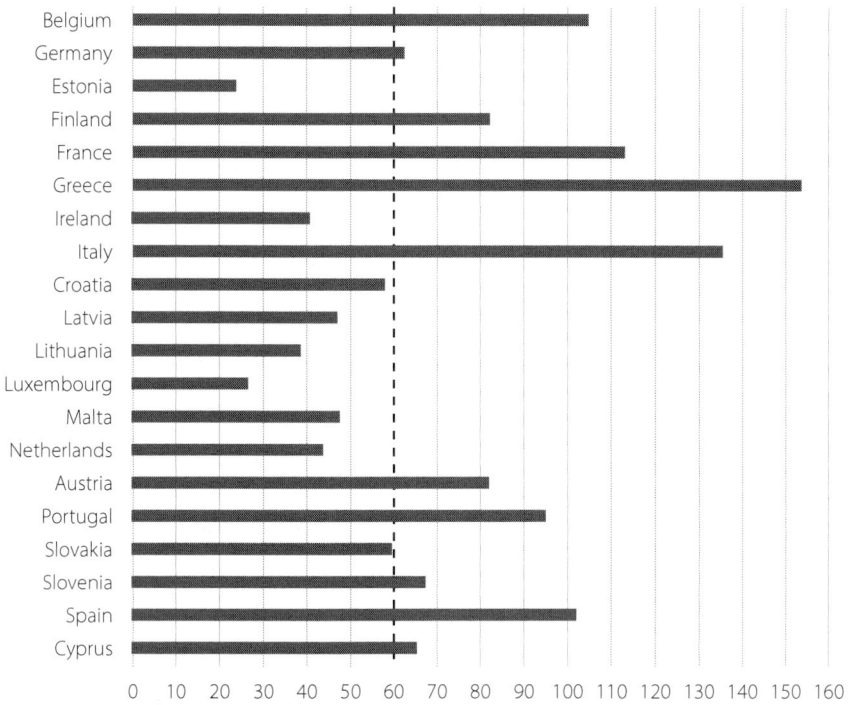

Fig. 64: Debt ratios 2024 (General government debt, % of GDP, data: ECB)

This list of requirements is the result of almost three decades of discussions evolving around the Stability and Growth Pact (▶ Ch. 3.4, 4.2 and 5.5.2). From the outset, critics of the fiscal rules complained that the 3 % and 60 % deficit and debt criteria were not only arbitrary with regard to the specific figures, but that the rules also tended to have a pro-cyclical effect and negatively impact public investment. If the governments of the member states were forced to reduce government spending (e. g., for infrastructure or education) and/or increase revenue during a period of economic weakness, this would not only exacerbate the crisis in the short term, but also reduce the long-term growth potential. Also, this effect would be even increased if a country had to pay fines for breaking the rules of the Stability and Growth Pact. In addition, critics argued that the rules had become increasingly complex over time. The fact that the rules were inconsistent and increasingly difficult to understand meant that they might no longer be accepted and ultimately be dismissed. Acceptance was also low, they argued, because the fiscal policy requirements had not been tailored to the situation of the individual member states, but rather been too general. Overall, the

7.4 The "NextGenEU" program and the future of fiscal policy in the monetary union

populations in the countries with high deficits and/or debt levels had perceived the guidelines from 'Brussels' as dictates and paternalism.

Those in support of a rule-based fiscal policy in the eurozone countries admit that the regulations, drawn up in the 1990s and continuously developed since then, have largely failed to achieve the two main goals of ensuring sustainable public finances in the eurozone and thereby ruling out fiscal dominance by the ECB's monetary policy. It should be noted that they do not generally doubt that fiscal rules are useful but in fact consider the requirements of the Maastricht Treaty and the original Stability and Growth Pact to be essentially appropriate. In their view, it is not the rules that are the problem, but rather the lack of compliance with them on the part of national governments. From the outset, critics argue, there had been too much room for interpretation, for example regarding when exactly the deficit of an individual eurozone member should be classified as 'excessive.' And even in cases in which the EU Commission had identified such an excessive deficit, it had not imposed any sanctions. According to critics, this failure was due to the absence of an appropriate automatic mechanism within the sanctions regime.

Advocates and critics of strict fiscal rules agree on one point, namely that the rules have become too complicated over the decades. At its core, the Stability and Growth Pact consists of just three elements:

- a preventive arm that defines a medium-term budget target. Eurozone countries that comply with it are less likely to breach the deficit and debt criteria.
- a corrective arm that specifies how to handle violations of the guidelines.
- and the sanction mechanism

A look at the history of the pact shows that the specific stipulations regarding these core elements have become increasingly detailed (▶ Fig. 65). The first version from 1997 (▶ Ch. 3.4) was revised in 2005 after Germany and France violated the deficit rules (▶ Ch. 4.2). The 2005 reform was a response to criticism that the rules of the pact had a pro-cyclical effect, were not tailored to the specific situation of the individual countries and contained no incentives to implement structural reforms. Accordingly, the medium-term budget target was changed: the structural budget balance replaced the unadjusted budget balance. In addition, the Commission was given more discretion when it came to taking into account the economic situation and economic policy of the individual member states in its decisions in the preventive and corrective arms. The financial and euro crisis from 2008 onwards led to the next revision of the Stability and Growth Pact. The amended version came into force in 2011 (▶ Ch. 5.5.2). It was a response to the criticism that the pact was a 'toothless tiger' because sanctions were very unlikely to be imposed. For this reason, from now on, if the Commission recommended that sanctions should be imposed, this would automatically be the case if the Council did not reject such measures with a 2/3 majority. In addition, the debt-to-GDP ratio gained center stage in the corrective arm, providing specific guidelines on how this ratio was to be reduced if it exceeded 60 %. In addition to the budget balance requirements, a spending rule was introduced to regulate the growth of government spending. The 2011 reforms brought innovations in the form of the Fiscal Compact and the European Semester, which were intended to supplement the Stability and Growth Pact and anchor its fiscal policy motivation more firmly in national policy. At the same time, a special matrix was introduced to map the structural policy efforts of the member states, and the Commission now also included foreign economic imbalances (defined as national current account balances as a percentage of GDP) in its assessment of national economic policies.

With the reforms of 2011, the heads of state and government attempted to incorporate the experience of the first fourteen years of the Stability and Growth Pact in the new version, taking into account the different positions of the member states. The result was a very complex set of rules that not only leaves considerable room for interpretation, but is also only understood by experts. Looking at the 1997, 2005 and 2011 versions of the Pact, two aspects can be noted: Firstly, the rules have not prevented the debt levels of many member states from moving further away from the 60 % limit than they were already in the 1990s. And secondly, despite numerous breaches of the rules (only two countries have never been subject to an excessive deficit procedure), sanctions have never been imposed. This does not necessarily mean that the Stability and Growth Pact has completely failed to achieve its objective because without it, the situation today might be even more problematic. It is possible that the true value of the fiscal rules was — and remains — to pressure member states to justify their fiscal policy. This is even more important given that the budgetary sovereignty of national parliaments must not be undermined. At the same time, the problem remains that the sustainability of public finances is perceived as a dictate because its implementation is not motivated by intrinsic motives but rather trough pressure 'from Brussels.' Ultimately, the Pact could therefore do more harm than good.

Fig. 65: Development of the Stability and Growth Pact

1997
• Target in the preventive arm: balanced budget in the medium term • Corrective arm: deficit procedure if deficit > 3 % of GDP • Limited exceptions: exceptional event, severe economic slump • Sanction decision by the Council on the recommendation of the Commission
2005
• Target in the preventive arm: structural deficit between 0 % and 1 % of GDP (specific target value depends on GDP growth and debt level) • If targets are missed, consolidation efforts must be made; stronger consolidation required in good economic situation, weaker consolidation required in poor economic situation. • Greater discretion for the Commission with regard to determining an excessive deficit, as, for example, the economic situation or structural reforms can be taken into account. • Sanction decision by the Council on the recommendation of the Commission

7.4 The "NextGenEU" program and the future of fiscal policy in the monetary union

Fig. 65: Development of the Stability and Growth Pact – Continuation

2011
• Target in the preventive arm: structurally almost balanced budget
• If the target is missed: countries with a debt level <60% of GDP must improve their structural budget balance by 0.5 percentage points per year, those with a debt level > 60% by one percentage point; in addition, expenditure growth must be below potential growth.
• Greater significance of the debt level: the difference to 60% must be reduced within three years by an annual average of 1/20 of the difference. If the 3% deficit target is exceeded, the structural deficit ratio must be reduced by at least 0.5 percentage points in the following year.
• Commission can (with a large margin of discretion) take into account the economic situation, investment expenditure, structural reforms, etc. when assessing national consolidation efforts.
• New sanction mechanism: Commission's sanction recommendation can be rejected by the Council by qualified majority.
• An exceptional case (extraordinary event, severe economic slump) can also be identified for the eurozone as a whole (general escape clause).
• New instruments to supplement the Stability and Growth Pact: Fiscal compact, European semester, matrix for assessing national reform efforts, current account balance to be taken into account.

2024
• Target in the preventive arm: If the two Maastricht criteria are not met, the development of net primary government expenditure must follow the multi-year adjustment path agreed upon with the Commission.
• Government debt ratio ought to move towards 60%.
• Debt sustainability analyses become an important basis for the Commission's recommendations. Control account records deviations from the agreed development of net primary expenditure.
• Failure to meet the agreed path of net primary expenditure can also trigger sanctions.
• Sanction mechanism remains unchanged.

Against this backdrop, the Stability and Growth Pact was further revised. The reformed version came into force in 2024, with a significantly changed preventive arm. Now, the focus is no longer on the structural budget balance and the 1/20 rule for debt reduction, but rather on the development of net primary government expenditure. This is government expenditure minus interest expenditure, cyclical expenditure (e.g., for the unemployed), expenditure for EU programs and certain one-time-only, temporary expenditure. that fail to meet the Maastricht fiscal policy criteria, agree upon a specific multi-year adjustment path for net primary expenditure with the Commission. If structural reforms are undertaken, that period can be extended. At the end of the adjustment path, the two Maastricht criteria should be met (again). In particular, the aim is for the debt ratio to fall over the period under review – i.e., to move towards the target value of 60%, as agreed upon in the Maastricht Treaty. Debt sustainability analyses play a central role here. If net primary expenditure develops differently than agreed upon, these deviations are recorded in a control account. Overruns of the agreed expenditure path must be offset later, while shortfalls can be offset against subsequent overruns. The main thrust of the corrective arm remains essentially unchanged, even if numerous changes have been made. The structural deficit must still be reduced by 0.5 percentage points annually if the 3 % limit is exceeded. What is new in the corrective arm is that a deficit procedure can also be initiated if the deviations from the path of net primary expenditure agreed upon are too great.

7.5   A 'digital euro'?

For a long time, many people took for granted the ECB's role as a monopolist in providing cash to private households and companies, as well as reserves to commercial banks. This is why this area was not the focus of attention. This has changed, first very slowly and gradually over the past decade and a half, but then drastically because the world of money was shaken up even in the eye of the general public in the summer of 2019: At that time, a consortium of companies, led by Facebook and including major technology groups and payment service providers, presented a plan to introduce a digital payment tool called 'Libra.' In return for depositing traditional money, users were to receive 'Libra' and to be able to use it cheaply and conveniently worldwide. Because they had direct access to billions of users, many observers were convinced that Facebook and the other members of the consortium had the potential to establish 'Libra' as a global alternative to national currencies. Yet the project failed quite quickly – not least because it faced massive political resistance from the outset. Nevertheless, the so-called 'Libra shock' has been a wake-up call that prompted most central banks (before 2019, only a few had already taken tentative steps in this direction) to take a closer look at the digitalization of money.

The year 2008, when the "Bitcoin White Paper" was published under the pseudonym "Satoshi Nakamoto," is regarded as the starting point for this development. This is an essay that describes the principle of the new "peer-to-peer electronic cash system." Bitcoin makes it possible to store and transfer digital value units and does not require the traditional participants in the payment system such as central banks or credit institutions. The technological basis of this new digital asset is the so-called blockchain. This blockchain is a decentralized database managed simultaneously and independently by the members of the system, in which entries are made with the help of an innovative cryptographic validation system ('proof-of-work'). Since its establishment, Bitcoin has developed into a much-noticed speculative and investment instrument, but it has not yet played a significant role in payment transactions. In the meantime, thousands of other so-called 'cryptocurrencies' have also emerged.

In addition to technological shortcomings, the use of Bitcoin in payment transactions suffers — among other things — from the strong price fluctuations to which the asset is exposed. The underlying reason is the fact that the algorithmically controlled supply of Bitcoin grows ever more slowly until it reaches its maximum of 21 million units in 2140. This means that the supply cannot always satisfy the sometimes strongly fluctuating demand, which results in the aforementioned sharp ups and downs of the Bitcoin price. To counter this shortcoming, so-called 'stablecoins' (such as 'Libra') were developed. These are digital assets as well that can be stored and transferred bypassing the traditional financial system. Unlike traditional 'cryptocurrencies,' however, their value is linked to that of a reference asset in order to ensure the greatest possible price stability. Most stablecoins currently in use are dollar-based. The money paid in when individual coins are issued is invested in a reserve from which repayments are made at face value in dollars when users return their coins. Stablecoins fulfill important functions in the universe of crypto assets – for example as a transaction vehicle and store of value – but, like the original 'cryptocurrencies,' have not yet been able to establish themselves in everyday business life.

In contrast to the 'Libra shock,' which hit governments, central banks and the financial world suddenly and largely unprepared, another important development in the monetary system is taking place more gradually: the declining use of cash for payment transactions. The proportion of payments made by debit or credit card continues to rise, while banknotes and coins are becoming increasingly unpopular. Cash provided by the central bank is losing importance in favor of commercial bank money in the form of current account deposits.

The ECB responded to these trends by launching a two-year "investigation phase" in 2021 to explore the possibilities and limits of a 'digital euro.' This initial phase is followed by a 'preparatory phase,' which has been running since 2023 and could – but, according to the ECB, does not have to – lead to the decision to introduce a "digital central bank digital currency" (CBDC) in the European Monetary Union at the end of 2025 or the beginning of 2026. Based on the results of the investigation phase, the digital euro as European digital central bank money could have the following characteristics:

- It would only be made available to private households and companies, but not to commercial banks. The digital euro would therefore be a kind of 'digital cash.'
- It would be introduced as a supplement to cash, not to replace it. The ECB intends to continue offering cash indefinitely.
- Intermediaries would provide wallets in which users could store their digital euros and with which they could dispose of them.
- In order to prevent an outflow of current account deposits and thus prevent danger to the business model of banks, there is to be an upper limit for the amount of digital euros that can be held in the wallet. Amounts exceeding this limit are automatically transferred to a current account linked to the wallet.
- Only permanent residents of the eurozone are to be able to use and hold the digital euro. A holding limit of zero euros applies to companies. Although they can receive payments in digital euros, they cannot store them in their wallet. Incoming digital euros are forwarded directly to the linked current account.

The ECB argues that the digital euro is necessary to ensure that all residents of the monetary union can safely participate in financial transactions and to guarantee Europe's technological independence and the functioning of European monetary policy in the digital age. According to the central bank, the declining use of cash makes citizens increasingly dependent on the payment transaction products of commercial banks and payment service providers. If there were to be disruptions in this sector, private households would no longer be able to access their bank accounts and would find it difficult to carry out everyday transactions. Currently, cash is still available as an alternative in crisis situations. It was unclear, however, how the cash infrastructure (stores that accept cash, ATMs, etc.) would develop if the popularity of cash continued to decline. Even if the ECB wanted to continue to offer cash, a situation might arise in which cash could no longer be used in large parts of the eurozone and could be difficult to obtain. In a world with ever decreasing cash usage, the ECB argues, the digital euro have to take on this role.

Furthermore, there is no truly European technological framework for cross-border payments within Europe. Whether a tourist uses an ATM abroad, an export company receives its proceeds by bank transfer or a citizen pays for an online order from another eurozone country by SEPA transfer: such transactions are almost always processed via non-European infrastructure. This infrastructure is primarily provided by the US credit card companies Mastercard and Visa. The ECB argues that such a dependence on profit-oriented providers that are based outside of Europe is no longer acceptable in view of the increasing geopolitical tensions. The digital euro could provide a remedy here as an independent pan-European payment infrastructure.

Last but not least, the ECB cites a more technical argument: With cash, the ECB offers private households and companies in the eurozone the ultimate form of liquidity. Cash can still fulfill its monetary functions (as a transaction medium, a unit of account and a store of value) if other forms of payment or value storage fail. Thus cash (together with the reserves for commercial banks) forms the basis of the European monetary order. It is the monetary anchor that ultimately lends stability to the eurozone's entire monetary system. Without this anchor, the ECB would no longer be able to guarantee stable prices and financial stability in the eurozone. Its policy would then come to nothing.

A significant part of the expert community cannot follow this line of argument. First of all, it is doubted that private households need a new payment technology. Most were likely to be satisfied with the options offered by cash, debit and credit cards on the one hand, and non-bank service providers such as PayPal on the other. According to the critics, it was therefore unclear whether the digital euro would be accepted to the necessary extent. Furthermore, the ECB's initial considerations regarding the design of the digital euro contained such far-reaching restrictions (holding limit, restriction to eurozone residents, severely limited use by companies, etc.) that the new money would not actually be able to fulfill the traditional functions of money. Money could only be money if its functions as a transaction medium, unit of account and store of value were unrestricted. This characteristic did not apply to the digital euro. And even if the digital euro could be used comprehensively, critics believed there was a risk that it would create more problems than it solved. In general, it was questionable whether there was a market failure in the payments market that required a comprehensive state solution as an alternative to the numerous private payment products. While it was true that the ECB had to react to the declining use of cash, the dependence on non-European infrastructure and the digitalization of the financial sector, the ECB should not embark on a very expensive large-scale project with an uncertain outcome. According to the critics, it should instead create the regulatory incentives and framework conditions for technology-open competition in the private sector. In this way, a market-based cross-border payments area could be created in Europe without the ECB having to take on considerable risks and costs.

7.6   When will the eurozone be complete?

More than 25 years after it was founded, the monetary union is still a work in progress, because it is unfinished in the following three respects:

Firstly, it is unfinished with regard to its geographical size. The fact that the single market, which was completed in 1993, brings enormous economic benefits to the EU has never been questioned. It is therefore very attractive for EU accession aspirants in Eastern and South-Eastern Europe. Even countries that do not want to become full members of the Union, such as Switzerland and Norway, are striving for the closest possible connection to the single market. Whether participation in the single market necessitates the adoption of the single currency is a question that can be answered in various ways. At this point, let us take a look at the UK as a case study. Like Denmark, the Maastricht Treaty exempted the UK from the obligation to adopt the euro if it met the convergence criteria. This specific passage did not prevent London from maintaining its position as the most important financial center in Europe (alongside Frankfurt and Paris) and even from increasing its lead over its European competitors after the start of monetary union. The country did not face serious economic problems until Brexit and the resulting exclusion from the single market. Also, altogether twenty of overall 27 remaining EU members (most recently Croatia in 2023) have adopted the euro. Bulgaria and Romania have been signaling their interest in joining the eurozone for several years. As of summer 2025, Bulgaria is set to join the currency union by January 2026. For Denmark, Sweden, the Czech Republic, Poland and Hungary, on the other hand, giving up their national currency does not appear to be an option, at least not at present. These five countries apparently consider the costs of accession to be higher than the potential benefits of a membership in the monetary union. Although this phenomenon is well-known in politics and academia, there is no real debate about what the underlying reasons are.

Secondly, the relationship between centralized and decentralized responsibility in policy areas that are crucial to the success of the monetary union remains de facto unresolved, even after decades of intensive debate. This is particularly true with regard to fiscal policy. The extent to which an extensive centralization makes economic sense remains controversial. Politically, steps towards more centralization are hard to take as long as "Europe" is viewed primarily through a national lens. Media coverage contributes to this challenge as there are no truly pan-European media (with any significant reach), and the national media continue to cover European politics mainly from the perspective of the respective country. If at all, a European political public sphere therefore only exists in the very early stages. As most citizens identify primarily as French, Cypriot, Portuguese, Latvian, etc. and only secondarily – if at all – as European, politicians therefore usually argue with a view to their respective domestic electorate. This became particularly obvious in the early stages of the COVID-19 pandemic, when there was a real scramble for masks, protective clothing and ventilators: In such a historic emergency situation, national egoisms clearly prevailed over the European solidarity that had regularly been invoked in Sunday speeches. Less drastic examples such as the French stance on the Mercosur agreement or the Polish government's position on the import of Ukrainian agricultural products also demonstrate this phenomenon: Not always, but very often, the interests of national lobby groups outweigh European concerns. Likewise, this is probably the root of the chronic non-compliance with fiscal rules. It is possible that the fundamentally changed geopolitical situation in the wake of the Russian attack on Ukraine and the second Trump presidency could bring about a change in this interplay between national and European interests in the medium and long term.

Thirdly, through the unconventional monetary policy it adopted in response to the financial crisis, the ECB has raised expectations that it may be unable to meet in the long term without compromising its primary objective of price stability. As the only institution that is capable and willing to act in the short term, the central bank has repeatedly taken on tasks that were highly controversial because it was unclear whether they were covered by its primarily monetary policy mandate, which is geared towards the primary objective of price stability. Over the years, the ECB has gradually allowed itself to be pushed into the role of 'policy maker of last resort.' In the event of any minor or major difficulties in the eurozone, the capital markets and the public expect it to be available to defuse the situation in a 'Whatever it takes' manner. This is a particular type of time inconsistency problem (▶ Ch. 3.3.1): The obligation to pursue the primary objective of price level stability and the ban on monetary state financing were credible at the point they were codified in the Maastricht Treaty; afterwards, however, the ECB and other institutions (including the European Court of Justice) faced challenges that made it seem rational from their perspective to back away from the promises made in the early 1990s.

The European Monetary Union remains a unique experiment in the history of money. Although it has survived extreme difficulties – from the financial and sovereign debt crisis to the COVID-19 pandemic – the experiment cannot automatically be considered a success. However, it has not failed either. Unlike ten years ago (when, in the year 2015, a temporary 'Grexit" was on the agenda), today there is no talk of individual members leaving or being excluded from the monetary union, not to mention of a complete collapse of the eurozone. At the same time, fundamental questions remain unanswered and the monetary union is still unfinished. As more countries prepare to adopt the euro, both 'Europe' and its member states must clarify their mutual relationship. At the same time, the issue of unsustainable public debt remains unresolved in many countries, and the European Central Bank faces the challenge of managing the enormous expectations associated with its role as the eurozone's ultimate rescue authority. The experiment continues.

Literature

Adamski, D. (2023): The Overburdened Monetary Policy Mandate of the ECB, in: Adamski D./Amtenbrink, F./de Haan, J. (eds): The Cambridge Handbook of European Monetary, Economic and Financial Integration, Cambridge Law Handbooks, Cambridge University Press 2023, pp. 155–174

Altavilla, C. et al. (2021): Assessing the Efficacy, Efficiency and Potential Side Effects of the ECB's Monetary Policy Instruments since 2014, ECB Occasional Papers, NO. 278, September 2021, https://www.ecb.europa.eu/pub/pdf/scpops/ecb.op278~a1ca90a789.en.pdf?f7eb7e959d0a797ec11cc20220315a09

Anon. (2012): The secret of 3% finally revealed, voxeurop, https://voxeurop.eu/en/the-secret-of-3-finally-revealed/

Baglioni, A. (2024): The European Central Bank. Twenty-five Years of Single Monetary Policy in the Euro Area, in: Baglioni, A. (ed.): Monetary Policy Implementation – Exploring the 'New Normal' in Central Banking, Springer Nature, pp. 93–145, https://link.springer.com/book/10.1007/978-3-031-53885-8,

Baldwin, R./Wyplosz, C. (2023): The Economics of European Integration, 7th edition, McGraw Hill 2023

Bank of England (2014): Money Creation in the Modern Economy, Quarterly Bulletin, Q1/2014, https://www.bankofengland.co.uk/-/media/boe/files/quarterly-bulletin/2014/money-creation-in-the-modern-economy

Bernoth, K. et al. (2024): ECB monetary policy – Past, Present and Future, Monetary Policy Dialogue Papers February 2024, https://www.europarl.europa.eu/RegData/etudes/IDAN/2024/755719/IPOL_IDA(2024)755719_EN.pdf

Bofinger, P./Haas, T. (2023): Der Digitale Euro – Nutzen, Kosten und Risiken, Gutachten im Auftrag der Bundessparte Bank und Versicherung der Wirtschaftskammer Österreich, Juli 2023, https://www.wko.at/oe/bank-versicherung/gutachten-digitaler-euro.pdf

Borio, C. (2024): Monetary Policy in the 21st Century. Lessons Learned and Challenges Ahead, BIS Annal Economic Report, June 2024, https://www.bis.org/publ/arpdf/ar2024e2.pdf

Bundesbank (1979): Das Europäische Währungssystem, Monatsbericht März 1979, pp. 30–39

Bundesbank (1990a): Die erste Stufe der Europäischen Wirtschafts- und Währungsunion, Monatsbericht Juli 1990, pp. 30–39

Bundesbank (1990b): Stellungnahme zur Errichtung einer Wirtschafts- und Währungsunion in Europa, Monatsbericht Oktober 1990, pp. 41–45

Bundesbank (1992): Die Beschlüsse von Maastricht zur Europäischen Wirtschafts- und Währungsunion, Monatsbericht Februar 1992, pp. 45–54

Bundesbank (1998): Stellungnahme des Zentralbankrates zur Konvergenzlage in der Europäischen Union im Hinblick auf die dritte Stufe der Europäischen Wirtschafts- und Währungsunion, Monatsbericht April 1998, pp. 17–40

Bundesbank (2017a): Die Rolle von Banken, Nichtbanken und Zentralbank im Geldschöpfungsprozess, Monatsbericht April 2017, pp. 15–36

Bundesbank (2017b): Design and Implications of the European Fiscal Rules, Monthly Report June 2017, pp. 29–44

Bundesbank (2021): The Eurosystem's Monetary Policy Strategy, Monthly Report September 2021, pp. 17–60

Busch, B./Kauder, B. (2021): Der Stabilitäts- und Wachstumspakt, IW-Analysen 142/2021, https://www.iwkoeln.de/fileadmin/user_upload/Studien/IW-Analysen/PDF/2021/IW-Analysen_Nr._142_Stabilit%C3%A4ts-und-Wachstumspakt.pdf

Buti, M./Corsetti,, G. (2024): The first 25 Years of the Euro, CEPR policy insight, Vol. 126, February 2024, https://cepr.org/publications/policy-insight-126-first-25-years-euro

Clostermann, J./Rauscher, A./Seitz, F. (2024): Der Digitale Euro: Notwendige Ergänzung oder unnötige Belastung des zukünftigen Geldsystems?, in: Knoppe, M. (eds): Unternehmerische Wertschöpfung neu aufstellen, Springer Gabler, Wiesbaden 2024, https://doi.org/10.1007/978-3-658-42270-7_5, pp. 121–143

Cochrane, J./Garicano, L./Masuch, K. (2025): Crisis Cycle – Challenges, Evolution and Future of the Euro, Princeton 2025

Committee for the Study of Economic and Monetary Union (1989): Report on Economic and Monetary Union in the European Community ('Delors Report'), April 17th, 1989, Brussels

de Grauwe, P. et al. (1992): In reply to Feldstein, in: The Economist, July 4th, 1992

de Grauwe, P. (1996): International Money – Postwar Trends and Theories, 2nd ed., Oxford 1996

de Grauwe, P. (2022): Economics of Monetary Union, 14th ed. Oxford 2022

Delors, J. (1989): Address given to the European Parliament, January 17th, 1989, https://www.cvce.eu/content/publication/2003/8/22/b9c06b95-db97-4774-a700-e8aea5172233/publishable_en.pdf

Draghi, M. (2012a): Speech at the Global Investment Conference, London, July 26th, 2012, https://www.ecb.europa.eu/press/key/date/2012/html/sp120726.en.html

Draghi, M. (2012b): Introductory statement to the press conference (with Q&A), September 6th, 2012, https://www.ecb.europa.eu/press/press_conference/monetary-policy-statement/2012/html/is120906.en.html

Draghi, M. (2013): Introductory statement to the press conference, July 4th, 2013, https://www.ecb.europa.eu/press/press_conference/monetary-policy-statement/2013/html/is130704.en.html

Dyson, K./Featherstone K. (1999): The Road to Maastricht – Negotiating Economic and Monetary Union, Oxford 1999

ECB (1998): A stability-oriented monetary policy strategy for the ESCB, 13 October 1998, https://www.ecb.europa.eu/press/pr/date/1998/html/pr981013_1.en.html

ECB (2001): The Monetary Policy of the ECB, Frankfurt 2001

ECB (2003): The ECB's Monetary Policy Strategy, May 8th, 2003, https://www.ecb.europa.eu/press/pr/date/2003/html/pr030508_2.en.html

ECB (2004): The Monetary Policy of the ECB, Frankfurt 2004

ECB (2011): The Monetary Policy of the ECB, Frankfurt 2011

ECB (2014): The ECB's forward guidance, ECB Monthly Bulletin, April 2014, https://www.ecb.europa.eu/pub/pdf/mobu/mb201404en.pdf, pp. 55–63

ECB (2021): The ECB's monetary policy strategy statement, https://www.ecb.europa.eu/home/search/review/html/ecb.strategyreview_monpol_strategy_statement.en.html

ECB (2023): A Stocktake on the Digital Euro. Summary Report on the Investigation Phase and Outlook on the Next Phase,18 October 2023, https://www.ecb.europa.eu/euro/digital_euro/progress/shared/pdf/ecb.dedocs231018.en.pdf?6fbcce71a4be7bb3b8fabc51fb5c7e2d

Eger, T./Wagener, H.-J. (2021): Die wirtschaftswissenschaftlichen Grundlagen der europäischen Integration, in: Hatje, A./Müller-Graff, P.-C. (Hrsg.): Enzyklopädie Europarecht, Bd. 1: Europäisches Organisations- und Verfassungsrecht, https://doi.org/10.5771/9783748908579, pp. 129–179

Eger, T./Wagener, H.-J. (2022): Ökonomische Herausforderungen einer unvollständigen Währungsunion, in: Hufeld, U./Ohler, C. (Hrsg.): Enzyklopädie Europarecht, Bd. 9: Europäische Wirtschafts- und Währungsunion, Baden-Baden: Nomos, 1. Auflage, 2022, pp. 239 – 295

Eichengreen, B. (2008): Globalizing capital – The history of the international monetary system, Princeton University Press, 2nd. ed., Princeton 2008

Eichengreen, B. (2012): European monetary integration with the benefit of hindsight, in: Journal of Common Market Studies, Vol. 50(1), 2012, pp. 123–136

Eichengreen B. (2023): Conceptual Foundations of Economic and Monetary Union: The Economic Dimension, in: Adamski D./Amtenbrink F./de Haan J. (eds.): The Cambridge Handbook of European Monetary, Economic and Financial Integration, Cambridge Law Handbooks, Cambridge University Press 2023, pp. 19–32

European Commission (1990): One Market, one Money – An Evaluation of the Potential Benefits and Costs of Forming an Economic and Monetary Union, European Economy, Vol. 44, October 1990

Feld, L./Wieland, V. (2020): The German Federal Constitutional Court Ruling and the European Central Bank's Strategy, Institute for Monetary and Financial Stability, IMFS Working Paper NO. 145, https://www.imfs-frankfurt.de/fileadmin/research/working_papers/imfs_wp_145.pdf

Feldstein, M. (1992): Europe's Monetary Union. The Case against EMU, in: The Economist, June 13th, 1992

Fremerey, M. et al. (2024): Zwischen Schuldentragfähigkeit und Investitionsbedarf – Vergleich und Anpassungsbedarf europäischer und deutscher Fiskalregeln, IW Policy Paper 11/24, https://www.iwkoeln.de/fileadmin/user_upload/Studien/policy_papers/PDF/2024/IW-Policy-Paper_2024-Europ%C3%A4ische_und_Deutsche_Schuldenregeln.pdf

Godschalk, H./Krüger, M./Seitz, F. (2024): Der digitale Euro aus Sicht des Verbrauchers, des Handels und der Industrie, Studie im Auftrag des Bundesverbandes der Deutschen Volksbanken und Raiffeisenbanken e. V. (BVR), August 2024

Görgens, E./Ruckriegel, K./Seitz, F. (2013): Europäische Geldpolitik. Theorie - Empirie – Praxis, 6. Auflage, Stuttgart 2013

Goodhart, C. (1995): The Political Economy of Monetary Union, in: Kenen, P. (ed.): Understanding Interdependence. The Macroeconomics of the Open Economy Princeton University Press 1995, pp. 156–202

Gros, D./Thygesen, N. (1998): European Monetary Integration, 2nd ed., Addison Wesley Longman 1998

Hannoun, H. et al. (2019): Memorandum on the ECB's Monetary Policy, 04 October 2019, https://centerforfinancialstability.org/research/Memorand.pdf

Hegemann, H./Wieland, V. (2025): ECB Policy and Strategy Review: Potential Improvements, European Parliament, Monetary Dialogue Papers, March 2025, https://www.europarl.europa.eu/RegData/etudes/STUD/2025/764185/ECTI_STU(2025)764185_EN.pdf

Hetzel, R. (2022): German Monetary History in the Second Half of the Twentieth Century – from the Deutsche Mark to the Euro, Federal Reserve Bank of Richmond Economic Quarterly, Vol. 88/2, Spring 2022

Ider, G./Kriwoluzky, A./Kurcz, F./Schumann, B. (2024): Friend, Not Foe – Energy Prices and European Monetary Policy, DIW Discussion Papers Nr. 2089, https://www.diw.de/de/diw_01.c.907121.de/publikationen/diskussionspapiere/2024_2089/friend__not_foe_-_energy_prices_and_european_monetary_policy.html

Ioannidis, M. et al. (2021): The mandate of the ECB. Legal considerations in the ECB's monetary policy strategy review, ECB Occasional Paper Series, NO. 276, Frankfurt 2021, https://www.ecb.europa.eu/pub/pdf/scpops/ecb.op276~3c53a6755d.en.pdf

Issing, O. (2008): Der Euro – Geburt, Erfolg, Zukunft, Verlag Franz Vahlen, München 2008

Issing, O. (2024): Von der D-Mark zum Euro. Erinnerungen des Chefökonomen, Verlag Franz Vahlen, München 2024

James, H. (1996): International Monetary Cooperation since Bretton Woods, Washington 1996

Jarchow, H.J./Rühmann, P. (2002): Monetäre Außenwirtschaft – II. Internationale Währungspolitik, 2. Auflage, Göttingen 2002

Krägenau, H./Wetter, W. (1993): Europäische Wirtschafts- und Währungsunion – Vom Werner-Plan zum Vertrag von Maastricht, Baden-Baden 1993

Krugman, P. (1993): Lessons of Massachusetts for EMU, in: Giavazzi, F./Torres, F. (Eds.): Adjustment and Growth in the European Monetary Union, Cambridge University Press 1993, pp. 241–266

Krugman, P./Obstfeld, M./Melitz, M. (2022): International Economics – Theory and Policy, 12th ed., London 2022

Kruse, D. (1980): Monetary integration in Western Europe – EMU, EMS and beyond, London/Boston 1980

Larch, M./Malzubris, J./Santacroce, S. (2023): Numerical Compliance with EU Fiscal Rules. Facts and Figures from a New Database, in: Intereconomics, Vol. 58, 1/2023, pp. 32–42

Marjolin, R. (1980): Report of the Study Group „Economic and Monetary Union 1980", Brüssel, March 8th, 1975

Markakis, M. (2022): The EU Fiscal Rules. Principle, Policy, and Reform Prospects, in: Adamski D./Amtenbrink, F./de Haan, J. (eds): The Cambridge Handbook of European Monetary, Economic and Financial Integration, Cambridge Law Handbooks, Cambridge University Press 2023, pp. 305–331

Mink, R. (2018): Eine griechische Tragödie – Staatsschuldenkrise und kein Ende? Marburg 2018

Mortagua, M. (2021): The Euro at 22 – economic crisis and political instability, Working Paper 04/2021, Instituto Universitario de Lisboa, https://repositorio.iscte-iul.pt/bitstream/10071/22662/1/WP_2021-04.pdf

Mundell, R. (1961): A theory of optimum currency areas, in: American Economic Review, Vol. 51 (4/1961), pp. 657–665

Polster, W. (2002): Europäische Währungsintegration – von der Zahlungsunion zur Währungsunion, Marburg 2002

Rösl, F./Seitz, F. (2022): CBDC and Cash in the Euro Area. Crowding out or Co-Circulation?, Weidener Diskussionspapiere Nr. 85, Oktober 2022, https://www.oth-aw.de/files/oth-aw/Aktuelles/Veroeffentlichungen/WEN-Diskussionspapier/WEN-DPs-PDF/DP85.pdf

Rostagno, M. et al. (2019): A tale of two decades – the ECB's monetary policy at 20, ECB Working Paper Series, NO. 2346, December 2019, https://www.ecb.europa.eu/pub/pdf/scpwps/ecb.wp2346~dd78042370.en.pdf

Rueff, J. (1950): L'Europe se fera par la monnaie ou ne se fera pas, in: Synthèses – Revue Mensuelle Internationale, Vol. 4, Fevrier 1950, pp. 267–271

Sachverständigenrat zur Begutachtung der gesamtwirtschaftlichen Entwicklung (1994): Jahresgutachten 1994/95, Drucksache des Deutschen Bundestages 13/26 vom 21.11.1994, Randnummer 183, p. 155.

Schäfer, S. (2022): Eine kurze Geschichte der Europäischen Währungsunion, in: Aus Politik und Zeitgeschichte, Vol. 72, Heft 18–19/22, pp. 32–39

Schleiminger, G. (1980): Europäische Zahlungsunion, in: Born, K. et al. (Hrsg.), Handwörterbuch der Wirtschaftswissenschaft, Vol. 2, Stuttgart et al. 1980, pp. 507–512

Schlesinger, H. (1991): „Eine europäische Währung muss genauso stabil sein wie die D-Mark", in: Handelsblatt vom 31.12.1991, p. 9.

Schubert, C. (2013): Wie das Maastricht-Kriterium im Louvre entstand, Frankfurter Allgemeine Zeitung vom 25.9.2013, p. 10

Schwarzer, Daniela (2015): Die Europäische Währungsunion – Geschichte, Krise und Reform, Stuttgart 2015

Siekmann, H./Wieland, V. (2013): The European Central Bank's Outright Monetary Transactions and the Federal Constitutional Court of Germany, Institute for Monetary and Financial Stability, Working Paper NO. 71, https://www.imfs-frankfurt.de/fileadmin/research/working_papers/imfs_wp_71.pdf

Solomon, R. (1982): The international monetary system 1945–1981, New York 1982

Sweeney, R/Garber, P./Pattison, J./Folkerts-Landau, D. (1992): The ECB: a bank or a monetary policy rule?, in: Grilli, V., Masson, P./Canzoneri, M. (eds.): Establishing a Central Bank. Issues in Europe and Lessons from the US, CEPR Press, Paris & London 1993, https://cepr.org/publications/books-and-reports/establishing-central-bank-issues-europe-and-lessons-us

Thygesen, N. (1989): The Delors Report and European Economic and Monetary Union, in: International Affairs, Vol. 65, NO. 4, Autumn 1989, pp. 637–652

Trichet, J.C. (2007): Introductory statement, Press conference, September 6th, 2007, https://www.ecb.europa.eu/press/press_conference/monetary-policy-statement/2007/html/is070906.en.html

Trichet, J.C. (2010): Introductory statement, Press conference, December 2nd, 2010, https://www.ecb.europa.eu/press/press_conference/monetary-policy-statement/2010/html/is101202.en.html

Ungerer, H. (1983): The European Monetary System – The Experience 1979–1982, International Monetary Fund, Washington, D.C., 1983

Ungerer, H. (1997): A Concise History of European Monetary Integration, Westport/London 1997

Werner, P. (1970a): Zwischenbericht an Rat und Kommission über die stufenweise Verwirklichung der Wirtschafts- und Währungsunion der Gemeinschaft, Luxemburg, 20. Mai 1970, Dokument 9.504/II/70-D

Werner, P. (1970b): Report to the Council and the Commission on the Realisation by Stages of Economic and Monetary Union in the Community, Supplement to Bulletin NO. 11 of the European Communities, Brussels 1970

Vanthoor, W. (1999): A chronological history of the European Union 1946–1998, Cheltenham 1999